A History of the Christian Tradition

From the Reformation to the Present

Thomas D. McGonigle, O.P.

James F. Quigley, O.P.

PAULIST PRESS

NEW YORK ◆ MAHWAH, N.J.

Cover design by Morris Berman Studio.
Maps by Frank Sabatté.

Book design by Nighthawk Design.

Copyright © 1996 by
Thomas D. McGonigle
and James F. Quigley

Library of Congress Cataloging-in-Publication Data

McGonigle, Thomas D., 1941–
  A history of the Christian tradition.
  Includes index.
  1. Church history. I. Quigley, James F., 1938– . II. Title.
BR162.2.M38 1988   270   87-35975
ISBN 0-8091-2964-7 (pbk.) Volume 1
    0-8091-3648-1 (pbk.) Volume 2

Published by Paulist Press
997 Macarthur Boulevard
Mahwah, New Jersey 07430

Printed and bound in the
United States of America

Contents

1

European Christianity—Sixteenth Century Protestant Europe

Germany

The outstanding figure of the complex social and religious movement known as the Reformation was undoubtedly Martin Luther. Born in Germany in 1483, he began his higher studies at the University of Erfurt in 1501. Within four years he had completed his studies and attained his master of arts degree. Although he originally planned to go on to study law, a religious experience in the summer of 1505 caused him to become a Hermit of St. Augustine. After his ordination to the priesthood in 1507, Luther began the study of theology and came under the influence of the teachings of William of Occam. He became a doctor of theology in 1512 and began lecturing on sacred scripture at the newly established University of Wittenberg.

Martin Luther was a very religious man who was deeply concerned about his own eternal salvation. His strict upbringing may have influenced the understanding of his relationship to God, for he was convinced that God was a strict parent and judge whom he could never please. Although he constantly strove to live a good Christian life, Luther's overwhelming sense of his own sinfulness led him to fear that he would be damned.

In his attempt to find peace of mind by his search for a gracious and forgiving God, Martin Luther tried all the usual remedies suggested by the late medieval church—acts of penance, frequent confession and constant prayer. None of these traditional spiritual remedies brought him the confidence in God's saving love for which he yearned. However, while lecturing on St. Paul's letter to the Romans, he came to the insight that salvation or justification comes by faith alone. This teaching of St. Paul freed Luther from his fears and anxiety because he now understood that salvation was a free gift of God's grace which could not be earned by good works. He felt that the church had deviated from this gospel message by emphasizing good works and devotional practices as necessary for salvation. Luther's conflict with the church began, however, not with his teaching about justification by faith but with his opposition to the traditional Catholic teaching on indulgences.

Medieval men and women believed that they could avoid hell, which they saw as a place of eternal punishment and pain, by living a good Christian life and by going to confession and receiving the sacrament of the anointing of the sick (formerly known as extreme unction) at the hour of death. But they also believed that most Christians, while escaping hell, would have to go to purgatory, an intermediate state of purification, before they could enter heaven. Dante's *Divine Comedy* vividly depicts the medieval understanding of purgatory as a place of punishment for forgiven sins and indicates why people had a real fear of going there after death.

The spiritual remedy offered by the church for avoiding purgatory was an indulgence, a complete or partial remission of the temporal punishment due for forgiven sins. By performing certain devotional practices and fulfilling other conditions laid down by the church—confession of sin, reception of holy communion and saying certain prayers—an indulgence could be gained which would lessen one's time in purgatory.

In October 1517 Luther posted his famous "ninety-five theses" on the door of the Castle Church in Wittenberg. By presenting these theses or propositions, he was offering to debate the various issues and abuses which he believed were involved in the teaching on indulgences. The immediate cause for Luther's action was the fund-raising effort launched by Pope Leo X (1513–1521) to reconstruct St. Peter's Basilica. Leo X, son of the great Florentine financier and patron of the arts Lorenzo de Medici, had authorized an indulgence to anyone who contributed funds for the reconstruction effort.

Among the preachers designated to promote this fund-raising effort was the Dominican John Tetzel, who apparently made extravagant claims about the indulgences that would be granted to those contributing money to the building fund. In the course of Tetzel's preaching tour of Germany, many became indignant at his claims because they seemed to suggest that one could sell and buy the remission of temporal punishment due to sin. By posting his "ninety-five theses," Luther challenged Tetzel's preaching of indulgences since he maintained that it was an exploitation of the fears and superstitions of simple people.

By the beginning of 1518, Archbishop Albert of Brandenburg (1490–1545), who had authorized Tetzel to preach the indulgence in Germany, lodged complaints against Luther in Rome. The Augustinian friar was ordered to appear before the papal legate, the Dominican Cardinal Thomas Cajetan (1469–1534), at Augsburg. Luther saw the meeting as an opportunity for an academic discussion of the question of indulgences, while Cajetan intended the occasion as the time when the professor from Wittenberg would obediently accept the traditional teaching of the church. Cardinal Cajetan's plans failed when Luther showed himself unwilling to accept the church's teaching authority and appealed to an ecumenical council of the church.

In challenging Tetzel's preaching of indulgences, Luther was not only offering a different theological perspective but also attacking the economic and political structures of late medieval society. By his actions he gained the support of several influential German princes and became a folk hero to the common people. As Luther's protests against the Roman Church gained momentum and support grew in all segments of German society, he felt the need to set forth his position clearly in three pamphlets which he wrote in 1520:

1) In his *Open Letter to the Christian Nobility of the German Nation*, Luther described the papacy's economic exploitation of the German people. He also taught that the teaching authority of the pope could be rejected because all Christians could authoritatively interpret sacred scripture for themselves.
2) In his *Babylonian Captivity of the Church*, he maintained that many of the doctrines taught by the Roman Church for the last one thousand years were invalid because they were contrary to the bible.
3) In his *Treatise on Christian Liberty*, Luther taught that true freedom came from being justified by faith and not by a rigid fulfillment of religious obligations.

Because his teaching was considered heretical and he refused to accept the teaching authority of the Roman Church, Martin Luther was excommunicated by Pope Leo X in 1520. The civil authority now intervened in the person of the emperor Charles V (1519–1556), who ordered the Augustinian friar to appear before the Imperial Diet in the city of Worms in 1521. At this great gather-

ing of German nobles, Luther refused to recant and was outlawed as
a heretic subject to the death penalty. On his return journey from
Worms, Luther's patron, the elector Frederick of Saxony
(1463–1525), took him into protective custody and hid him in the
Wartburg Castle. He remained there until 1523 when he returned
to Wittenberg, where he was able to live the rest of his life promoting the Reformation under the protection of his supporters among
the German princes.

Luther spent the years from 1523 until his death in 1546 translating the bible into German and writing numerous polemic, liturgical and pastoral works. Luther's translation of the bible was a
literary masterpiece and profoundly affected the development of the
German language. Although his intent had been to reform the late
medieval church as he knew it, Luther in fact unleashed forces that
would divide western Christendom to the present day.

The full religious and political impact of Luther's reform movement was first felt in Germany at the Diet of Speyer in 1526 when
the princes divided themselves into two parties, those supporting
the pope and the emperor and those supporting Luther. Those
aligned with Luther were sufficiently strong to ensure that each
German prince could choose for or against the new reform movement in his own territory. At the Diet of Speyer in 1529 those
upholding the papacy tried to reimpose the old ways throughout
Germany. However, six German princes, supporters of Luther,
protested this action and thus came to be called "Protestants."
Germany was now divided into Catholic and Protestant camps.

After a nine year absence from Germany, Emperor Charles V
returned in 1530 and called the Imperial Diet to meet at Augsburg
to discuss the current religious crisis. Luther's colleague at
Wittenberg, Philipp Melanchthon (1497–1560), presented a document which contained an understanding of the Christian faith from
the perspective of Luther and his supporters. This important statement, which came to be called the Augsburg Confession, became the
basis for the Lutheran profession of Christian faith.

Because he needed the support of the Protestant princes against

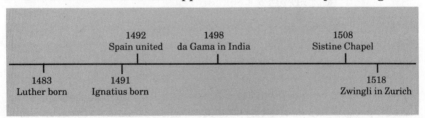

| 1492 | 1498 | 1508 |
| Spain united | da Gama in India | Sistine Chapel |

| 1483 | 1491 | | 1518 |
| Luther born | Ignatius born | | Zwingli in Zurich |

the Turks and the French, Charles V agreed to the Truce of Nuremberg in 1532, which stipulated that Protestant princes could practice the Lutheran faith in their own territories, but that areas that were currently Roman Catholic had to remain so. Protestantism, however, continued to advance, especially in northern and eastern Germany. The final settlement of the religious question in Germany came with the Peace of Augsburg in 1555. Each ruler was to determine whether the Catholic faith or the Lutheran faith would be practiced within his region. His subjects could either accept that decision or emigrate to another area. The princes now became the effective religious leaders of their territories, which meant that in Protestant areas the ruler was now the equivalent of a bishop because he was the de facto head of the state church within his own domain.

Protestant Christianity took a variety of forms over the next four hundred years, and many of these forms were never envisioned by Luther when he began his program of reform in 1517. He was truly a traditional man and a conservative Catholic who only sought to restore the evangelical basis of the ancient faith, which he thought had been distorted by medieval accretions. While his intention was to restore the Catholic Church and not to begin separate forms of Christianity, he did in fact become the articulator of the major tenets of Protestant Christianity. The basic teachings of Luther, which stand at the heart of the new Protestant vision of Christianity, include the following:

1) The bible is the ultimate source of authority in Christian life, rather than the church or tradition, because in it God's Word of salvation, Jesus Christ, is ever revealed.
2) The saving action of God through the death and resurrection of Jesus Christ forgives all sins and calls human beings to newness of life. The sinful human being is justified by the free gift of God's grace through faith alone, and this justification cannot be merited or earned by good works.
3) By reason of the gift of God's justifying grace in baptism, all

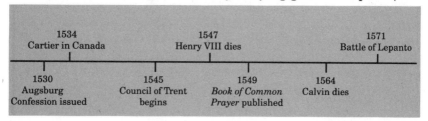

| 1534 | 1547 | 1571 |
| Cartier in Canada | Henry VIII dies | Battle of Lepanto |

1530	1545	1549	1564
Augsburg	Council of Trent	*Book of Common*	Calvin dies
Confession issued	begins	*Prayer* published	

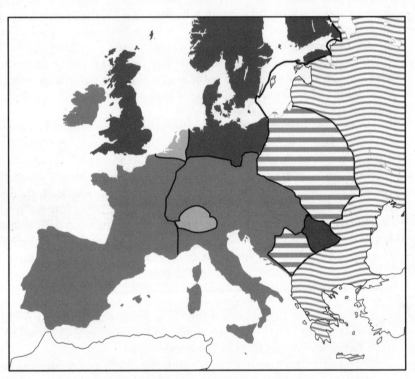

The Protestant Reformation

Protestant regions

Catholic regions

Mixed Catholic and Protestant

Orthodox regions

Mixed Catholic and Orthodox

Islamic regions

Christians become priests and do not need any human mediator before God. Thus the priesthood of all believers replaces
the ministerial priesthood.

4) Baptism and the holy eucharist are the only two sacraments
instituted by Christ. Although confession is a salutary practice, it is not a sacrament nor is it necessary for salvation.

5) Christ is truly present in the bread and wine of the eucharist,
but the elements are not transubstantiated into his body and
blood.

6) The pope is meant to be a symbol of the unity of all local
churches, but does not have authority over national churches.

7) Doctrinal teachings which have no basis in the scriptures
include: a) the mass as a sacrifice; b) purgatory; c) indulgences;
d) the primacy of the pope; e) the vows of religious life.

8) Liturgical customs which have no basis in the scriptures
include: a) private masses without a congregation; b) reserva-
tion of the eucharist in a tabernacle; c) obligatory private confession; d) the use of Latin in public worship.

9) Devotional practices which have no basis in the scriptures
include: a) veneration of the Virgin Mary and the saints; b)
honoring relics; c) going on pilgrimages to religious shrines; d)
using religious objects, such as rosaries.

Scandinavia

The Protestant princes of Germany used the Reformation as a way
to separate themselves from the forced unity and identity represented by the Roman Catholic Church and the Holy Roman Empire,
so that they could forge new religious and political identities at the
local and regional levels. In a similar way the peoples of
Scandinavia took up the Reformation as a way to throw off the yoke
of foreign or oppressive rulers and begin a new way of life as distinct
or renewed nation states.

When the Reformation began in Germany, King Christian II
(1513–1523) ruled over something of a united kingdom that included
Denmark, Norway and Sweden. From his base of power in Denmark,
King Christian sought to consolidate his political control of Sweden
by having himself crowned king in Stockholm. The bloody military
campaign which he waged against his enemies culminated in the
1520 "massacre of Stockholm." The ensuing rebellion forced King

Christian to flee, and he was eventually defeated and imprisoned by his uncle and successor Frederick I (1523–1533).

Frederick I supported the Reformation in Denmark and Norway as a way of forging a new sense of national identity between the two countries. By the time of his death in 1533 most of the population in both Denmark and Norway had become Lutheran. The new Protestant state church used the confiscated wealth of the religious orders to insure the loyalty of the nobles in its program of national reform. The new Lutheran vernacular liturgy played a significant role in the development of Danish and Norwegian culture.

Following the "massacre of Stockholm," Gustavus Erikson Vasa (1523–1560) led the national rebellion against the Danish occupation under Christian II. After a series of successful military campaigns, he was elected king at Strangnas in 1523. Convinced of the advantages offered by the Reformation for consolidating royal authority and national loyalty, Gustavus encouraged the Wittenberg-trained preacher Olav Pedersson (1493–1552) to reform the Swedish church according to the Lutheran model. By the time of Gustavus' death in 1560, Sweden had become a Protestant nation, but it retained the episcopal form of church government and maintained many of the outward appearances of the late medieval Catholic Church in its worship and traditions.

Switzerland

Ulrich Zwingli

The early leader of the Reformation in Switzerland was Ulrich Zwingli (1484–1531). Ordained to the Roman Catholic priesthood in 1506, he served as a chaplain for a time to Swiss mercenary soldiers who had been recruited to serve in Italy. Zwingli's military experience convinced him that Swiss involvement in foreign mercenary service was detrimental to true Christian life. Hence he left the army and became a chaplain at the shrine to the Virgin Mary at Einsiedeln. However, his growing sense of opposition to any religious practices not mentioned in scripture soon led to his dismissal from his post because of his preaching against pilgrimages and devotion to the saints.

In 1518, Zwingli was invited to become the pastor and preacher at the Old Minster (the major church) in Zurich. The reforming efforts of Zwingli in Switzerland paralleled those of Luther in Germany. Both opposed the teaching of the Roman Church and preached reliance on the bible as the ultimate authority in religious matters. Zwingli was also strong in his condemnation of devotional practices such as pilgrimages and veneration of the saints, which he felt were non-scriptural creations of the clergy to exploit the credulity of ordinary believers.

Zwingli persuaded the city council of Zurich to pass an ordinance in 1523 which forbade the preaching of any doctrine or the continuance of any religious practice not explicitly mentioned in scripture. This resulted in the removal of images from churches, the suppression of monasteries and convents, the abolition of the mass and even the prohibition of organ music in the simple communion service that was now the center of worship.

Switzerland's thirteen cantons or independent districts soon became bitterly divided over the question of the Reformation. Some supported Zwingli and his reforming efforts while others chose to remain loyal to the Roman Catholic tradition. After 1525, the Reformed and the Catholic cantons organized defensive leagues. Five Catholic cantons attacked Zurich in 1531 and Zwingli was killed in battle near Kappel. Subsequently it was agreed that each canton was free to choose either to adopt the reform or to remain Catholic. To the present day some Swiss cantons are strongly Protestant while others are strongly Catholic.

While agreeing with Luther in his opposition to many teachings of the Roman Catholic Church, Zwingli also differed from the great German reformer in his presentation of some aspects of the Christian faith. Zwingli is the first representative of what is known as the Reform tradition within Protestant Christianity. The principal tenets of Zwingli's teaching include the following:

1) Because he is all-knowing, God determines from all eternity who will be saved and who will be damned by a divine decree of predestination.
2) The bible is the sole authoritative norm of faith.
3) Because worship ought to be simple and scriptural, all church art and elaborate forms of music are forbidden.
4) The eucharist is a memorial of Christ's passion, and hence he is only spiritually present in the bread and wine and not physically present as Roman Catholics and Lutherans maintained.
5) Secular rulers are independent of the jurisdiction of religious authorities in civil matters.

The Anabaptists

Some Swiss Christians believed that a more radical renewal of Christian life and society beyond that envisioned by either Luther or Zwingli was necessary. This group of reformers constitutes the radical Reformation or the Anabaptist movement. The Anabaptists—from the Greek word meaning rebaptizers—rejected infant baptism; hence, they rebaptized adults. In Anabaptist understanding salvation happened through an adult conversion experience which was sealed by a lifelong commitment to the search for holiness symbolized by baptism through immersion.

In 1525 the leaders of the Anabaptist movement in Switzerland, Conrad Grebel (1498–1526) and Felix Mantz (1500–1527), began to experience the opposition of more conservative Protestants. The town council of Zurich imposed the penalty of drowning on anyone who was rebaptized. When Felix Mantz was so punished in 1527, many of the Anabaptists fled and took refuge in other parts of Europe, especially Germany and Holland.

One group of Anabaptists settled in the city of Münster in Germany in 1534. Under the direction of John of Leyden, who had apocalyptic and communistic notions, they set up the kingdom of Sion and expelled both Catholics and Protestants. Eventually the city was recaptured by the local princes and the militant Anabaptist leaders were killed. This tragedy led Anabaptists to become pacifists and to separate themselves from any participation in civil society. It also caused Catholics and Protestants alike to be suspicious of the Anabaptist movement.

In 1536 a former Dutch Catholic priest, Menno Simons (1492–1559), joined the reconstituted Anabaptist movement and guided them in the ways of strict pacifism so that they were considered subversive by many authorities for refusing military service. Simons' disciples, the "Mennonites," scattered throughout Europe and Russia and eventually emigrated to North America.

John Calvin

The principal theologian of the Reform tradition, John Calvin (1509–1564), was born in France and studied humanities at the University of Paris and law at the University of Orleans. Influenced both by his humanist studies and by the Reformation movement, Calvin left the Catholic Church in 1535. Since the French government was persecuting Protestants, he left his native land and went into exile in Switzerland. Settling at first in the city of Basel, he spent his time studying and writing. In 1536 he published the first edition of his theological masterpiece, *The Institutes of the Christian Religion*, which would eventually encompass a full treatment of the Christian faith in four books and eighty chapters in the final edition of 1559.

While passing through Geneva on his way back to Basel after a brief visit to France in 1536, Calvin was persuaded by Guillaume Farel, a leading reformer, to assist him in his teaching and preaching. In a disagreement over discipline with civil authorities, Calvin and Farel left Geneva in 1538. However, Calvin was recalled to Geneva in 1541 and became the architect of a model Christian life in which civil and religious officials were co-responsible for ordering the lives of citizens in accord with the gospel.

Through his *Institutes* Calvin emerged as the great systematizer of the Reform tradition within Protestant Christianity. His influence spread from Geneva to Holland, France and Great Britain. The English supporters of Calvin, the Puritans, had a profound impact on the development of the values and ideals of the American spirit through their colonies in New England. The teachings of the Reform tradition articulated by Calvin include the following:

1) We truly know God only through revelation as presented by the scriptures.
2) From all eternity God predestines some to be saved and others to be damned.
3) Every human person is totally corrupt by reason of original sin.
4) The true church of Christ is an invisible reality whose members are known only to God because they are predestined to salvation. The institutional church is a visible reality whose members include both those destined for salvation and those destined for perdition.
5) There are only two sacraments established by Jesus Christ for his church, baptism and the holy eucharist.
6) The eucharist does not contain the actual body and blood of Christ which is in heaven, but is a memorial of Christ's passion which unites the believer spiritually to the risen Christ.
7) The church is governed according to a presbyterian form of polity in which ordained presbyters or pastors share responsibility for the life and good order of the community with lay elders.
8) The state or local government is obliged to conduct itself in accord with the gospel norms proposed by the church.

Great Britain

England

The issues faced by the English church at the beginning of the six-teenth century pertain more directly to the royal succession than to the ideas of the reformers. Six children had been born from the mar-riage between Henry VIII (1509–1547) and Catherine of Aragon, but only one daughter, Mary Tudor, survived infancy. Because it was essential to have a male heir, Henry sought to obtain an annul-ment of his marriage to Catherine. When Pope Clement VII (1523–1534) refused his request, Henry broke with Rome and secretly married Ann Boleyn after the archbishop of Canterbury, Thomas Cranmer, declared his marriage with Catherine invalid in 1533.

When the pope excommunicated Henry in 1534, parliament responded with the "Act of Supremacy" which declared the king to be the supreme head of the Church of England. Maintaining that there was no true marriage between Henry and Catherine, parlia-ment also declared that Ann's children and not Mary Tudor were the legitimate heirs to the English throne.

All office-holders were now required to take an oath which acknowledged Henry as head of the English church and Ann's chil-dren as legitimate heirs. When Sir Thomas More (1478–1535), lord chancellor of England, refused to take the oath, he was imprisoned in the Tower of London and eventually executed. At the time of his death he declared that he was "the king's good servant but God's first."

Although he had severed his allegiance to the pope, Henry remained a conservative Roman Catholic for the whole of his life. Archbishop Thomas Cranmer (1489–1556), however, was a strong supporter of the views of the reformers as were Henry's subsequent wives. The influence of the advocates of the Reformation became increasingly stronger in the final years of Henry's reign.

When Henry died in 1547, his only male heir, Edward VI (1547–1553), son of Jane Seymour, Henry's third wife, succeeded to the throne of England. Since Edward was only ten years old at the time, he was under the regency of the duke of Northumberland, who quickly moved with Thomas Cranmer to introduce Reformation ideas. Celibacy was no longer a requirement for priestly ministry; images were removed from churches and the cup was administered to the laity at the eucharist. Worship was now conducted according to the *Book of Common Prayer*, carefully drawn up by Cranmer in

1549. Revised in 1552, the *Book of Common Prayer*, which was a masterpiece of liturgical composition and language, became the hallmark of the life and spirituality of the new Protestant church of England, the Anglican Church.

Mary Tudor (1553–1558), the oldest surviving daughter of Henry VIII, succeeded to the throne at Edward's death in 1553. As the daughter of Catherine of Aragon, she was fiercely committed to the Roman Catholic Church. Mary was determined to undo the Reformation ideas and practices introduced under Edward and restore Catholicism. England returned to obedience to Rome in 1554, but Mary's persecution of leading Protestants, which included the execution of Thomas Cranmer and four other bishops, alienated many of the English people. The five year reign of "Bloody Mary" unintentionally prepared the way for the return of the English church to Protestantism.

Elizabeth I (1558–1603), the daughter of Henry VIII and Ann Boleyn, succeeded to the throne at the death of her half-sister, Mary Tudor. She was a moderate Protestant who rejected both Roman Catholicism and the extreme form of Anglicanism represented by the Puritan party. In 1559, Parliament declared that Elizabeth was the "supreme governor" of the Church of England. Worship according to the *Book of Common Prayer* was restored in all English parishes.

In 1563 Elizabeth published the "Thirty-Nine Articles," a kind of credal statement of the English church, which clearly placed Anglicanism within the Protestant traditions by rejecting such Catholic teachings as purgatory, indulgences, private confession and transubstantiation. The profession of Roman Catholicism was now illegal in England and practicing Catholics were subject to severe penalties. As Mary had persecuted and executed Protestants, Elizabeth now did the same with Catholics. A seminary was established at Douai in France in 1568 to train priests who could be secretly smuggled into England to minister to the remaining Catholics. An English translation of the bible, known as the Douai-Reims version, was prepared for the use of Roman Catholics in 1609 at this seminary in exile.

The Puritan party within the English church felt that the moderate reforms introduced by Elizabeth did not go far enough in purifying the Christian faith from medieval Catholic teaching and practices. Preferring a more Calvinist approach, they objected to the continuance of the episcopal form of church order and some of the patterns of worship permitted by the *Book of Common Prayer*. Although they remained within the state church, they continued to demand further reforms and became a very powerful political force in the seventeenth century.

Scotland

The centuries-old rivalry between England and Scotland took a new turn during the Reformation period when James VI of Scotland, son of Mary Stuart, ascended the English throne in 1603 as the successor of Elizabeth I. The event was the culmination of a complex set of happenings that surrounded the introduction of the Reformation into Scotland. John Knox (1513–1572), the leader of the Scottish Reformation, was ordained to the priesthood in the Roman Catholic Church in 1540, but embraced the teachings of the reformers, especially Calvin, in 1544. He was forced to flee to Geneva in 1547 after the French allies of Queen Mary Stuart (1542–1587) were victorious over the Scottish nobles who had espoused the Protestant cause.

The Protestant forces, however, rallied and were strong enough to establish the Reformed Church of Scotland in 1562 according to the theology and pattern of John Calvin. The Catholic cause suffered many setbacks because of the amorous affairs of Queen Mary Stuart, who was finally forced to abdicate in 1567 in favor of her Protestant son, James VI (1567–1625). The victorious Protestants now reorganized the Church in Scotland under the leadership of John Knox, who had returned from exile in 1559.

The First Book of Discipline, written by Knox in 1560, clearly espoused the Reform tradition of Protestantism, which opted for the presbyterian rather than the episcopal form of church order. Knox also composed the worship book for the Scottish Presbyterian Church, *The Book of Common Order*, before his death in 1572. Although the Church of Scotland was presbyterian in orientation, the episcopal structure of church order perdured until 1690. This state of affairs occurred because of the union of England and Scotland in 1603 when James VI Stuart, king of Scotland, the closest blood relative of Elizabeth I, became James I, king of England. Only at the deposition of the last of the Stuart kings, James II, in 1688 were Scottish Protestants finally able to complete the Reformation and establish a presbyterian form of church order.

Ireland

In 1537 Ireland, because it was under the political control of the English kings, gave nominal assent to the supremacy of Henry VIII as head of the church in England and Ireland. The reforming efforts under Edward VI had little impact and the Irish people rejoiced at the restoration of Roman Catholicism under Mary Tudor. During the reign of Elizabeth I, the Irish parliament was compelled in 1560 to establish the Church of Ireland, which was Anglican in theology and church order. The new national Protestant Church was rejected by the vast number of the Irish people, who remained staunchly loyal to the Catholic faith. Persecution only galvanized the resistance of the Irish Catholics, who saw themselves involved in a life or death struggle not only to maintain their faith but to regain their land from their English overlords.

France

Francis I (1515–1547), because of his bitter opposition to the German emperor, Charles V, at times supported the Protestant princes of Germany for his own political purposes. However, he remained committed to Roman Catholicism and did not tolerate the spread of the teachings of the reformers within France. Supporters of the Reformation in France were known as "Huguenots," a word of uncertain origin. Influenced by the theological ideas of John Calvin in Geneva, the Huguenots organized themselves into a church in 1555 and four years later produced a confession of faith and a book of discipline and church order.

Under Francis I's son, Henry II (1547–1559), Huguenot power began to grow steadily in some parts of France. While the ordinary people remained attached to the old faith, some of the nobles and members of the middle class converted to Protestantism both for personal reasons and also as a way of establishing a new power base in opposition to the growing control of the French kings over all aspects of societal life. Although Henry II continued his father's policy of persecution, the Huguenot movement increased in strength, fueled by its new political aspirations.

Under Henry II's three weak sons, France was convulsed by civil war between Catholics and Huguenots from 1562 until 1589. The most awful atrocity of this terrible period of religious wars was the St. Bartholomew's Day massacre on August 24, 1572, when thousands of Huguenots in all parts of the country were brutally murdered. Only with the succession of Henry IV (1589–1610), brother-in-law of the last of Henry II's sons, was there some resolution to this religious fratricide. Although he was a Protestant when he became king in 1589, he converted to Roman Catholicism because it was the religion of the majority of the French people. He is supposed to have said: "Paris is worth a mass."

In 1598 Henry IV published the Edict of Nantes which granted freedom of worship to Huguenots in specified towns and regions. The way was now open to peace in France. However, the religious wars had produced, as evidenced by the thought of Michel Montaigne, a spirit of cynicism and mistrust toward Christianity in general and the Roman Catholic Church in particular. The disastrous results of the religious wars would become fully evident in the Jansenist struggle of the seventeenth century and the Enlightenment writers of the eighteenth century.

The Low Countries

The geographical area that embraces modern Belgium, the Netherlands and Luxembourg was under the political authority of the Hapsburg family when its principal representative, Charles V, became holy Roman emperor in 1519. This territory, known as the Seventeen Provinces, was divided culturally into the French-speaking south, the Dutch-speaking north and an intermediate Flemish-speaking zone.

Erasmus of Rotterdam (1469–1536), the great northern humanist, personified the openness of this area to the idea of church reform. When Lutheran preachers entered this area in the 1520s, they found sympathetic listeners. However, it was the theology of Calvin that eventually provided the major impetus for the development of Protestantism within the Seventeen Provinces.

Both Charles V and his son Philip II (1556–1598), ruler of Spain and the Low Countries, tried to halt the spread of Protestantism. The repressive measures employed by the Spaniards caused the Calvinists in the Seventeen Provinces to rise in revolt under the leadership of Prince William of Orange (1533–1584). Although the Spaniards triumphed in the ten southern provinces, the seven northern provinces declared their independence from Spain in 1581. The war dragged on until a truce was finally signed in 1607. As a result of the treaty, the ten southern provinces became Catholic Belgium and Luxembourg, while the seven northern provinces became Protestant Holland.

At the end of the sixteenth century, not only was western Europe divided into Protestant and Catholic countries and areas, but the

Protestant Christians themselves were further divided into Lutheran, Calvinist, Anglican and Anabaptist churches. In the early years of the Reformation, most people still thought of themselves as belonging to a single universal church that was struggling for renewal. Only when the reformers found themselves persecuted by the ecclesiastical authorities of the Roman Church or when they began to disagree among themselves about the nature of the reform itself did the various groups come to understand themselves as separate ecclesial communities.

Distinct doctrine, worship, discipline and church order as well as outside political and social forces contributed to the development of this denominational awareness. Diverse interpretations of the Christian message coupled with a sense of their own orthodoxy and orthopraxis soon led to antagonism and strife between the different ecclesial communities. When these powerful religious differences were tied into political, social and economic struggles, the result was the terrible period of the religious wars that began in the mid-sixteenth century and continued until 1648. The common heritage of the gospel of Christ yielded to polemics and armed conflict in the name of the reform of the abuses of late medieval Christianity. The ecumenical movement of the twentieth century is now trying to heal the wounds that have painfully marked the church for more than four hundred years.

2

Sixteenth Century
Catholic Reform and
Counter- Reformation

The church or the *ekklesia* is the gathering together of people throughout history and throughout the world who profess belief in Jesus Christ as Lord. From the perspective of the Christian faith, the church is a community enlivened by the presence of the risen Christ in and through the Holy Spirit. As a mystery it is the locus for encounter between God and the people of God. It is also a community of men and women who organize their life together as they journey toward salvation.

Because it is a human institution, the church must constantly renew and reform itself to exist authentically as the people of God and the body of Christ. Historically, therefore, the church always lives in tension—the tension between sanctity and sinfulness, between the Spirit-filled community and the human institution, between leaders and the faithful, between universalism and a tendency to nationalism.

Abuses and corruption at the time of the Reformation made a program of renewal and reform absolutely essential if the church was to witness to the holiness of life to which it was called. While the efforts for reform and renewal led many away from the Roman Catholic Church, others attempted to renew and reform the church in accord with traditional doctrine and discipline.

Spain

At the end of the fifteenth century, when Martin Luther was still a young man, the reform and renewal of Catholic life in Spain was already underway. From 1479 to 1515 Ferdinand of Aragon and his wife, Isabella of Castile, worked to unite their nation and to reform the church as the primary instrument of national unity and identity. The architect for the reform of the Spanish church was the Franciscan archbishop of Toledo, Francisco Ximénez de Cisneros (1436–1517). His program of reform envisioned educated, morally upright and zealous priests and bishops, who would be assisted and encouraged in their ministry by men and women religious who were deeply committed to their vowed life of prayer and service.

Like the northern humanists, Ximénez was committed to a program of renewal that included study of the bible in Hebrew and Greek. He founded the University of Alcala, near Madrid, as a center for humanist studies in 1508. Important Spanish intellectual and religious leaders, such as Miguel de Cervantes (1547–1616) and Ignatius Loyola (1491–1556), were educated in the classics at this great center of learning. In 1517 Cardinal Ximénez published a multilingual edition of the bible, the *Complutensian Polyglot*, in Hebrew, Greek and Latin.

By the concordat or agreement between the rulers of Spain and the papacy in 1482, the king was the de facto head of the church in Spain with the right to appoint bishops and the powers necessary to reform all aspects of church life. As a result, the church in Spain, although it would not tolerate doctrinal reform, was more involved in educational and disciplinary reform than any other part of the church in western Europe at the beginning of the sixteenth century.

The Inquisition

The Inquisition was a tribunal or court established by Pope Gregory IX in 1231 to root out heresy, which in medieval Christian society was both a religious and a civil crime. A repentant heretic could be sentenced to life imprisonment and an obstinate heretic could be sentenced to death. The severity of the punishment for heresy was due to the belief of medieval society that the heretic by his or her rejection of the Catholic faith was an enemy of the common good. Thus in cases of capital punishment the accused was turned over to the civil or secular authorities for punishment. Because of their theological training, Dominicans and Franciscans were often chosen as inquisitors or judges.

Although a court or tribunal to judge the orthodoxy of individuals made sense to the minds of the leaders of medieval Christian society, it certainly does not accord with our ideas of the inviolability of conscience and religious freedom. The church strove to be just and fair in the inquisitorial process, but abuses often entered the system and the rights of the accused were at times ignored. Disregard of the rights of individuals that eventuates in torture and death is certainly reprehensible. However, over the course of time certain myths have developed in popular and literary imagination that exaggerate the horror and distort the role of the church in the Inquisition. While condemning injustice in all forms, students of history must always strive to interpret institutions within their own historical perspective and try to understand why the leaders of the church and civil society acted as they did in a particular cultural situation.

Ferdinand and Isabella established the Inquisition in Spain in 1478 and named the Dominican, Tomás de Torquemada, as inquisitor general. They saw Roman Catholicism, the religion of the majority of the Spanish people, as the cohesive force that could bring the emerging nation together. Thus one of the purposes of the Spanish Inquisition was to monitor the orthodoxy and conduct of Jewish and Muslim converts. In 1492 Granada, the last Islamic center in Spain, was captured and Jews who refused to convert to Catholicism were expelled. The 400,000 Jews who had become converts to Catholicism, the *Conversos* or *Marranos*, as well as the converted Muslims, the *Moriscos*, were always of concern to the Spanish Inquisition.

The original work of the Spanish Inquisition, then, was to maintain the orthodoxy of Jewish and Muslim converts as a way of ensuring national unity and cultural cohesiveness. The ideas of the Protestant reformers made little headway in Spain because the Inquisition broadened the scope of its religious oversight to include anything that threatened Spanish unity and identity by moving people away from the traditional doctrines and practices of the Roman Catholic Church.

New Religious Orders

Within Christianity, as a movement leading women and men to salvation, there is another movement, religious life, which seeks to live the gospel in a more intense way. By their vowed life, women and men religious throughout the centuries have tried to serve the needs of the Christian community at particular times and places in a variety of ways.

The sixteenth century witnessed the foundation of new orders or groups of religious women and men who sought to renew the Catholic Church as a place of evangelical life and service. They also sought in different ways to defend the church against those ideas of the Protestant reformers which undermined traditional doctrine and practice.

The great Spanish mystic and spiritual writer, Teresa of Avila (1515–1582), founded a Discalced (barefoot) Carmelite convent for women in 1562 and in cooperation with John of the Cross (1542–1591) a Discalced monastery for men in 1568. The lifestyle of the Discalced Carmelites emphasized renewed dedication to prayer within the context of a simple gospel life of poverty and penance. Teresa traveled throughout Spain establishing Discalced Carmelite convents and monasteries, which became centers of reform and renewal first for the church in Spain and subsequently for the church in all parts of the Catholic world.

Teresa furthered the reform of the Roman Catholic Church not only by her religious foundations but also by her literary efforts. In her books, *The Interior Castle*, *The Book of Her Life* and *The Way of Perfection*, she wrote of her own spiritual journey. By detailing her own personal experiences of God and the interior life, she provided inspiration for countless men and women who were concerned about deepening their own lives of prayer and service. St. Teresa's colleague in the Carmelite reform, St. John of the Cross, also contributed to the development of our understanding of the search for God by his spiritual classics, *The Ascent of Mt. Carmel*, *The Dark Night of the Soul*, *The Spiritual Canticle*, and *The Living Flame of Love*.

Matteo di Bassi of Urbino, who died in 1552, began a reform of the Franciscan Order by insisting that the friars return to the simple ideals of St. Francis of Assisi (1181–1226). Known as the Capuchins, because of the pointed hood (*cappuccio* in Italian), which they wore as part of their religious habit, these reformed Franciscans lived in very simple dwellings and spent their time in preaching and working with the poor. Initially they settled in rural areas and de-emphasized the intellectual life. However, as the Capuchin reform expanded, they undertook a significant urban ministry and adopted a strong commitment to study as an essential component of their preaching ministry. Eventually the Capuchins, along with the Jesuits, became the great preachers of the Counter-Reformation, defending and communicating the truths of the Catholic faith throughout Europe.

Numerous other groups of religious men and women were founded in the sixteenth century to live the ideals of the gospel in a reformed

Catholic Church and to serve the pastoral needs of their contemporaries. Education in general and the education of women in particular was a very significant need. St. Angela Merici (1447–1540) responded to this need by establishing the Ursulines, a community of women religious who committed themselves to education and charitable work among women of all ages and social classes. The witness of these dedicated women religious served as a powerful example of the impetus that a life of dedicated service could have for the renewal of Christian society.

The Theatines, founded in 1524 by St. Cajetan (1480–1547), emphasized the reform of clerical life. Theatines were to exercise their priestly ministry as true shepherds of their parishioners by living among their people as men of prayer and pastoral care. Similar ideals were articulated by St. Philip Neri (1515–1595) who established oratories or meeting places for prayer where priests and laity could meet to receive and give mutual support to one another in their common search for holiness and gospel service.

The Jesuits

The founder of the Society of Jesus, the Jesuits, was Ignatius Loyola (1491–1556), a Spanish nobleman. After a serious leg wound had ended his military career, he spent his convalescence reading the lives of the saints. Moved by their heroism, Ignatius resolved to become a soldier of Christ and spent a year making a retreat at Manresa, where he composed his *Spiritual Exercises*. These exercises constitute a four week retreat which seeks to produce consecration to Christ through a life of self-control and discipline.

Between 1524 and 1534 Ignatius studied the humanities and theology at various centers of learning in Spain and at the University of Paris. With six friends in 1534, he vowed to live in poverty, chastity and special obedience to the pope as the representative on earth of Christ the King. The members of the Society of Jesus dedicated themselves to serve the church by defending the truths of the Catholic faith under the direction of the pope. The order was approved by Pope Paul III in 1540, and by 1556 there were more than a thousand members of the society scattered throughout Europe, Asia and the new world.

The Jesuits dedicated themselves to preaching, spiritual direction and missionary work, but their special apostolate was education in the tradition of Renaissance humanism. Catholic rulers and bishops who wanted a school or university in their sphere of influence called on the Society of Jesus. Although they taught all classes of people, the Jesuits were especially concerned about training those who would become the leaders in the renewal of Catholic life in European society. Their impact on education was immense as evidenced by their four hundred colleges in 1623 and their eight hundred colleges by 1749.

During the second half of the sixteenth century, the Jesuits were the principal agents of the Counter-Reformation in Germany, Austria and Poland. Their beautiful baroque churches in Bavaria and the Rhineland are wonderful examples of the way in which their places of worship became centers of Catholic preaching and spiritual renewal. St. Peter Canisius (1521–1597) published a catechism in 1555 in which he used scriptural quotations to present the Catholic faith clearly and precisely. This catechism became an important sign of the revival of the Catholic faith in southern Germany, where Canisius labored arduously to enlist the support of the local princes and to establish educational institutions.

The Jesuits' vow of obedience to the pope made it possible for them to be deployed anywhere in the world where their services were needed. Their desire to extend the kingdom of Christ beyond western Europe by the preaching of the gospel made them powerful missionaries in the New World and the Far East. When he left Lisbon for India in 1541, the great Jesuit missionary, Francis Xavier (1506–1552), became the first of a long line of members of the society who would dedicate themselves to preaching the gospel throughout the world.

Reforming Popes

The reform-minded Dutchman Adrian VI (1522–1523) succeeded the renaissance pope, Leo X, at his death in 1521. His very short reign made it impossible for him to carry out the strict program of reform that he envisioned as necessary to renew the life of the church in accord with the gospel as Luther and the other reformers were asking.

The powerful Medici pope, Clement VII (1523–1534), involved himself deeply in European politics and eventually was taken prisoner and detained in the Castel San Angelo by the troops of Emperor Charles V in 1527 for seven months. The complex political situation and the actions of the major European rulers severely limited Clement's ability to accomplish any real reforms. For example, Henry VIII appealed to him for an annulment of his marriage to

Catherine of Aragon at the very moment that her nephew, Charles V, was besieging the city of Rome.

Clement's successor, Paul III (1534–1549), sought to implement the long delayed reform of the church by appointing a commission of outstanding cardinals. Some, such as Gasparo Contarini (1483–1542), hoped to come to an understanding with the Protestant reformers, while others, like Giovanni Carafa (1476–1559), believed that there should be no compromise with those promoting heretical doctrine. After long and serious negotiations, Pope Paul was eventually able to call a general council of the church, which opened on December 13, 1545, in the city of Trent.

When Pope Paul III died in 1549, he was succeeded by Pope Julius III (1550–1555). As a cardinal, the new pope had been an active participant in the Council of Trent and believed that any serious efforts at reform had to begin by reorganizing the Roman curia, the central papal bureaucracy. In the sixteenth century, the curia had often attracted greedy and ambitious careerists who were more interested in advancing their own interests than in serving the pastoral needs of the church. Although Pope Julius did not live to see the completion of his reform of the curia, he appointed only reform-minded men to high office in the church.

Cardinal Marcellus Cervini was elected pope in 1555, but died after only twenty-two days in office. He was succeeded by the formidable Cardinal Giovanni Carafa, Pope Paul IV (1555–1559), who with fierce determination and absolute confidence in his approach set out to reform the church singlehandedly. Instead of reconvening the Council of Trent, which had been suspended in 1552, he moved on his own and used the powers of the papacy and the Roman Inquisition to initiate reform and to extirpate heresy. One of the tools employed by Pope Paul IV to defend orthodox Catholic teaching was the *Index of Forbidden Books*.

The Fifth Lateran Council in 1515 had required that authors of books on religious topics obtain permission for the publication of their works. Each book would be read by censors and then, if acceptable from the perspective of Catholic doctrine, it would be given an *imprimatur*, a Latin word meaning "let it be printed." In 1559 Paul IV further extended this control over religious literature by publishing an index or list of books which were judged to be either contrary to or dangerous for an orthodox understanding of the Catholic faith. The Catholic faithful were forbidden to read these books, which included not only the works of the reformers but also the writings of critical Catholics such as the humanist Erasmus. The *Index of*

Forbidden Books was periodically updated and became a permanent feature of post-Tridentine Catholic life until it was abolished in 1966.

The reforming popes of the sixteenth century had a new vision of the church that differed from that of their renaissance predecessors. The latter wanted a powerful and sophisticated papacy, which ruled the church from a Rome gloriously restored as the center of art and culture for the whole of Europe. The reforming popes, on the other hand, hoped to form the church into a highly organized and dedicated group of men and women who would mold society in accord with gospel norms under the direction of the papacy. Their model was the Society of Jesus. However, they would meet active resistance in the implementation of this model from the rulers of Catholic Europe, who intended the church to be an integral part of their own nationalist ideals and not an international body under the direction of the papacy.

The Council of Trent

The nineteenth ecumenical council of the church met at Trent, Italy, in twenty-five sessions over a period of eighteen years (1545–1563). Because the challenge of the Protestant reformers included the whole range of Catholic doctrine and life, the agenda of the council was very broad. Thus disciplinary decrees that regulated the day to day living of the faith were promulgated as well as dogmatic decrees that specified the official teaching of the church on a particular doctrine. The most significant teachings of the council were the following:

1) St. Jerome's Latin translation of the bible, the Vulgate, was to be used as the authoritative version of the scriptures by Roman Catholics.
2) The Catholic bible included some books which had been rejected by the reformers, for example, Tobit, Judith, Wisdom, Ecclesiasticus, Baruch and 1 and 2 Maccabees.
3) The church and not the individual believer was the authoritative interpreter of the scriptures.
4) The basic truths of the Christian faith were to be found both in the bible and in the tradition of the church as they were interpreted by the pope and the bishops under the guidance of the Holy Spirit.
5) Justification by faith alone was not sufficient for salvation. Faith must be a living reality which manifests itself in hope and love through good works.

6) Although original sin wounded human nature, it did not totally corrupt it as the reformers maintained.

7) Grace, as a free gift of God, which was necessary for salvation, has healed human nature and elevated the human person to participation in the divine life.

8) There are seven sacraments instituted by Christ to give
grace: baptism, confirmation, eucharist, penance (reconciliation), extreme unction (anointing of the sick), holy orders and
matrimony. These sacraments truly confer the grace they sig-
nify.

9) Baptism removes the stain of original sin and penance is the
remedy for all post-baptismal sins. The sacrament of penance
(reconciliation) requires: a) sorrow for one's sins with a firm
purpose of amendment; b) confession to a priest; c) the perfor-
mance of the assigned penance.

10) The mass is truly a renewal of the sacrifice of Calvary and
can be offered for the spiritual welfare of both the living and
the dead. Private masses are valid.

11) The body and blood of Christ are truly present in the
eucharist under the appearances of bread and wine, and the
real presence of Christ continues in the reserved Blessed
Sacrament even after the celebration of mass.

12) Since the whole body and blood of Christ are present in the
bread as well as the wine, it is not necessary for the laity to
receive the cup.

13) The mass would continue to be celebrated in Latin.

14) Preaching was to be a part of the eucharist on all Sundays
and holy days.

15) Careful rules of life were laid down for bishops, priests and
religious.

16) Students for the priesthood were to be trained in seminaries.

17) The philosophy and theology of St. Thomas Aquinas were
embraced as a true and exemplary presentation of the
Catholic faith.

The Council of Trent envisioned that the pope through the curia
and the bishops, utilizing national and diocesan resources, would be
able to implement the various decrees. However, implementation
required the cooperation of the Catholic rulers as well, and as a
result the process of renewal was very slow in many parts of
Europe. The Dominican reform pope, Pius V (1566–1572), furthered
the post-Tridentine renewal by issuing a new Roman catechism in

1566, a new breviary in 1568 and a new missal in 1570. The institutional self-understanding of the church articulated at Trent dominated the experience of Roman Catholics for the next four hundred years. Only with the Second Vatican Council (1962–1965) has a new understanding of the church's relationship to the modern world emerged.

Baroque Art

A new art form expressive of the ideas and mentality of the Counter-Reformation emerged at the end of the sixteenth century—the baroque. Grandeur, passion, drama and mystery, themes close to Catholic thought and practice, emerged as dominant motifs in baroque art. As one can see in a great baroque church, such as that of the Gesu, the central Jesuit church in Rome, there is an attempt to integrate architecture, scripture and painting as a way of achieving a unified religious experience.

Massive and emotional statues of the saints were meant to evoke a desire to imitate the fidelity of the heroes and heroines of the past to the Catholic faith. The elaborate and majestic tabernacle, as the focal point of the worship space, proclaimed the Catholic belief in real presence of Christ in the reserved sacrament. The enormous and highly decorated pulpit in the nave of the church emphasized the Catholic commitment to preaching the scriptures rightly interpreted by the church. The beautifully constructed organ, usually in the back choir loft, gave credence to the Catholic belief that all of created reality, such as music and singing, could be sacraments or signs of the divine presence. Richly colored ceiling and wall murals testified to the grandeur of God that filled the whole of creation with life and grace.

Under the artistic genius of painters and sculptors such as Giovanni Bernini (1598–1680) and Peter Paul Rubens (1577–1640), baroque art spread throughout Catholic Europe and the new world. Baroque churches became symbols of the renewed, post-Tridentine Roman Catholic Church.

3

Sixteenth Century Missions

The church by its very nature is missionary since its task or purpose is to continue the mission of Christ, which is the establishment of the kingdom of God throughout history. St. Paul, at the beginning of the church's history, stands as the first great missionary who spent his life engaged in preaching the gospel to those who had not yet heard the good news of Jesus Christ.

After the conversion of the Roman empire to Christianity in the fourth century, the church turned its attention to preaching the gospel to the newly arrived Germanic peoples and those who lived outside of the geographical boundaries of the Roman empire. The period from A.D. 500 to 1000 saw numerous missionaries, such as St. Augustine of Canterbury (d. 604) and St. Boniface (680–754), engaged in establishing new Christian communities throughout Europe. By 1300 the few remaining areas that had continued to remain pagan, such as the Baltic region, had entered the church.

As the monks had been the primary agents of missionary activity between A.D. 500 and 1000, the mendicant friars, especially the Franciscans and the Dominicans, became the great missionaries in the high middle ages. Their extensive activities began in 1220 in the Middle East, Africa and the Orient. However, they came to an abrupt halt as a result of the bubonic plague (1347–1350), which killed almost one-third of the population of western Europe. Missionary activity resumed in the fifteenth century at the dawn of the "age of European exploration."

Spain and Portugal

While in the service of Ferdinand and Isabella of Spain, Christopher Columbus (1451–1506), an Italian from Genoa, in 1492 landed in America, which he named the West Indies since he thought the islands were part of Asia. By this event Spain joined Portugal as a principal participant in the "age of exploration." The objectives of these two maritime powers were conquest, settlement of the lands and evangelization of the peoples they encountered. The indigenous peoples of these lands were open to exploitation by European colonists and they were to become converts to Roman Catholicism.

The Line of Demarcation

To settle disputes about ownership of their newly conquered lands, Spain and Portugal had recourse to Pope Alexander VI in 1493. Pope Alexander drew a line of demarcation from north to south one hundred leagues west of the Azores and the Cape Verde Islands. Under this arrangement, all newly explored lands west of the line belonged to Spain and all lands east belonged to Portugal. The line was redrawn two years later, with the result that all of Central and South America, with the exception of Brazil, belonged to Spain.

When Ferdinand Magellan (1480–1521) circumnavigated the globe in 1521, it became necessary to draw a similar line of demarcation through the Pacific. In this process of division, Portugal became the dominant power of the Far East with the Philippines, named after King Philip II (1556–1598), being assigned to the jurisdiction of Spain.

Latin America

The occupation of the West Indies by the Spanish took place in less than twenty-five years from 1492 to 1515. Within ten years of Columbus' arrival in the Bahamas, there were already twenty-five hundred colonists on the island of Hispaniola (modern Haiti and the Dominican Republic).

In 1521 Hernando Cortes (1485–1547) conquered the great Aztec ruler of Mexico, Montezuma II, and founded Mexico City to replace the former capital, Tenochtitlan. A decade later between 1532 and 1535, Francisco Pizarro (1470–1541) overthrew the Inca leader, Atahualpa, and in 1535 established the city of Lima, Peru. While the Spaniards were involved in their conquest of the Aztec and Inca empires, the Portuguese under Pedro Cabral (1460–1526) were involved in the conquest of Brazil. The city of São Paolo was founded in 1553–1554. Later in the sixteenth century, the Spaniards went on to occupy the regions of the La Plata River (modern Argentina and Paraguay).

The line of demarcation granted Spain and Portugal monopoly over missionary work in the geographical areas assigned to them. The *Patronato Real* gave the Spanish kings considerable power over the church in the new world, including the authority to establish dioceses and to appoint bishops. As the Catholic monarchs of Spain had organized the *reconquista* against Islam, so they now launched the *conquista* against the native religions of Latin America. Indians who would not recognize the authority of Spain and convert to Roman Catholicism were liable to severe penalties. Conquered land was seen as a royal fief, *encomienda*, and the Indians were forced to work the land in return for protection and the basic necessities of life.

The methods of evangelization utilized by the Spanish missionaries followed from the theology of the time. Since baptism was necessary for salvation, conversion to the Catholic faith was the goal of missionary activity. Because they wanted the natives of the new world to be saved, the Franciscan and Dominican missionaries who accompanied the *conquistadores* often risked their lives in preaching to the indigenous peoples. Although large numbers of the population received baptism as a result of the work of the missionaries, they often had only the most superficial understanding of the Christian faith.

The early missionaries made valiant efforts to learn the native languages of their converts and tried to teach them at least the rudiments of reading and writing. Beyond the basic level of education, the missionaries also established institutions of higher learning in Mexico in 1544 and in Peru in 1600.

The Europeans viewed the native peoples as inferior, however, when it was a question of full participation in the sacramental life of the church. The missionaries allowed them to receive the sacraments of baptism, penance and matrimony. But only the bishop could permit someone to receive holy communion after he had ascertained that the individual truly understood what he or she was doing.

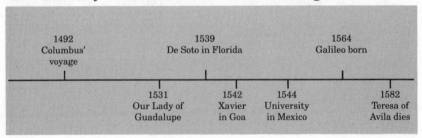

| 1492 | 1539 | 1564 |
| Columbus' voyage | De Soto in Florida | Galileo born |

| 1531 | 1542 | 1544 | 1582 |
| Our Lady of Guadalupe | Xavier in Goa | University in Mexico | Teresa of Avila dies |

A similar attitude prevailed in regard to the sacrament of holy orders or priesthood. The lack of enthusiasm for an indigenous clergy would have serious ramifications for the long-term development of the Latin American church. In 1555 a local synod or council in Mexico forbade ordaining Indians, mestizos (half Indian/half Spanish) or mulattoes (half Spanish/half negroid) to the priesthood. A local synod in Lima in 1585 allowed local bishops to decide the question for their own dioceses, but in fact only a few mestizos and no Indians were ever ordained. Mestizos and mulattos were finally being admitted to the priesthood throughout Latin America by 1772, but the first Indian was not ordained to the priesthood until 1794.

Bartolomé de Las Casas

While some missionaries protested the injustices perpetrated by the *conquistadores* upon the native people, others preferred to ignore the situation or to remain silent out of fear. One of those who chose to speak out in defense of the rights of the Indians was Bartolomé de Las Casas (1474–1566). Originally a lawyer, Las Casas experienced the *encomienda* system first-hand in Cuba. Impressed by the protest against the abuse of the natives by some Dominican missionaries, Las Casas decided to enter the Order of Preachers and was the first priest ordained in the new world in 1510.

Las Casas crossed the Atlantic fourteen times in an effort to correct the evils of an unjust colonial policy and to better the lot of the indigenous peoples. He argued forcefully against the opinion that certain individuals or races were naturally inferior to others. The fiery Dominican was successful in influencing Emperor Charles V to pass new laws in 1542–1543 which prohibited Indian slavery and recognized them as being equal to the colonizers under the law. Many colonists bitterly opposed the work of Las Casas because they saw it as weakening the *encomienda* system. Las Casas also maintained that the rights of the natives should be respected by the missionaries so that they would not be forced to convert to Roman Catholicism.

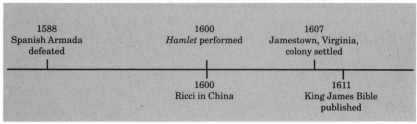

1588	1600	1607
Spanish Armada defeated	*Hamlet* performed	Jamestown, Virginia, colony settled
	1600	1611
	Ricci in China	King James Bible published

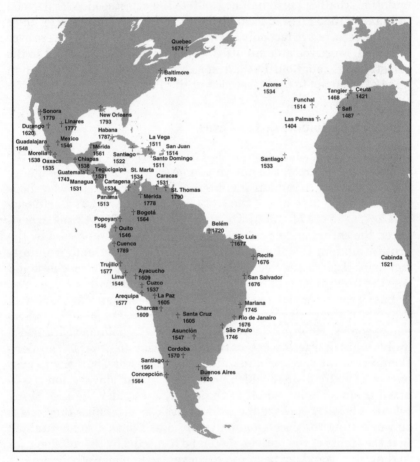

16th – 18th Century Missions

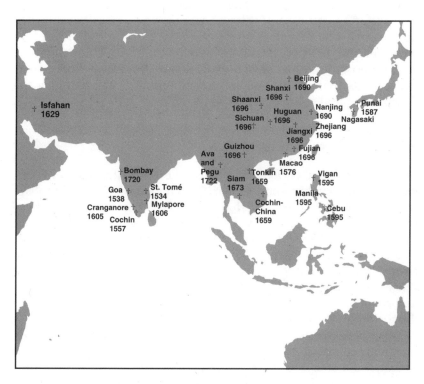

16th – 18th Century Missions

Named bishop of Chiapa in 1543, he worked diligently to see that the new laws were enforced, but he was only partially successful in these efforts. In 1552 Las Casas returned to Spain where he spent the rest of his life writing letters and treatises in defense of the rights of native peoples. Because he denounced the evils perpetrated against them and sought to defend their dignity, Las Casas has been called the "Apostle to the Indians." Although he was a man of justice and integrity, he was also given to exaggeration and generalization when making his case against the *conquistadores*. Unfortunately, historians of this period have sometimes used his works without sufficient objectivity to render harsh and negative judgments on the Spanish colonial enterprise as a whole.

The Reductions

During the colonial period, missionaries at different times and in different places sought to protect Christian native peoples by establishing villages or "reductions" for them. The most famous of these reductions were those run by the Jesuits in Paraguay. Gathered into their villages, which were separated from the mainstream of the lives of the colonists, the natives were able to have control over their own lives under the oversight of the missionaries. With a parish church, schools and workshops in each village, they lived and worked as free and community-oriented Christians. The reductions were eventually destroyed by those who wished to reduce the natives to slavery in order to maintain the work force necessary for the *encomienda* system.

While the reduction system was at times patronizing and authoritarian, it did offer a humane alternative to the structural brutalities present in the *encomienda* system. The Spanish missionaries in Latin America and the Portuguese missionaries in Brazil often strove heroically to make the good news of the gospel a lived reality for the people whom they served. Their ministry certainly had its share of failures, but there were also some splendid examples of true Christian love of neighbor given by countless men and women in their proclamation of the gospel, as evidenced by the Dominicans, St. Rose of Lima (1586–1617) and St. Martin de Porres (1579–1639).

Africa

The church that flourished in North Africa in the first six centuries of the Christian era had been reduced by the Islamic conquests of the seventh century to a few struggling communities in Egypt and Ethiopia. In the fifteenth century, the Portuguese made their first exploratory visits down the coast of West Africa. Bartolomeo Diaz (1450–1500) sailed around the Cape of Good Hope in 1486–1487, and Vasco da Gama (1469–1524) sailed up the coast of East Africa and reached India in 1498.

The Portuguese directed their energies primarily toward trade and had little interest initially in missionary efforts. For them Africa was only a stop on the way to the Indies, so they did not penetrate the African interior but simply established forts and trading posts along the coast. The names given by the Portuguese to the coastal areas—Gold Coast, Ivory Coast and Slave Coast—point to their reason for being in Africa and also indicate why the natives would be resistant to subsequent missionary efforts.

The first mission to the Congo set out in 1490. Although the missionaries were successful at first, the bad example of the Portuguese traders and the involvement of the missionaries in the slave trade eventually destroyed the mission. The Portuguese slave trade was a serious barrier to missionary work. Between 1575 and 1591 more than fifty-two thousand slaves were exported from Angola. Nevertheless, even in the midst of this injustice, the church was established in Angola in 1558 and in Mozambique in 1612.

Asia

In 1500 Pedro Cabral, accompanied by missionaries, landed in southern India. There they encountered a Christian community— the Thomas Christians—who traced their religious origins back to St. Thomas the Apostle, who in their belief was the first to preach the gospel in India. Since they had been isolated from the rest of the Christian world for centuries, they had no links to the church in western Europe. After the Portuguese had established Goa as their commercial and ecclesial base in India, the archbishop of Goa was able to bring the Thomas Christians into communion with the Roman Catholic Church.

In 1542 the great Jesuit missionary, St. Francis Xavier (1506–1552), arrived in Goa. Before his arrival many of the natives along the Coromandel coast had been baptized *en masse*—a common pastoral practice among the early missionaries. Xavier spent his time visiting the local villages trying to instruct these new converts and preparing others to receive baptism. After seven years of missionary activity in various parts of Asia, he decided to focus his attention on Japan.

When he arrived in 1549, Xavier encountered a highly civilized culture that looked with suspicion upon foreigners. Previously missionary strategy had assumed that Christianity and western culture would simply replace the customs and traditions of the indigenous peoples. However, Xavier quickly realized that in many ways Japanese culture was superior to that of western Europe. Hence the church had to be separated from its European perspective and to take on the positive aspects of Japanese culture if the gospel was to be proclaimed. Through such a process of cultural adaptation or inculturation, Xavier and his fellow Jesuit missionaries were able to make many converts among both the nobility and the common people of Japan.

By respecting Japanese culture and customs, the Jesuits evangelized all levels of society and even established a native clergy between 1549 and 1587. Political changes and the arrival of Spanish Franciscan and Dominican missionaries altered the government's attitude toward Christianity, however, and missionaries were ordered to leave Japan. The profession of the Christian faith now became a capital crime and thousands of Japanese Christians were put to death between 1597 and 1637. Although a handful of Christians were able to preserve their faith in secret from generation to generation, Japan closed itself off from Western influence and Christian missionaries from 1640 until 1859.

Although he had hoped to bring the gospel message to China, St. Francis Xavier died on the island of Sancian, off the China coast, in 1549, with his dream unfulfilled. The Portuguese established a trading colony on the island of Macao at the mouth of the Canton River in 1557. From here another great Jesuit missionary, Matteo Ricci (1552–1610), fulfilled Xavier's dream by entering China in 1600. Through his knowledge of European scientific instruments, such as clocks and maps, he was able to gain the support of Chinese officials, who permitted him to establish a small Christian community.

Like the Japanese, the Chinese had a highly sophisticated culture and mistrusted any foreign influences within their society. Hence Ricci faced the challenge of inculturation in his missionary activity. In establishing the church within Chinese culture, he allowed his new converts to retain any customs that were not contrary to the basic tenets of the Christian faith. Since the Chinese viewed veneration of their ancestors as a civil duty and not an act of religious worship, Ricci permitted his converts to continue practices associated with such veneration, including the homage paid to Confucius.

Spanish missionaries began establishing the church in the Philippine Islands soon after their discovery by Ferdinand Magellan in 1522. Here the missionaries did not find a highly developed civilization as they had in India, Japan and China, so they used an approach similar to that employed in Latin America. They established village mission stations that included schools and hospitals where the population could be introduced to European culture as well as the Christian faith. The Filipinos were a welcoming and peaceful people, who very quickly embraced the Catholic faith that the missionaries presented to them, and they soon constituted the single largest Catholic population in the Far East. Manila, the capital of the Philippines, became an archdiocese in 1595, and the Dominicans established the University of Santo Tomás in 1619.

4

Seventeenth Century Christian Europe

By the beginning of the seventeenth century, denominational stances had hardened and Europe was now deeply divided by religious differences. The various Protestant traditions had now incarnated themselves in state and local churches with their own doctrines, forms of worship and organizational structures. Following the completion of the Council of Trent in 1563, the Roman Catholic Church had embarked on an aggressive program of reform and renewal that was successful not only in Catholic countries but also in areas that had opted for the Reformation.

England

James I Stuart (1603–1625), successor of Elizabeth I, strongly insisted on the divine right of kings, and in so doing he alienated various groups within the parliament. The king made a significant contribution to the Anglican tradition when he authorized the publication of the King James version of the bible in 1611. In an attempt to ameliorate their situation as a persecuted minority, some Catholics plotted to overthrow the government. In 1605 the rebels planned to blow up the houses of parliament and then seize control of the government. The authorities became aware of the plan, known as the Gunpowder Plot, and the leader of the rebels, Guy Fawkes, was captured and executed. Because of this act of treason committed by Catholics, the persecution of adherents of the old faith intensified during the reign of James I.

Puritans, who had grudgingly conformed to Anglicanism during the reign of Elizabeth I, hoped that James would be more attuned to their goal of further purifying the state church of its more Catholic elements and moving in a Calvinist direction. They were, however, to be disappointed, for James was fully committed to the Catholic elements, such as the episcopacy, within the Anglican tradition.

In their dissatisfaction with the state church, a number of Puritans broke away and formed their own independent congregations; hence they came to be called Congregationalists. Persecuted in England, they fled to Holland and eventually immigrated in large numbers to New England. Thomas Helwys (1550–1616), a Puritan who had fled to Holland with his co-religionists, split away from the group in 1612 and returned to England. With his followers he formed the first congregation of English Baptists. Adhering to Calvin's theology and practicing adult baptism, these Protestant Christians became a significant new religious movement in England.

By 1640 the Puritans who remained in England had gained sufficient political power to be able to dominate the English parliament. Civil war broke out in 1642, pitting Puritans against Anglicans. The Puritan forces were victorious under their leader, Oliver Cromwell (1599–1658), and King Charles I (1625–1649) was beheaded in 1649. During the rule of Oliver Cromwell, known as the Commonwealth (1649–1660), both Catholics and Anglicans were subject to severe legal penalties.

George Fox (1624–1691) was an outspoken critic of Cromwell's bloody tactics. After a long inner struggle, in 1646 he experienced what he called the "inner light of the living Christ." He subsequently founded the Society of Friends, later known as the Quakers, who were strong advocates of non-violence.

After the death of Cromwell, the son of the executed King Charles I was restored to the English throne. Charles II (1660–1685) was a strong supporter of the Anglican Church and tolerated Roman Catholics. He was succeeded by his brother, James II (1685–1688), who had become a convert to Roman Catholicism in 1670.

Determined to restore the Roman Catholic Church in England and Scotland, James II failed to perceive the depth of the commitment of the majority of the people to the Protestant faith. His enthusiasm for restoring Catholicism only served to galvanize the resistance of his enemies, and after three years he was overthrown by parliament. James was replaced by his Protestant daughter, Mary, and her husband, Prince William of Orange (1689–1702). The new Protestant rulers were tolerant toward the various Protestant denominations that now existed in England and Scotland, but never again would a Roman Catholic be permitted to come to the throne.

The Anglican Church was now firmly established as the state church of England. The Puritan cause had been severely weakened by events during the period of the Commonwealth, but two important Puritan literary works continued to be read widely: John Bunyan's *Pilgrim's Progress* and John Milton's *Paradise Lost*.

France

Implementation of the decrees of the Council of Trent in France centered on a strong concern for the education and reform of the clergy. Jean-Jacques Olier (1608–1657) founded the Society of Saint Sulpice in 1642 to educate future priests. The seminary at Saint Sulpice became a model for training future pastors in the ideals of the Catholic reform inaugurated at the Council of Trent. Another strong advocate of clerical reform, St. John Eudes (1601–1680), was, along with St. Margaret Mary Alacoque (1647–1690), deeply committed to promoting devotion to the Sacred Heart of Jesus. This devotion challenged the Protestant rejection of symbols and earthly realities as proper media for the communication of divine truths.

The author of the *Introduction to the Devout Life*, St. Francis de Sales (1567–1622), cooperated with St. Jane Frances de Chantal (1572–1641) in establishing the Visitation Nuns, who engaged in education. St. Vincent de Paul (1580–1660) founded the Daughters of Charity to provide for the needs of the sick and the poor. Both these religious communities of women were influential in reviving the vitality of French Catholicism in the seventeenth century.

The reforms of the Council of Trent encountered opposition when they moved beyond the ordinary educational and charitable ministries of the church and addressed the appointment of bishops or the relation between the church and the French monarchy. Louis XIV (1643–1715) espoused the theory of the divine right of kings and opposed any outside interference in French internal affairs including oversight of the French or Gallican church. He insisted on his rights and resisted any attempts by Rome to intervene in religious matters. In 1682, under pressure from the king, the French clergy issued the "Four Gallican Articles." In this document they affirmed the absolute rights of the monarch over all aspects of the life of the church in France and saw the pope only as a distant sign of Catholic unity, who had no real power over the Gallican church.

In 1685 Louis XIV repealed the Edict of Nantes that had guaranteed religious toleration to French Protestants (Huguenots). This led to a mass exodus of members of the Huguenot community and deprived France of some her most gifted citizens.

Jansenism

The Council of Trent condemned the teaching of John Calvin which maintained that human nature was absolutely corrupt and that God willed to damn some individuals. In the second half of the sixteenth century, a theological controversy arose between the Dominicans and the Jesuits over the question of predestination and God's grace. Jesuits accused Dominicans of being Calvinists, and Dominicans accused Jesuits of being Pelagians, who believed that the human person could gain salvation without the assistance of God's grace.

Another stage of the controversy began in 1640 when *Augustinus*, a work on St. Augustine's doctrine of grace, written by Cornelius Jansen (1585–1638), bishop of Ypres, was published posthumously. Although Rome condemned the work because it seemed to espouse Calvinist teachings, the convent of reformed nuns at Port Royal in France became a center for Jansenist spirituality. Under the leadership of Mother Angelique Arnauld (1591–1661), the life of the sisters was very severe and penitential since they believed that it was absolutely necessary to try to control corrupt human nature. The Jansenist supporters of Mother Angelique severely criticized the Jesuits for being too lenient in their spiritual teaching because they believed in the basic goodness of human nature and the freedom of human activity. One of the popularizers of the Jansenist outlook was the philosopher, Blaise Pascal (1623–1662), who constantly attacked the Jesuits for their supposed laxism.

Eventually King Louis XIV moved against the Jansenists and closed Port Royal in 1709 because he saw them as a threat to the political and religious unity of France. Although the Jansenist movement itself eventually died out, within Roman Catholic spirituality it left a legacy of distrust of human nature, fear of freedom and the need for harsh penance as part of Christian life.

The Thirty Years War

By the beginning of the seventeenth century, the Holy Roman Empire was deeply divided along denominational lines. The Peace of Augsburg in 1555 had accepted the principle that each ruler could decide the religion of his territory. People who did not wish to accept the religion of the ruler were free to move. While Austria and Hungary remained predominantly Catholic and the Scandinavian countries were Lutheran, Switzerland, Bohemia and Germany were divided between Catholics, Lutherans and Calvinists. In such a volatile religious situation, a single incident could easily ignite this powder keg of denominational antagonism.

Such an incident occurred in 1606 when a Catholic religious procession was attacked by Protestants in the city of Donauworth. A year later, Maximilian, the Catholic duke of Bavaria, conquered the city and forced Protestants to convert to Roman Catholicism. To protect themselves, Protestant rulers organized the "Evangelical Union" and Catholic rulers followed suit by forming the "Catholic League." War broke out in 1618 when Protestant nobles in Bohemia threw the imperial commissioners out of the windows of the Hradschin Palace—an event known in history as the Defenestration of Prague—and drove out the Jesuits as a sign of their revolt against Austria.

The Bohemian nobles invited Frederick V, the Calvinist ruler of the Palatinate in Germany, to be their ruler. The Catholic League invaded Bohemia, and after conquering the rebellious forces, their leaders forced all Protestants either to convert to Roman Catholicism or to leave the country. It is estimated that during the course of the Thirty Years War the population of Bohemia dwindled from three million to eight hundred thousand.

Eventually the war came to involve the major European nations. The Protestant rulers of Germany, Sweden, Denmark and England were joined by Catholic France, who feared the growing power of the Catholic Hapsburgs in Spain and Austria. Although peace was finally concluded by the Treaty of Westphalia in 1648, Germany was left in ruins. Through the treaty, France and Sweden extended their territories, and for all practical purposes the Holy Roman Empire became a fiction.

The treaty once more adopted the principles of the Peace of Augsburg so that rulers and people were allowed to choose to be Catholic, Lutheran or Calvinist. The fact that religion had been the cause of so much destruction and cruelty posed a serious question for many thoughtful people. With the Treaty of Westphalia, the modern secular state began to develop as it became clear that the civil power could not be involved in defending the claims of diverse religious groups by armed conflicts.

5

Seventeenth Century Missions

The Congregation for the Propagation of the Faith

During the sixteenth century, missionary work had been more or less turned over to the two Catholic nations who had pioneered the age of exploration, Portugal and Spain. The *Patronato* in Spain and the *Padroado* in Portugal gave the government almost total control over all aspects of church life in the newly explored lands. This system led to abuses such as dioceses being left vacant for years so that either the king could use their revenues or bishops could remain at court and never actually go to their dioceses.

In an attempt to regain control over the church's missionary efforts and to reform abuses, Pope Gregory XV (1621–1623) established the Congregation for the Propagation of the Faith in 1622. The pope hoped to limit the power of secular governments over the missions so that Christianity would not be seen as another aspect of colonialism. The congregation began naming bishops, often called vicars apostolic, to mission dioceses to offset royal patronage. Because the missionary efforts of the different religious orders often became the occasion for scandalous competition, the congregation recruited diocesan priests for the missions and established special seminaries for their training. The congregation was also concerned for the development of an indigenous clergy so that the church would not be a foreign institution in its pastoral leadership.

India

Along with Francis Xavier and Matteo Ricci, Robert de Nobili (1577–1656) was one of the great pioneering missionaries of the Orient. When Nobili arrived in southern India in 1604, there was great reluctance on the part of members of the higher caste to associate with Christianity because of its identification with the lower castes. Like Ricci in China, Nobili believed that people should not have to abandon their culture in order to become Christians. In the spirit of inculturation, he adapted himself to the Indian way of life by learning the language and following Hindu customs. His approach was very effective because many high caste Indians, Brahmins, who had thus far rejected the gospel, asked for instruction in the Christian faith. By 1609 he was able to build a church for his new converts.

Feeling that Christianity was not compatible with a caste system, many criticized Nobili's methods of evangelizing. He responded by suggesting that different missionaries be trained for work among the various castes with the hope that common participation in the faith by members of all castes would eventually work toward remedying the injustices which the system involved. It is estimated that Nobili's converts numbered one hundred thousand.

China

The German Jesuit, Adam Schall von Bell (1591–1666), succeeded Matteo Ricci in working among the Chinese at the imperial court. Schall was a learned astronomer and was appointed to the board which regulated the Chinese calendar. Although a period of confusion and persecution of Christians followed the collapse of the Ming Dynasty in 1644, the missions in China experienced a new period of growth and development around the middle of the seventeenth century.

In 1647 Rome named Lo Wen-Tsao to be the vicar apostolic for northern China. He was the first Chinese priest to be named a bishop until the twentieth century. Many of the more traditional missionaries worried that, as a native Chinese, the bishop would be more tolerant of the accommodation to Chinese culture that the Jesuits had been developing, such as the celebration of the mass in Chinese. The struggle between traditional and progressive

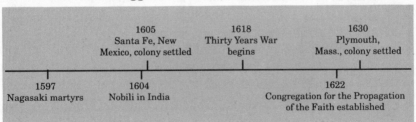

	1605 Santa Fe, New Mexico, colony settled	1618 Thirty Years War begins	1630 Plymouth, Mass., colony settled
1597 Nagasaki martyrs	1604 Nobili in India		1622 Congregation for the Propagation of the Faith established

approaches to missionary activity came to a head in the "Chinese Rites" controversy.

The Jesuits had labored for many years in China and were respected by the upper classes for their scientific knowledge. Members of the Society of Jesus made every effort to learn Chinese and to accommodate the gospel to the legitimate customs of the culture. However, they would not permit any practices that were clearly in conflict with the Catholic faith. When the Spanish Franciscans and Dominicans arrived in the 1630s, they pursued traditional methods of evangelization and accused the Jesuits of making unwarranted adaptations of the faith in order to gain converts. Fearful of the progressive approach of the Jesuits, Rome issued a decree in 1704 which condemned their method of evangelization and forbade the veneration of ancestors and Confucius. The more conservative approach of the Franciscans and the Dominicans, which often confused Christianity with western European culture, became the rule in missionary practice for the next two centuries.

Southeast Asia

The work of Christian missionaries in Asia was extremely difficult not only because the physical conditions were harsh but also because of the hostile reception which the missionaries received from local rulers. Torture and martyrdom were not uncommon for those who "went to the ends of the earth" to preach and baptize. In India, China and Japan, the missionaries encountered not only sophisticated cultures but also the ancient world religions of Hinduism, Confucianism and Buddhism.

In 1623 Alexander de Rhodes, a Spanish Jesuit, began missionary work in South Vietnam. After he was expelled from there, he journeyed to North Vietnam. By the time he was permanently expelled from the north in 1645, he had made an important contribution toward the establishment of an indigenous church in Vietnam.

Rhodes' great contribution to missionary work was his use of

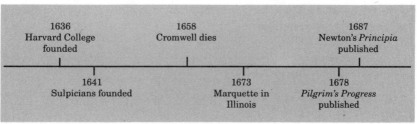

| 1636 Harvard College founded | 1658 Cromwell dies | 1687 Newton's *Principia* published |
| 1641 Sulpicians founded | 1673 Marquette in Illinois | 1678 *Pilgrim's Progress* published |

native catechists. He trained his first converts to become preachers and teachers of their new faith so that they could share the gospel they had received with their own neighbors. These catechists prayed together, lived celibate lives and shared their goods in common. After Rhodes was finally expelled, these lay catechists continued their work of evangelization and kept the faith alive until the next wave of missionaries arrived.

Africa

Missionary activity in Africa during the seventeenth century met, at best, with mixed results. Poor climate, unhealthy living conditions and the need to travel vast distances often proved injurious to the health of even the strongest missionaries. The traditional approach of importing western European culture with Christianity and the identification of the missionaries with the colonial powers seriously limited their ability to convince the native population of the good news of the gospel.

Missionary work in Muslim north Africa was usually limited to ministry among European traders and captured Christian slaves. Missionaries were forbidden to preach to the Muslim population, and rarely would a Muslim even think about converting to Christianity since such an act would make the new convert liable to the death penalty.

The main impediment to the work of missionaries in the Portuguese colonies on the west African coast was the slave trade. Although some bishops and missionaries protested this injustice, at times church officials participated in the system by having slaves on their own lands. The slaves there, however, were treated well so that the social institution of slavery itself was not often questioned.

Although Portuguese missionaries initially did some evangelization in south Africa, the arrival of Dutch Protestants in the seventeenth century ended preaching in that area. The Dominicans and the Jesuits worked in east Africa in what would be modern Zimbabwe and Kenya, but their efforts were hindered by the spread of Islam in those regions.

Latin America

The interference of the state in the affairs of the church in Latin America during the seventeenth and eighteenth centuries was a major obstacle to effective evangelization. The extension and implementation of the *Patronato Real* not only negated Rome's authority over church life but also prevented the development of an indigenous clergy. The church in Latin America was almost totally dependent on clergy coming from Spain. When they arrived from Spain, they were often frustrated in their pastoral efforts by a lack of cooperation on the part of civil authorities and by restrictive government regulations.

In Brazil the original settlements had been on the coast, and only gradually did the Portuguese move into the interior of the country. The problems of the church in Brazil involved not only the difficulties resulting from *Padroado* but also the injustices flowing from slavery. Missionaries sought to minister to the slaves and to protect the indigenous peoples from the system. Enslavement of the Indians was finally forbidden in 1758, but enslavement of the black Africans continued until the end of the nineteenth century.

A great deal of thought was given to the issue of the natural rights of the native peoples and the responsibilities of the church and civil government to protect these rights. The Christian faith recognized that the "Indians" were the children of God and deserved to be treated with dignity and respect.

During the Spanish colonial period in Latin America from 1519 to 1821, European art and architecture flourished. The baroque style of architecture was used in numerous cathedrals, churches, monasteries and convents.

The church in Latin America was responsible for education and social welfare and hence played a very significant role in the life of the people. During the colonial period, twenty-five universities and fifty-six colleges were founded. But because the church was dependent on the Spanish government for personnel and finances, it was also in danger of simply becoming the education and welfare department of the state. Church and state had become so intertwined, for example, that the seal of confession did not bind if the matter confessed concerned the life of the king or his representative. The full implications of this complicated pattern of relationship between the church and the Spanish government would become very evident in the nineteenth century as the nations of Latin America declared their independence from Spain.

New Spain

In 1526 the Spaniards founded a colony in what is now the state of Virginia, but it did not succeed. The first permanent colony was established at St. Augustine in Florida in 1565. The area that is now the continental United States formed part of New Spain, which extended from Panama up through California. Since the heart of the Spanish empire in the New World was Central and South America, the North American part of New Spain received less attention. However, exploration and colonization did continue.

Don Juan de Onate claimed the territory that is now the southwestern United States for the king of Spain when he founded a colony in New Mexico in 1598. Missionaries soon began their efforts to preach the gospel to the natives of Texas, New Mexico, Arizona and California. Franciscan and Jesuit missionaries used the traditional Spanish approach to evangelization by building churches, schools and clinics.

One of the most famous of the early missionaries was the Austrian Jesuit, Eusebio Kino, who arrived in Mexico in 1681. He labored for twenty-four years in the southwestern United States, where he baptized over four thousand people. In his missionary tours, he carefully mapped the terrain that he traveled and was the first European to discover that lower California was a peninsula and not an island.

In 1690 a Franciscan friar, Damian Massonet, founded the mission of San Francisco de Los Tejas in Texas, but it was soon abandoned. A permanent mission, the Alamo, was established at San Antonio a few years later. Although the *padres* worked very hard, they found it difficult to make many converts among the Comanches and the Apaches.

While the Jesuits began missionary work at a very early date in lower California, upper California remained virtually forgotten until 1741. When the Russian explorer, Vitus Bering, claimed the area for the czar in the mid-eighteenth century, the Spaniards were spurred to establish their own claims by colonizing the territory. Part of the strategy used by the Spanish in their colonizing efforts was the establishment of twenty-one missions from San Diego in the south to San Francisco in the north. The first of these missions, San Diego de Alcala, was founded by the Franciscan Junipero Serra (1713–1784) in 1769. Father Serra was a holy and dedicated missionary, but he was also a man of his times who treated the natives in a paternalistic way. The chain of missions founded by Serra, with their characteristic style of architecture, became important centers of evangelization and culture. The work of Spanish missionaries in what is now the United States spanned over three centuries from 1520 to 1854. By the latter date, all Spanish land which would become part of the continental United States, had been annexed, purchased or conquered.

The major symbol of the heritage of Spanish Catholicism within the United States is Our Lady of Guadalupe. From the perspective of the Catholic faith, the Blessed Virgin Mary appeared to an Indian, Juan Diego, near Mexico City in 1531 and asked him to build a church in her honor on the site. Since he needed a sign, she told him to pick the roses which had grown out of season on the hillside and take them to the bishop of Mexico City. When he opened his cloak containing the roses in the presence of the bishop, all saw an image of the Virgin with the features of an Aztec woman etched on the inside of the cloak. The cloak with the image of the Blessed Virgin was later enshrined above the altar of the great church which was built on the site of the apparition. Our Lady of Guadalupe came to be a symbol of God's protection and love for the native people and the Spaniards who called New Spain their home.

New France

Although Jacques Cartier claimed what is now Canada for the king of France when he sailed into the Gulf of St. Lawrence in 1534, exploration and colonization did not begin until the seventeenth century. Only after peace had been restored, following the sixteenth century wars of religion was it possible for France once more to look to the new world. In 1608 Samuel Champlain (1567–1635) founded the city of Quebec as the first French colony in Canada. French missionaries, especially members of the Society of Jesus, labored to implant the church in this vast new land by preaching to the native peoples of the region: the Hurons, the Algonquins and the Iroquois.

The missionary work of the Jesuits was seriously hindered by the hostility that existed between the various tribes, such as the Hurons and the Iroquois. Among the victims of the war between the Iroquois and the Hurons in 1648–1649 were St. Jean de Brebeuf and his four Jesuit companions. The Hurons were finally forced to leave the northeast, and the Jesuit missionaries went with them to the Wisconsin area. In 1673 a Jesuit missionary working in the Great

Lakes region, Fr. Jacques Marquette, and his companion, Louis Joliet, became the first Europeans to discover the Mississippi River.

The Jesuits also attempted to work among the Iroquois, but with little success. In 1643 the Iroquois captured and tortured St. Isaac Jogues and several companions. Although Jogues escaped, he chose to return to his efforts at evangelizing the Iroquois, but they blamed him for a crop failure and he was martyred near Auriesville, New York, in 1649.

A young Mohawk girl, Kateri Tekakwitha, was received into the church by the Jesuit missionary, Fr. Jacques de Lamberville, on Easter Sunday, 1676. She died four years later with a reputation for great holiness and heroic charity in the midst of persecution. This remarkable native woman was declared blessed by Pope John Paul II in 1980. Other remarkable women, who witnessed to the values of the Christian faith in New France, were Marie of the Incarnation, an Ursuline nun, who came to Canada in 1639, and Marguerite Bourgeoys who founded a community of religious, the Sisters of Notre Dame, to educate women.

The first bishop of Canada, François Montmorency de Laval (1623–1708), arrived in Quebec in 1659. A strong leader and pastor, Laval did all he could to strengthen the faith of his small flock and founded a seminary to train priests for his vast diocese. The staunch loyalty to the church which he inculcated in his people was to be a mainstay of French-speaking Catholics after Canada became part of the British empire in 1759.

From 1699 through 1766, New France also eventually came to include territory which now constitutes the states of Louisiana and Mississippi. Because slavery came to be part of the lifestyle of the French colonists in this area, the church was always hindered in its missionary efforts. Although the church worked hard to better living and working conditions for slaves, it did not actually challenge slavery as an institution.

Creole society in Louisiana was composed of French, Spanish and Acadians. The latter were French men and women driven out of Nova Scotia by the British, who settled eventually in Louisiana where they became the ancestors of today's Cajuns. The large number of black slaves, who had come from Africa via the Caribbean, and the settlers of European descent became part of a new cultural experience when Louisiana was purchased by the United States in 1803. The Catholicism of Louisiana, visible in New Orleans and the Cajun country, and the vital and active church in eastern Canada stand as strong witness to the toil and devotion of countless missionaries, who often gave their lives in an attempt to preach the gospel in New France.

New England

Sir Walter Raleigh attempted in 1585, without success, to establish a colony in the territory of Virginia, so named in honor of the virgin queen, Elizabeth I. The first colony was finally established at Jamestown, Virginia, in 1607. While the principal motive for the colony was economic, the English were also concerned that the Anglican Church serve as a bastion for the Protestant faith in the new world. The soil of Virginia was ideal for growing tobacco, and in 1619 the colonists began importing African slaves to work in the tobacco fields. Like the Catholic Church in the new world, the Church of England tried to mitigate the worst aspects of slavery, but it did not oppose slavery as such.

The other English colonies founded in the south, such as the Carolinas and Georgia, which were intended to stop the advance of the Spanish from Florida, were settled mainly by Anglicans. Some French Huguenots, English Baptists and Quakers settled in the south, but the main opponents of the established church, the Puritans, looked farther north to find a place for their own colonizing efforts.

The first group of Puritans to reach the new world, the Pilgrims, landed at Plymouth, Massachusetts, in 1630. King Charles I had chartered the Massachusetts Bay Company in 1629, and by 1641 at least twenty thousand Puritans had immigrated to New England, founding towns all along the rugged Massachusetts coast. Settlements in Connecticut made New Haven an important center for Puritan life and thought.

Strong in their theological opinions, the Puritans permitted no divergence from the established patterns of thinking. Because they thought of themselves as the sons and daughters of light in a world filled with darkness and the power of Satan, they were especially on the watch for anything that seemed to indicate the presence of the evil one in their midst. Idol gossip in Salem, Massachusetts, led to the deaths of fourteen women and six men for witchcraft.

Because they opposed the rigidity of the Puritan way of life and thought, many who came to the new world to find religious freedom left Massachusetts to establish their own settlements. Roger Williams founded a colony at Providence on Narragansett Bay in

1636 as a place for religious freedom. Similar foundations were soon made at Portsmouth and Newport. In 1644 Williams obtained recognition for his colony of Rhode Island and Providence Plantations from the English parliament. The church which Williams established soon became Baptist in faith and served as the mother church for many other Baptist churches in the colonies.

Pennsylvania

William Penn (1644–1718) used land given him by King Charles II to establish a colony in 1682 that would be a "holy experiment" based on true religious tolerance. He intended this colony to be a haven for his persecuted co-religionists, who were members of the Society of Friends, popularly known as Quakers. The Society of Friends had been established in England in 1652 by George Fox (1624–1691).

Fox rejected most of the elements of organized Christianity, such as creeds, sacraments, and ministers, and concentrated on the "inner light of the living Christ" by which a person truly experienced God. Only through this light could the scriptures be understood. Worship was not meant to be preaching or celebration of the sacraments, but a simple meeting of "friends" who listened together in silence and waited upon the inspiration of the Holy Spirit to enlighten them. At their meetings, the "friends" often began to tremble as they felt themselves to be moved by the Holy Spirit and sought to witness to the inspiration they had received. Thus they came to be called Quakers because of their religious enthusiasm.

In founding the Society of Friends, Fox intended that they would be deeply committed to the service of others and to a life of non-violence. The pacifism of the Quakers and their refusal to swear oaths or uncover their heads before anyone but God caused them to be persecuted because they were seen not only as opponents of the Church of England but also as subversive of the good order of the nation. It was persecution that led Quakers under the leadership of William Penn to try to find a place where they could live their faith in peace. In calling the capital of his new colony Philadelphia, the city of brotherly love, William Penn indicated his hopes for this "holy experiment" upon which he and the other members of the Society of Friends had embarked.

Maryland

In 1632 King Charles I granted land in the new world to Cecil Calvert, Lord Baltimore, as a place of refuge for the harassed Catholics of England. The first Catholic colonists arrived in 1634. Because their number was small, the Catholics were soon outnumbered by Protestants, who had also come to Maryland. By the end of the seventeenth century, Anglicanism was the official religion of the colony and the Catholics found themselves in a situation of disenfranchisement similar to that which they had known in England. Only after the American revolution would the small Catholic population in the thirteen English colonies know what true religious freedom meant.

By 1690 the total population of the English colonies was about two hundred and fifty thousand. Most of this number professed either Anglicanism or Puritanism although there were also Baptists, Quakers, Catholics, Scottish Presbyterians, French Huguenots and Swedish and German Lutherans scattered throughout the population. Of these religious groups, the Puritans were to have the most profound effect on the development of the American ethos.

The Puritans believed that they were an elect people of God called to establish a new covenant based upon biblical doctrine and righteous living in a land free of the superstitions of medieval Catholicism and the authoritarianism of the Church of England. Puritans were Calvinist in theology and presbyterian in church government, so they believed in predestination, hard work and success as a sign of God's blessing upon their lives. They rejected any kind of civil or ecclesiastical authority imposed from above, believing that people should determine civil and ecclesial structures for themselves democratically. Devotion to family, work and the community within this world led to true holiness of life. Hence frugality, patriotism and civic responsibility were virtues to be cultivated. The ethos of seventeenth century Puritanism did much to create some of the best aspects of the American character, but it also formed an outlook that needed the values of the immigrants, who were yet to come, to form the basis for a truly whole and balanced life.

FOR FURTHER READING AND REFERENCE

Sydney E. Ahlstrom, *A Religious History of the American People*, Vol. 1 (Garden City, New York: Image Books, 1975).

Enrique Dussel, *A History of the Church in Latin America* (Grand Rapids, Michigan: William B. Eerdmans Publishing Company, 1981).

Hubert Jedin, ed., *History of the Church*, Vol. V: *Reformation and Counter Reformation* (New York: Crossroad Publishing Company, 1980).

_____, *History of the Church*, Vol. VI: *The Church in the Age of Absolutism and Enlightenment* (New York: Crossroad Publishing Company, 1981).

Stephen Neill, *A History of Christian Missions* (Middlesex, England: Penguin Books, 1964).

6

Eighteenth Century European Christianity to the French Revolution

The Renaissance of the fifteenth and sixteenth centuries reawakened in Western consciousness a new appreciation of human potential and the ability of the human mind to understand the workings of the natural world around us. The new value placed upon reason and science, that constitutes the core of the eighteenth century approach to life, was the development of that outlook. The emphasis upon science as an important key toward understanding the meaning of life, unfortunately, often found itself in conflict with organized religion in a battle for the loyalty of the men and women of the eighteenth century.

Galileo Galilei

Born in Pisa, Galileo Galilei (1564–1642) began his academic career as a student of medicine, but he eventually became a lecturer in mathematics and science at the University of Pisa. Methodologically Galileo often found himself in conflict with his Aristotelian colleagues in philosophy, who were more interested in studying past texts than in investigating empirical questions. Because he believed that it was essential to explore the reality of the world around us, he resigned his chair in mathematics and began to work in the field of astronomy.

At that time the prevailing understanding of the world was the view of Aristotle and Ptolemy that the earth was a motionless sphere at the center of the cosmos. However, the Polish astronomer, Nicolaus Copernicus (1473–1543), had offered the theory in a book

entitled *De Revolutionibus Orbium Coelestium* that the sun and not
the earth was the center of the universe, and that the earth as well
as all the other heavenly bodies traveled in an orbit around the sun.
Galileo hoped to be able to demonstrate the scientific truth of
Copernicus' theory through his own research.

Because it contradicted the geocentric view of reality presented
by Aristotle and the bible, the new astronomy met serious opposition from traditional thinkers. Realizing that he could be in the difficult situation of seeming to place reason and science in opposition
to faith and revelation, he sought the support of more progressive
intellectuals within the church. Initially he received support from
the Jesuit astronomers at the Collegio Romano and the great Jesuit
theologian, St. Robert Bellarmine (1542–1621), who maintained
that indeed many passages of scripture could not be interpreted literally from a scientific perspective.

The more conservative forces within the academic and ecclesiastical communities began to assert their influence, and the Roman
authorities were asked to give some ruling on Galileo's theory.
Eventually church officials handed down the verdict that Galileo's
belief that the sun was at the center of the universe was philosophi-
cally unsound and contrary to the teaching of the bible. Although he
was forbidden to continue teaching his theory, Galileo pursued his
research and tried once more to prove the validity of his position in
a book he published in 1632 entitled: *Dialogue on the Two Great
World Systems*. The official response of the church was to ban the
book and to place Galileo under house arrest for the rest of his life
as a penalty for maintaining heretical opinions.

The Enlightenment

The *Enlightenment* is a term used to describe the scientific, philosophical, religious and political developments of the eighteenth century. Important themes emphasized by the thinkers of the
Enlightenment include:

1) a supreme confidence in human reason;
2) a demand for freedom of thought and speech;
3) a reliance on mathematics and the scientific approach as ways
   of knowing reality;
4) an enlarged vision of the world that recognized the values of
   non-Western cultures;

5) a criticism of religious dogmatism and political authoritarianism;

6) an emphasis on the uniqueness of the individual and the importance of the subjective;

7) a mistrust of any form of knowledge that cannot be measured or quantified.

From the centers of the Enlightenment in England, France and Germany, ideas that incarnated these themes spread throughout western Europe and the Americas.

The Enlightenment view is well-exemplified in the empiricism of the English philosopher, John Locke (1632–1704). He believed that knowledge was based upon experience and that religious faith, because it flowed from revelation, did not have the same certainty as conclusions drawn from reason. Locke believed that Christianity should be based upon a reasonable interpretation of scripture that moved away from complex dogmatic questions and emphasized the work of God in creation and the exemplary modeling of human life given by Jesus Christ.

Deists

Locke's simplification of Christianity was a reaction against the theological debates and the religious warfare that had marked the sixteenth and seventeenth centuries. The "deists," thinkers who emphasized belief in what could be known about God by reason, maintained that all human beings had an innate knowledge of God and basic moral principles. From this innate knowledge one could reasonably conclude that God should be worshiped and that actions contrary to basic moral principles were wrong and liable to punishment by the supreme lawgiver. Anything beyond these fundamental religious truths was an illegitimate accretion which had obscured a true Christianity based on reason. Deism taught that the basic purpose of the bible was to present a moral message that emphasized the virtuous life and the loving service of others.

While the deists were optimistic about the role of reason as the basis for religion, the Scottish philosopher, David Hume (1711–1776), maintained that reason was much more limited than some thought. He said that any proofs for the existence of God were based upon concepts such as cause and effect, which were simply creations of the human mind. As a skeptic, Hume maintained that religion pertained to the domain of faith and was not something that could be based upon reason.

The French Roman Catholic philosopher, René Descartes (1596–1650), felt that he could prove the existence of God by philosophizing from a position of universal doubt. Since the idea of a perfect being could not be produced by the mind itself, it must have a basis in reality outside the mind and, therefore, for Descartes, God exists. As a profoundly religious man, he saw no opposition between faith and reason, religion and science. A later generation of French intellectuals, the *philosophes*, did not share Descartes' perspective.

While the Enlightenment was primarily an intellectual movement in England, it had political, social and religious overtones for the *philosophes* of France led by François-Marie Arouet (1694–1778), better known as Voltaire. A philosopher, playwright, mathematician and businessman, Voltaire was a severe critic of *l'ancien régime*. In his literary career, which lasted for more than sixty years and produced masterpieces such as *Candide*, he constantly attacked the political, economic, social and religious systems created by the absolutist monarchs, Louis XIV (1643–1715) and Louis XV (1715–1774).

Voltaire is often associated with the phrase, *ecrasez l'infame* (crush the infamous thing), which presents his disdain for the Roman Catholic Church in France. As a deist he believed in a God who had created an orderly and harmonious universe in which rational and free beings were meant to be agents of social progress and the abolition of evil where possible. Voltaire saw a natural religion which inculcated basic human values as preferable to a revealed religion, such as Catholicism, which had become a participant in maintaining oppressive social and political structures.

A major undertaking of the intellectuals of the French Enlightenment was the publication of a multi-volume encyclopedia edited by Denis Diderot (1713–1784) and Jean D'Alembert (1717–1783). While Voltaire maintained that belief in God was essential for upholding the basis for moral behavior, Diderot thought that belief in God was not necessary for preserving the moral fabric of society. In his opinion, atheists could certainly be good citizens.

Jean Jacques Rousseau (1712–1778) taught that God had created humankind in a state of natural innocence and that Christianity undermined an appreciation of the goodness of human nature by its overemphasis on original sin. Rousseau maintained that humankind had fallen from its first innocence through the corrupting influence of societal structures, but that innocence could be restored by the creation of a just and free society based upon reason. The ideas of Voltaire, Diderot and Rousseau would come to full flowering in the thought and action of their disciples during the French Revolution.

The Enlightenment in Germany reached its apex with the publication of two works by Immanuel Kant (1724–1804), the *Critique of Pure Reason* (1781) and the *Critique of Practical Reason* (1788). In the latter work, he challenged the deists by arguing that pure reason cannot prove the existence of God or immortality. Kant taught that it is through practical reason, which has to do with the moral life, that a person can know both the existence of God as the judge of all action and that immortality is the ultimate reward of a life of integrity.

The age of reason or Enlightenment of the seventeenth and eighteenth centuries affected religion in general and Christianity in particular in a number of ways. Emphasis on reason improved religious instruction and catechesis by challenging anything that implied superstition, magic or the miraculous. The liturgy also benefited when the Enlightenment thinkers critiqued sentimentalism and formalism in Christian worship. However, reliance on the power of reason and the scientific method also undermined essential elements of the faith such as revelation, tradition and church authority. Rationalism attacked the heart of the Christian message when it taught that faith manifested an infantile stage in the development of humanity and that human progress required that the world move beyond religion.

Christianity in the Holy Roman Empire

The Treaty of Westphalia (1648) made the Holy Roman Empire a patchwork of three hundred independent territories of various sizes. Although all were theoretically under the authority of the emperor, they were in fact self-governing entities. During the eighteenth century the most powerful states were Saxony, Bavaria, Brandenburg and Prussia, which was under the leadership of Frederick the Great (1774–1786). The next stage of development in Germany would occur when the Holy Roman Empire came to an end in 1806 during the Napoleonic era.

The effective power of the Hapsburg emperors was limited to Austria. Under the leadership of Emperor Joseph II (1765–1790), the absolutist claims of the secular state culminated in a program,

later called Josephinism, that sought to bring the church totally
under state control. Josephinism called for the following:

1) The emperor would nominate all bishops in Austria and in the
   empire's provinces, which included parts of Italy.
2) Clergy would become state employees.
3) Seminaries would be under the direction of the state to insure
   that Enlightenment ideas were part of the curriculum.
4) Jurisdictional ties between religious and their superiors in
   Rome would be severed.
5) Contemplative orders would be suppressed as being useless for
   the social development of the state.
6) Money realized from the sale of monastic properties would be
   used as pensions for the displaced monks and nuns and for the
   construction of new parishes.

As a result of this program, eight hundred and seventy-six monasteries and convents were closed and seven hundred and seventy-
four were sold. The church had now become a department of the
state.

The scandal of division between Protestants and Catholics led
many to believe that reunion could come only by a return to a sim-
pler form of Christianity that accorded with the church as described
in the New Testament. In this spirit of ecumenism, Bishop Nikolaus
von Hontheim (1701–1790) of Trier, Germany, writing under the
pseudonym of Febronius, developed a new ecclesiological perspective. He taught the following:

1) Christ had not given the papacy the power which it claimed.
2) The church was not meant to be a monarchical structure.
3) The papacy existed only to be the sign and servant of church
   unity.
4) An ecumenical council could be called by the pope, the emperor
   or the bishops.
5) Infallibility resided in the whole church, and only the consent of the bishops made the pope's pronouncements bind-
   ing.

Although the intention of "Febronianism" was to enhance the role of
the local bishop and further Christian unity, it had the potential of
creating more national churches separated from Rome. The
Enlightenment rejection of any claim to universal authority, the

influence of secular absolutism and the influence of Gallicanism were all at work in the development of Hontheim's theory.

England

For almost a century after the Glorious Revolution of 1688, which brought the Protestant rulers, William and Mary (1689–1702), to the throne, penal laws prevented Catholics in England from voting, practicing law or inheriting land. Toward the end of the eighteenth century, parliament passed a series of relief acts which somewhat eased state discrimination against the seventy thousand Roman Catholics who remained in England. At the outbreak of the French Revolution in 1790, a large number of Catholic bishops and priests fled to England to escape persecution. Since religious houses that had been established for English Catholics in France were now being closed, many monks and nuns returned to their homeland. Although Catholic worship in public was still prohibited, the Catholic Emancipation Act of 1829 restored basic civil rights to those practicing the old faith.

Methodists

The eighteenth century Anglican Church, which had rejected the extremes of Roman Catholicism and Puritanism, was in need of revitalization. The Enlightenment in England had suggested an abbreviated form of Christianity that was based on reason and promoted moral behavior. Many, however, felt that what was needed was a return to a more inspirational and experiential form of Christianity that preserved the traditions of the church. John Wesley (1703–1791) and his brother Charles (1707–1788) were to be the leaders of this evangelical revival movement.

While studying at Oxford University, John established the "Holy Club" or "Methodists" whose members agreed to pray together, to read the bible, to lead good lives and to assist those in need. After ordination to the Anglican priesthood, both John and Charles went to Georgia in 1735 to work as missionaries. Their preaching was not well received and they returned to England within two years. Feeling the need for a deeper commitment to the Christian faith, John made contact with the Moravians in Germany since he had come to know something of their evangelical spirituality while in

America. As a result of their visit to the Moravians, both John and Charles underwent a conversion experience in 1738.

Listening to readings from Martin Luther, both sensed a "warming of the heart" and became convinced experientially that Christ had truly saved them from their sins by his death on the cross. Empowered by their conversion, the brothers began to preach everywhere, proclaiming their new method of experienced grace for living the Christian life. When local churches would not give them a place to preach, they moved out into the open air, often drawing large crowds, especially from the working class poor. It was not the intention of the Wesleys to begin a new Christian denomination. Rather they hoped to renew the Anglican Church by recapturing the evangelical enthusiasm of the New Testament period.

The brothers organized their followers into societies for prayer, bible reading and community service. Charles wrote more than five thousand hymns for Methodists to use in their worship services. The societies were organized into circuits, and a traveling preacher, the circuit rider, would travel from one gathered community to another. Women as well as men became leaders and preachers in these small communities.

These local community leaders and circuit preachers were not ordained at first because the Wesleys saw them as leaders of prayer groups within the Anglican Church. Only when the authorities of the Church of England refused to recognize the validity of the Methodist approach did John Wesley begin ordaining his followers, thus establishing a separate church with its own bishops and pastors. Methodism was most successful among the working classes of England who had moved to the newly developing industrial cities in the latter part of the eighteenth century. Because they often lived in utter poverty and were scorned by the local Anglican parishes, these urban poor found in Methodism a source of hope and strength to face their daily lives.

Scotland

The Counter-Reformation made little headway in Scotland because the people felt that the Presbyterian form of Christianity well suited their own religious needs and their democratic outlook on life. In 1690 the Scottish parliament ratified the Presbyterian form of church government, thus distinguishing themselves from their Anglican brothers and sisters in the British Isles. Although Catholic missionary activity continued during the seventeenth and eighteenth centuries, the Catholic population continued to decline because of emigration to other English-speaking countries, such as Canada. This downward trend in the Catholic population was only reversed in the early nineteenth century with the arrival in Scotland of many Irish Catholics fleeing persecution and famine in their homeland.

Ireland

During the Commonwealth (1649–1660), Catholics in Ireland underwent severe persecution. Catholic clergy were liable to death for saying mass, and the Catholic laity were deprived of their land and their civil rights. Although their situation changed during the Catholic restoration of James II (1685–1688), after the Glorious Revolution of 1688 they were once more subject to penal laws. This new persecution led to an even deeper identification of Irish Catholicism with Irish nationalism. In the eighteenth century, Irish Catholics increasingly called for more independence from England, as did Scotch Protestants living in Ireland. The outbreak of the French Revolution intensified the call by both Catholics and Protestants for political reform. Fearing the excesses in France, many Irish Catholic bishops took a conservative stance and condemned a revolt in 1798, which sought to establish a free Ireland; that revolt was crushed by England. Eventually, however, members of the hierarchy did become supporters of the move for Irish independence in the nineteenth century.

France

Besides Jansenism and Gallicanism, the Catholic Church in France had to struggle with the internal problem of quietism in the seventeenth and eighteenth centuries. In 1675 Miguel de Molinos (1640–1697), a noted Spanish spiritual director living in Rome, published his *Spiritual Guide* in which he advocated the abandonment of any attempt to grow in the spiritual life and insisted instead on the need for total passivity and surrender to God. Molinos' teaching was a reaction to an overly organized approach to the spiritual life, but his critics accused him of bypassing the sacramental life of the church and avoiding any engagement in active works of charity toward others.

Rome condemned the spiritual teachings of Molinos in 1687, and he was imprisoned for the rest of his life. Quietism, however, was taken up in France by a deeply religious woman, Madame Guyon (1648–1717). Through her book, *A Short and Simple Means of Prayer*, she influenced many, including the saintly bishop of Cambrai, François de Fénelon (1651–1715). Opposition to this French form of quietism came from the celebrated theologian and preacher, Jacques Bossuet (1627–1704). As a result of Bossuet's efforts, Madame Guyon was condemned and imprisoned for a time, while Bishop Fenelon was exiled from his diocese for the rest of his life in 1697. The condemnation of quietism contributed to the formalism of eighteenth century Catholicism by its seemingly negative evaluation of contemplation and the spiritual life.

The Catholic Church in eighteenth century France was ill-prepared to respond to the criticisms of the Enlightenment thinkers. The bishops were aristocrats who were more interested in life at the court of Versailles than in being pastors of the dioceses entrusted to them. The parish priests were from the lower classes and often lacked the education necessary to deal with the new ideas about reason and freedom that were being discussed in the salons of Paris. The one group that might have been able to revitalize eighteenth century French Catholicism and respond to the thinkers of the Enlightenment was the religious orders in general and the Society of Jesus in particular. But religious life was under attack in all the Catholic courts of Europe, and the Jesuits were involved in a life and death struggle for their very existence.

The Suppression of the Jesuits

By the eighteenth century, the Society of Jesus was a powerful force in European society, and its influence and prestige, as well as its unqualified support of the papacy, had elicited the animosity of the supporters of Gallicanism, Josephinism and Febronianism. The most bitter opponents of the Jesuits in France were the Jansenists and the Enlightenment thinkers.

In 1759 Portugal expelled the Jesuits and confiscated their property at home and in all the Portuguese colonies throughout the world. France declared the Society of Jesus to be illegal in 1764, but did not force the three thousand members of the society into exile. Spain expelled five thousand Jesuits from its territories in 1767 and confiscated their property.

Not satisfied with the suppression of the Society of Jesus in their own countries, the kings of Portugal, Spain and France pressured Pope Clement XIII (1758–1769) to suppress the Jesuits throughout the world. Although he was able to resist their efforts, his successor, Clement XIV (1769–1774), bowed to their wishes in an attempt to safeguard the greater good of the church. Declaring his desire to maintain peace within the church, Clement declared the suppression of the Society of Jesus on July 21, 1773. Because Catherine II of Russia (1762–1796) refused to publish the decree of suppression in her domains, the society continued to exist there until it was restored to full worldwide existence again in 1814 by Pope Pius VII (1800–1823).

In the interim, former Jesuits joined the diocesan clergy or became members of other religious communities. John Carroll (1735–1815), the first bishop of the Roman Catholic Church in the United States, and many other eighteenth century Catholic clergy in the new nation were former Jesuits. As the suppression of the Jesuits brought about a weakening of the educational and missionary efforts of the church in the eighteenth century, so their restoration indicated a new surge of interest in the educational and missionary apostolate of the church in the nineteenth century.

7

Eighteenth Century
North American Christianity
to the New Republic

The Colonies

Religious diversity has characterized the United States since the days of the original thirteen colonies. After the Church of England achieved official status in the colony of Virginia as early as 1619, Anglicanism found its home, especially during the seventeenth century, in the south. Due, however, to the lack of economic support, few ministers and a scattered population, it was difficult to maintain the Anglican way. Still, by the middle of the eighteenth century, there were over one hundred churches of the Anglican communion in the colony.

The Anglican Church planted roots also in the Carolinas, Georgia, and Maryland. By the time of the American Revolution, Anglican Christianity was the predominant religious expression in the southern colonies, with its greatest strength in the tidewater region of Virginia.

The major centers established by the Puritans in New England were in the colonies of Massachusetts and Connecticut. They organized themselves as "Congregationalists," having separated themselves from the Church of England or the Anglican Church. The churches in their communities were served by caring and well-educated ministers who were prepared at such Congregationalist schools as Harvard (1636) and Yale (1701).

The maverick colony of Rhode Island was founded by Roger Williams, a Puritan, who was expelled as a troublemaker from the Massachusetts Bay Colony. Although he established the Baptist Church in his colony, Williams insisted on religious tolerance in the colony of Rhode Island and Providence Plantations. Religious freedom allowed Quakers, who were often persecuted in the other New England colonies, to settle in Rhode Island, especially at Newport.

The middle colonies (New York, New Jersey, Pennsylvania, and Maryland) witnessed great religious diversity. The Dutch brought the Dutch Reformed Church (Calvinism) to New York and New Jersey, and established their college, Rutgers, in 1766. Presbyterians from Scotland and Ireland populated the area as well. The Quakers (Society of Friends), persecuted in England and in many of the English colonies, founded Pennsylvania as a safe haven for those seeking religious freedom. Their city, Philadelphia, or the City of Brotherly Love, was founded by William Penn in 1682. Many German Lutherans settled in Pennsylvania, as did also a tiny number of English Roman Catholics, who experienced persecution in Maryland, their original place of settlement.

The religious map of the thirteen original colonies depicts a variety of Protestant churches—Congregationalists, Presbyterians, Anglicans, Dutch and German Reformed, Lutherans, and Quakers. Roman Catholics were a very small minority.

The Great Awakening

Religion is a complex reality and has been defined or described as an entire world view or way of understanding the human person, human community, human destiny, and how to achieve that destiny. In a word, religion is the pattern of a person's relationship to an absolute, often named God. As such, religion informs all of life and needs to be experienced as both intellectually and emotionally satisfying, thus anchoring a person in reality. At times throughout history emphasis has been placed on the intellectual dimension of religion. The great schools of theology have been an example of the studied effort to understand faith and revelation. Another emphasis, often in reaction to a cerebral religion, places great importance on the emotional or the feeling dimensions of religion. The eighteenth century saw an emphasis on that emotional dimension of Christianity in both Europe and the American colonies.

One of the forerunners of eighteenth century religious enthusiasm was the pietist movement in Germany. Around 1670, a German pastor, Philipp Jakob Spener, began founding groups in Frankfurt called Colleges of Piety. To encourage in people a vibrant, personal faith, Spener preached the need to listen to and study the bible with great reverence. Believing that laity, as well as clergy, were called by God to sanctity, Spener called Christians to live a devout life with enthusiasm and not merely do the minimum required by the church, that is, the Lutheran Church. Spener himself interpreted the Book of Revelation in the New Testament literally and so saw the end of the world as imminent (apocalypticism).

Although it had its critics within the church, the pietist movement took roots in the German Lutheran tradition. It spread as well to the Reformed Churches or churches in the Calvinist tradition. Pietism spread particularly because of its emphasis on missionary activity and through the use of popular religious hymns.

In Scandinavia, pietism was supported by the king of Denmark. Similarly, the movement made inroads in the Moravian community through Spener's godson, Count Nikolaus von Zinzendorf. As a reaction to a cold and brittle dogmatism, the pietist revival emphasized conversion and personal faith, as well as commitment to Christ. It was characterized by small prayer meetings, bible reflection, and sharing of the Christian experience. The movement restored vitality to the Protestant Christian church by seeking to return to the original enthusiasm of the sixteenth century reformers.

The pietist movement influenced a community known as the Bohemian Brethren, the heirs of John Huss in Bohemia and Poland. This group, who would later be called the Moravian Brethren or the United Brethren, settled in 1722 in Saxony, Germany, on the estate of Count von Zinzendorf.

The emphasis of this revivalist community was "heart religion." One cannot know God except through the Son, and the Son reveals God to those whom he chooses. One knows the Son through a personal relationship or experience. Christian religion essentially is a religion of love, which casts out fear. Salvation could not be a question or in doubt when one loved; hence death is simply a "going home."

The Moravian enthusiasm soon spread from Germany to England. There, it lived on its own right and influenced others, chief

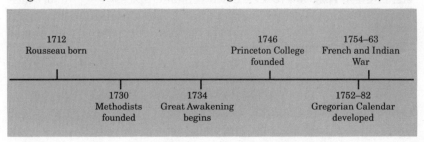

1712 Rousseau born		1746 Princeton College founded	1754–63 French and Indian War
	1730 Methodists founded	1734 Great Awakening begins	1752–82 Gregorian Calendar developed

among whom were the brothers, John and Charles Wesley, the founders of Methodism.

At the beginning of the eighteenth century, there were approximately 250,000 inhabitants in the thirteen colonies. For the most part they were British and heavily Congregational or Presbyterian. However, they were soon joined by other European immigrants, especially German Lutherans, many of whom had been touched by the pietist movement.

By the beginning of the eighteenth century, the religious fervor of the founding colonists had cooled. The Puritan vision of society ruled by God became clouded by a certain materialism due to commercial success. In 1734, a religious revival began in Northampton, Massachusetts, under the aegis of Jonathan Edwards (1703–1758), the pastor of the local Congregationalist church.

Edwards had undergone a profound religious experience of absolute dependence on God, which he described as "awakening" in his book *Personal Narrative* (1739). This fitted well with his Calvinist theological understanding of predestination and the absolute corruptness of human nature due to original sin.

In 1735, Edwards began preaching in a powerful and moving way on justification by faith and the need for personal conversion to Jesus Christ and the gospel. His sermons were listened to with great attention and enthusiasm, and his hearers often experienced their own "awakening."

The enthusiasm and revival of the Protestant Christian experience in New England was further assisted by the English preacher, George Whitefield. The Calvinist-Methodist Whitefield often preached in the open air. His themes were justification, original sin, and personal conversion. Over twenty thousand persons attended his farewell sermon before he returned to England.

The religious revival or "Great Awakening" spread throughout the colonies. Other denominations, for example, the Baptists in the southern colonies, caught the fervor and enthusiasm of the moment. Churches were renewed and a kind of inter-church cooperation

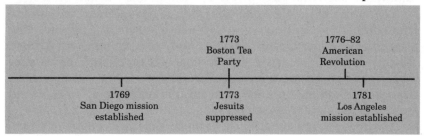

	1773 Boston Tea Party	1776–82 American Revolution
1769 San Diego mission established	1773 Jesuits suppressed	1781 Los Angeles mission established

developed among those participating in the awakening. The movement encouraged higher education, and Princeton College in New Jersey opened as a result of the revival. In January 1758, Jonathan Edwards became the president of the College of New Jersey at Princeton, that is, today's Princeton University.

The "Great Awakening" had varied results on American Protestant life:

1) It underlined and contributed to the diversity of Protestantism in the American colonies.
2) Such denominational variety militated against the domination of any one church.
3) The experience of "awakening" crossed denominational lines, thus promoting inter-church understanding and religious toleration, at least among Protestants.
4) Religious affiliation was chosen and voluntary rather than compulsory.
5) Religious ecumenism crossed colonial boundaries, giving birth to a kind of nascent national understanding.

Revivalism thus made its own contribution to the American Revolution.

Catholics and the American Colonies

Roman Catholicism during the colonial period was principally present in Maryland and to a lesser extent in Pennsylvania and New York. In 1632, King Charles I presented a charter to the second Lord Baltimore, Cecil Calvert, for lands that would become the colony of Maryland. In 1634, the *Ark* and the *Dove* brought sixteen to twenty Roman Catholic gentlemen and between two and three hundred Protestant workers to the shores of the Potomac River. While all religions initially were tolerated in the colony of Maryland, soon that gave way to Protestant and Puritan control.

The future of the Catholic Church in Maryland reflected the fortunes and treatment of the Catholic Church in England. The Dominican pope, Saint Pius V, had excommunicated Queen Elizabeth in 1570. Legislation subsequently prohibited the practice of Catholicism in the country. A Catholic seminary was opened at Douai in Flanders in 1568 to train diocesan priests who would return to England as missionaries.

The newly founded Society of Jesus was also concerned about the persecuted Catholics of England, and in 1580 Edmund Campion and Thomas Parsons became the first of a long line of dedicated Jesuit missionaries to go to England. Campion became the object of an intensive manhunt. Eventually he was captured and imprisoned in the Tower of London. Finally after weeks of torture, he was charged with treason and hanged, drawn, and quartered at Tyburn on December 1, 1581. He was canonized by Pope Paul VI in 1970, as one of forty English and Welsh martyrs. Campion was one of a number of clergy and laity who gave their life for the Catholic faith in England, including Thomas More, John Fisher, Cuthbert Mayne and Margaret Clitherow.

The Jesuit presence and influence in England overflowed to Maryland. There, the Jesuits served settlers in parishes and inaugurated missionary work among such native Americans as the Piscataways. By 1708 there were approximately three thousand Catholics in Maryland, many of whom were people of means. However, the so-called Glorious Revolution (1688–1689) in England had put the Catholic Church, both in England and in Maryland, at a disadvantage. Because Catholics were harassed and discriminated against, the Catholic Church in the colony struggled for existence during most of the eighteenth century.

In 1674, James, duke of York, established a policy of religious toleration in the New York colony, and Catholic governors there assisted the work of the church by inviting Jesuit missionaries to the area. However, by 1691 the climate had changed. Catholics in the colony could not vote or hold office, priests were denied entry into the colony, and for seventy-five years there was no public place for Catholic worship. Mass was occasionally celebrated in secret in a house on Wall Street by a Jesuit from Maryland.

Catholics enjoyed religious toleration in Pennsylvania under the regime of William Penn. Under Queen Anne (1705), however, Catholics were prohibited from voting or holding office. In 1733, Saint Joseph's Church was erected in Philadelphia, the first public Catholic Church in the English colonies. By 1757, there were about thirteen hundred Catholics in Pennsylvania.

During the colonial period, the Roman Catholic Church was but a small minority group. While at times it enjoyed toleration, if not acceptance, for the most part it was a persecuted community. Individual Catholics suffered discrimination, clergy were impeded from their ministry, and institutional presence (e.g., schools and churches) was non-existent. The situation reflected the plight of the

Catholic Church in England. Some of this changed, however, with the American Revolution.

The American Revolution

At the time of the Revolution there were roughly two and a half million colonists. Many Anglican clergy and Anglican laity of the north and middle colonies supported the loyalists or English side during the Revolution. So, also, did some members of other Protestant groups, for example, wealthy Quakers. By and large, however, church people or religious people increasingly viewed English rule with disfavor. More important than any activity of a religious institution or individuals was the contribution to the independence movement of a religious world view.

As a result of Enlightenment thinking and philosophy, the patriots developed a distinct understanding of God, the human person, the rights of the individual, natural law, equality and freedom. These views melded with Protestant Puritan theology and biblical interpretation to produce a political theory. The individual was the subject of rights and more important than the state; liberty and freedom were more important than obedience.

The morale of the churches during and after the war of independence was indeed low. People were apathetic or engaged in political rather than religious issues. Clergy had fled or were scarce, and church life was disorganized. Many had lost enthusiasm for religion, at least for a time. One exception was the religious movement of "deism." This natural religion suggested that reason and science provided a person with all that he or she needed for a religious and ethical life. A revealed religion was either accepted alongside a natural religion or deemed unnecessary. A great propagandist of deism was the patriot Thomas Paine, as was Ethan Allen of Vermont. Thomas Jefferson (1743–1826), a rationalist, took his philosophy of religion and his political theory and provided what has become key to the American religious experience, that is, the separation clause or the separation of church and state.

The Anglican Church suffered a great exodus of both clergy and laity during and after the war. These loyalists returned to England, emptying parishes. King's College in New York (later Columbia University) and the University of Pennsylvania lost their connection or identity with the Anglican Church. Where the Anglican Church was the established or official church of a colony, it was subsequently disestablished. Still, the Anglican Church survived in

America as the Protestant Episcopal Church with lay participation in church government, elected bishops, and strong vestries or local parish councils. Similarly, the Methodist Church after the war became independent of England.

Congregationalism or the Calvinist Puritan movement had contributed to the revolution and so was not negatively affected by the war. However, these Reformed Churches faced internal division. The Presbyterian Church grew after the revolution because of the arrival of large numbers of Scotch-Irish peoples. The Baptist movement similarly prospered, especially in the southern colonies or states. In 1764, a charter was approved by the colonial assembly establishing a Baptist college in Rhode Island. The charter was rather liberal, stating that a portion of the trustees could be from other denominations, and officers and students need not be Baptist. In 1804, the college changed its name to Brown University in honor of a local patron who had made money indirectly from the slave trade.

The small number of Roman Catholics in the colonies meant a minor role for them in the Revolution. There were about twenty-five thousand Catholics at the time, out of a population of two and a half million. There were twenty-three priests in Maryland and Pennsylvania, all former Jesuits, and a few others ministered in other states. In 1773, Pope Clement XIV had abolished the Society of Jesus; subsequently, most Jesuit priests chose to become diocesan clergy. After the suppression of the Society of Jesus, a Marylander, John Carroll, decided to return to his homeland, to minister there as a diocesan priest.

In general, an anti-Catholic climate prevailed in the colonies. Maryland produced, however, a competent and wealthy Catholic patriot in the person of Charles Carroll, a signer of the Declaration of Independence and a cousin of Father John Carroll. Other individual Catholics served on the patriot side during the war. An outcome of the American Revolution was religious toleration and a refusal to establish any official church. Roman Catholicism was a beneficiary of this official policy even though hostility toward the Roman Catholic Church continued to prevail in many quarters.

8

European Christianity 1789–1815

The French Revolution

A serious step in the secularization of European thought came at the end of the seventeenth and the beginning of the eighteenth century—*la crise de la conscience europenne*. Most of the usual arguments against Christianity were then coined. Only "science versus religion" awaited another era.

With the Enlightenment, a new world view was born, competing with a religious world view. The Roman Catholic version of that view had its roots in the Aristotelian-Thomistic synthesis of the Middle Ages. There, a person was understood to be created in the image of God, capable of doing good and empowered to do so by grace. Christ was the universal savior, leading all persons of good will to salvation. In a word, such a view was upbeat and optimistic.

The various Protestant versions of the Christian world view generally emphasized the terrible, corrupting effects of original sin on the human person. This view leaned heavily on the Platonic theology of St. Augustine. Salvation was by no means guaranteed and, in fact, probably would not be the destiny for the majority of persons. A Christian life was test, trial, and dependence totally on the gratuitous action of God. John Calvin, for instance, taught a double predestination, whereby some were predestined for heaven, while, sadly, others were predestined to hell.

Both world views, whether optimistic or not, were thoroughly religious. The human person was created by God, and hopefully would share everlasting life with God in heaven. The moral, virtuous life was expected and possible because of grace. The creator intervened in history through Christ, the savior and redeemer and, thus, original creation was renewed and set free from the power of original sin.

The tenor of the Enlightenment favored natural religion and emphasized the role of human reason. The person was naturally good and could achieve natural happiness and completion without recourse to something beyond the self. To do this one needed knowledge and education, thereby freeing oneself from superstition. Similarly, one needed liberty from oppressive authority, whether civil or ecclesiastical. Perhaps Jean-Jacques Rousseau's (1712–1778) "noble savage" serves as a metaphor for the Enlightenment person. Human perfectibility and progress characterized this optimistic vision.

The intellectual currents of the day challenged religion. In fact, they provoked the churches to renew pastoral activities, for example, liturgical reform, biblical study, religious education. At the same time, Enlightenment ideas fomented discontent with the status quo. France, in particular, came to disdain the old order or *l'ancien régime,* and the idea of a modern secular state came into vogue.

France Immediately Before the Revolution

Roman Catholicism was the only official religion of France. While the Edict of Nantes (1598) had granted toleration to French Protestant Calvinists (Huguenots), that had been revoked by King Louis XIV in 1685. Curiously, King Louis XVI in 1787, on the eve of the revolution, granted freedom of religion to French Protestants. This latter group was something of an intellectual and economic elite, often distrusted by the poorer Catholic classes. Louis XVI's move was applauded by the philosophers of the Enlightenment as a strategic way of lessening the power of the Catholic Church.

The church or Christian community, universal or local, is always in need of reform. The community needs constantly to look to the gospel as to a mirror. The point of church membership is to relate to Christ and through Christ to God in and through the Holy Spirit. The Christian community in eighteenth century France truly needed renewal and reform.

The church or Catholic community of the time, through its institutions, offered the population many services (education, care of the poor, et al.). Nevertheless, some of the clergy or "the first estate" lorded it over people. As a class they enjoyed privileges such as exemption from taxation. They possessed or controlled at least ten percent of the land in France. Parish priests or *curés* generally came from poorer backgrounds, worked hard to serve their people and were thus respected. Bishops and abbots of monasteries often came from aristocratic families, enjoyed power and wealth, and were often resented by both people and parish clergy. Religious orders, for example, the Benedictines and Dominicans, were similarly often not respected because they seemed to lack pastoral zeal and to be more concerned about living a secular lifestyle than preaching the gospel.

There was a loyalty on the part of many people to the Catholic Church, and there were, indeed, serious criticisms by them of sectors of the church which needed reform and renewal. Catholic practice often lacked enthusiasm and fervor. At this point in time, there was absolutely no intention of smashing the church or replacing it. However, that is exactly what happened a few years later.

The French Revolution
Phase I: An Ill-Fated Experiment in Civil Religion

King Louis XVI convened a meeting of the Estates-General, which opened on May 5, 1789, with a candlelight procession. Representatives of the various classes of society or "estates" chose delegates to the Estates-General (the members of the first estate were the clergy; the members of the second estate were the nobles; the members of the third estate were lawyers and professional people). Of the two hundred and ninety-six members of the first estate or the clergy, two hundred and eight parish priests were elected. This indicated a strong antagonism to the aristocratic church leaders and religious as well as a real appreciation for the hard-working, committed parish clergy. These lower class clerical representatives shared the grievances of the third estate against the upper classes. On June 17, 1789, the three estates united to form the National Constituent Assembly.

Circumstances, individuals, and political agendas soon moved the assembly in directions not foreseen by many at the outset. The church experienced growing hostility. Efforts were soon made to separate the French church from the authority of the pope by creating a national church, subject to civil law, as opposed to a universal church subject to the pope. On November 2, 1789, Bishop Talleyrand of Autun suggested that the wealth of the church be appropriated by the state. Considerable church holdings were sold, often to the bourgeoisie and wealthy, thus aligning these classes to the growing revolutionary movement.

In February of 1790, the assembly moved against religious orders (Benedictines, Dominicans, Franciscans, etc.). Religious vows were forbidden; priories, monasteries and convents were closed. Those religious priests, brothers, and nuns who wished to continue their vowed religious life were forced into exile. Many believed that these measures were designed to reform and renew an independent French church and, therefore, were acceptable and needed measures. Events changed dramatically with the passage of the Civil Constitution of the Clergy on July 12, 1790.

The constituent assembly had completely reorganized the government of France. It sought to bring the church into line with that reorganization. Parish and diocesan boundaries were redrawn. Bishops and priests were elected by state officials or parish members. The pope was simply to be notified of clerical elections. Clergy, in effect, became civil servants. What was created, therefore, was a national civil religion within a schismatic church, that is, one broken away from the one universal Roman Catholic Church in union with the pope.

On November 27, 1790, the assembly imposed an oath of allegiance on the clergy to the civil constitution. Only seven out of one hundred and sixty bishops took the oath; about half of the priests did. Those who refused to take the oath (the non-jurors) were soon replaced by those who did take the oath (the jurors or constitutionals). The non-juring priests and nuns were ordered to leave France (roughly thirty thousand to forty thousand departed) or were persecuted, hunted down, imprisoned and executed (two thousand to five thousand perished).

For many, this was the point where the Revolution went wrong. The measures against the church turned King Louis XVI against the movement. In 1791, Pope Pius VI condemned the constitution. Many clergy and laity became bitter enemies of the Revolution. The Jacobin government (called Jacobin because their headquarters was the former Dominican convent of St. Jacques in Paris) severed all relations with the Holy See in 1791.

Phase II: The Radicals

The situation for the church, clergy and laity, gradually deteriorated. The attempt to "de-Christianize" the country led to virulent anti-Catholicism. King Louis XVI was executed on January 21, 1793. Churches were closed and worship was forbidden. A large number of priests and their lay supporters were arraigned before revolutionary tribunals and condemned to death; for example, one hundred and thirty-five priests were shot to death in Lyons, sixteen Carmelites were executed in Compiegne, and thirty-six nuns were martyred in Orange. The "cult of reason" was set up as a new civil religion, and Notre Dame Cathedral in Paris was declared the "temple of reason." Saints' names were forbidden, and even the religiously inspired calendar of Pope Gregory was replaced by a revolutionary calendar without Sundays or feast days. Hatred against Catholicism raged out of control during this Reign of Terror (September 1793 to July 1794). Even the leader of the rebels, Maximilien Robespierre, opposed the excesses of the terror by promoting the need for deism and the concomitant morality it promoted.

Phase III: Separation of Church and State

In 1794, the French republican army met military success, occupying Belgium, the Rhineland, and parts of Italy. They put legislation regulating religion into place in these Catholic areas. Priests were deported and convents were closed. The French even abducted Pope Pius VI from Rome and held him prisoner until the eighty-one-year-old pontiff died at Valence on August 24, 1799. The record shows his death recorded as: "Jean-Ange Bisasche, exercising the profession of pontiff."

Catholicism, nevertheless, did not die in France nor in French occupied territory. Worship and the eucharist continued to be celebrated in secret or quite openly in some geographical areas which resented the Revolution, for example, Brittany and the insurgent area of the Vendee. The resistance of whole sectors of the population to "de-Christianization" eventually won the day. With the fall of Robespierre in 1794, the revolutionary government fell into disfavor.

In 1795, the directory form of government, a ruling council of five, was inaugurated. It proposed a separation of church and state and toleration of all religions. In practice the government's approach to religion was inconsistent. For instance, it moved from toleration, to accommodation and then to renewed persecution of the Catholic Church. Between 1797 and 1799, the directory attempted once more to extirpate the Catholic Church from France.

As early as 1796, some directors wanted the young general in Italy, Napoleon Bonaparte, to march against the Holy See. He refused, sensing the loyalty of Italians to the Catholic Church. His successor in Italy did move against Rome and took the pope, Pius VI (1775-1799), prisoner. However, on November 9-10, 1799, General

Bonaparte in a *coup d'état* seized power as first consul and within two years religious peace returned to France.

Napoleon and the Church

Napoleon Bonaparte was born August 5, 1769, on the island of Corsica. He was brought up as a Roman Catholic, attended military schools, and, as was the custom, was forced to practice his religion. Without much money, he spent time reading and studying, especially the works of the French rationalists of the Enlightenment, for example, Voltaire and Rousseau.

Napoleon possessed great military talents and achieved early recognition and success. He was named a general of the army at the age of twenty-two. While in charge of the French campaign in Italy, he refused the directory's order to crush the papacy, thus winning for himself Catholic support in Italy as well as in France. This convinced him of the wisdom of a rapprochement with the Catholic Church and the absurdity of "de-Christianization."

In 1799, Bonaparte became first consul and almost immediately restored religious freedom to France. Religiously, while a baptized Catholic, Napoleon was more of a deist along the lines of Voltaire. Religion was valuable for the nation and so ought to be professed freely. However, churches needed some government supervision. Always politically astute, Napoleon also realized that an alliance with Rome would make it easier for him to rule a heavily Catholic empire. To this end in 1801, he entered into a concordat or treaty with Pope Pius VII (1800–1823) restoring the Catholic Church in France. It granted freedom of worship to the church, affirmed the right of the pope to name bishops, and provided salaries for the clergy. The treaty did not recognize the Catholic Church as the official religion of the French nation nor did it return confiscated property to the church. Religious orders, such as the Benedictines and Dominicans, were not restored. The Concordat of 1801 remained in force until 1905.

Bonaparte was extraordinarily popular with the people of France. On December 2, 1804, Pope Pius VII came to crown him emperor at Notre Dame Cathedral in Paris. In fact, the pope merely watched as Napoleon placed the crown on his own head. Symbolically, this event has come to be interpreted positively as freeing the papacy from secular control. At the time, however, the event was not so favorably understood.

In 1806, serious conflict arose between the pope and Napoleon.

The pope refused to honor France's blockade of trade with England. When the emperor annexed the Papal States to the French empire, the pope excommunicated the perpetrators. Napoleon retaliated, and on July 6, 1809, his general arrested the pope and brought him to Savona in northern Italy as a prisoner. Pius remained there until transferred to Fontainebleau, near Paris, in June 1812. Pope and emperor battled until Napoleon set Pope Pius free on June 21, 1814, as military defeat in Russia and elsewhere overwhelmed him. In exile on St. Helena, Napoleon requested the sacraments of the church—viaticum, which is the eucharist or holy communion and anointing of the sick (extreme unction) given when one is in danger of death. Pope Pius VII personally requested clemency for Napoleon but was turned down. Pius forgave Napoleon the insults he had experienced on the emperor's orders. Napoleon died May 5, 1821.

Aftermath

The French Revolution ushered in a new era of church-state relations. It signaled the collapse of *l'ancien régime* in France where the Catholic Church was identified with the ruling class and, therefore, with the state. That in itself prophesied what would happen eventually in the rest of Europe and the west. What Constantine began would come to an end with the modern experience of separation of church and state. Today, while this relationship is generally the case with Catholicism, it is not universal, as seen in many Islamic republics, the Jewish State of Israel, and certain Protestant nations.

Roman Catholicism survived the radical attempts to destroy it during the Revolution. Notwithstanding abuses in the church and practices open to criticism, rank and file Catholic laity and many good religious and priests fiercely maintained their faith commitment. In fact, a strong case can be made that the church emerged from the reign of terror stronger, purified, freer, and better able to meet the modern age. The Christian religion was ultimately a meaningful world view or way of living offered to human persons and not only an institution with all its human foibles.

The Revolution had weakened the efforts in Catholic countries to establish national churches free from the authority and pastoral care of the pope. The end of the Revolution saw division and differences of opinion in Europe and in the church. Some espoused the ideas and ethos of the Revolution—liberty, equality, fraternity—the rights of individuals. They could forgive the excesses of the

Revolution or at least disclaim them. Others saw the liberal agenda, born in the Enlightenment, as pernicious—the relativism of truth, subjectivism, the challenge to legitimate authority. The church would struggle with these ideas, theologically and pragmatically, for the next century and a half. The question was: How to be the authentic church of Jesus Christ in the modern world?

9

European Christianity
1815–1848

The unusual overemphasis on reason and natural religion promoted during the French Revolution ran its course. With the defeat of Napoleon, a new era, the time of "restoration," began in European history. At the Congress of Vienna (1815), the superpowers of the day, that is, England, Russia, Austria, and Prussia, set out to re-establish the old order which had been displaced. The French borders were set as they were before the Revolution, and Louis XVIII, of the house of Bourbon, became king. Other leaders, deposed by Napoleon, were restored.

There was great division among people over the central ideas proposed during the Revolution. The so-called reactionaries, who wanted to return or go back to *l'ancien régime* or the old order with its values of hierarchy, morality, and authority, experienced a temporary victory in 1815. The so-called liberals, who supported the principles of liberty, equality, and rights, would have to wait until later in the nineteenth century for their agenda to gain ascendancy once more.

In the Europe of 1815, there were about one hundred million Catholics, forty million Orthodox, thirty million Protestants, and nine million Anglicans. The "restoration," at least for the Catholic Church, proceeded differently in various countries.

France

King Louis XVIII ascended the restored French throne in 1814. He was succeeded by his brother, Charles X, in 1824. Both hoped to return to the old regime, although by this time the monarchy was controlled by an elected assembly. Louis, however, did make Roman

Catholicism once again the official state religion. While the "restoration" in France made many royalists very happy, it also alienated intellectuals and younger urban professionals. They saw the church as opposing liberty and equality and bent on regaining its privileged, landed status. Liberals grew increasingly anti-clerical and viewed the institutional church as a reactionary force.

Religion and Catholicism, from a less political perspective, seemed to come to life again after the Revolution. Protestant churches witnessed the same phenomenon in their revival movements. People, it seemed, were unhappy with the rationalism of the day and sought more comfort, focus, direction, and personal meaning for daily living from religion. Even intellectuals were caught up in an appreciation for the romanticism of religious faith and, in particular, for the Catholic medieval tradition. In France, François Chateaubriand (1768–1848) produced his famous work, *The Genius of Christianity*, which praised the values and contributions of Christianity to society. His thesis was that the church had, in fact, saved civilization.

The "restoration" agenda heavily promoted the recruitment and education of clergy. The number of ordinations to the priesthood went from nine hundred and eighteen nationally in 1815 to two thousand three hundred and thirty-seven in 1830. In 1815 there were fourteen thousand two hundred and twenty-six sisters in forty-three congregations; by 1830, there were twenty-four thousand nine hundred and ninety-five sisters in sixty-five different congregations. The number of religious brothers, often dedicated to Catholic education, likewise grew, and new groups, such as the Marist Brothers, were founded. Religious orders and congregations were established to meet specific apostolic needs, for example, work with the poor or with the sick. In 1814 Pope Pius VII restored the Jesuits, who had been suppressed by Pope Clement XIV in 1773. The Society of Jesus, however, had never fully ceased to exist, since it had continued during suppression in Russia under the protection of the empress Catherine the Great. The center for Catholic life and spirituality traditionally revolved around a local community or parish, and increased numbers of priests allowed for the establishment of a large number of new parishes throughout France.

Charles X was crowned at Rheims Cathedral in September 1824. He brought to the throne a zealotry for Catholicism that played into the hands of the "ultras" or "reactionaries," that is, those who supported a return to the old order. Such a position was, of course, calculated to alienate those who supported a liberal position.

The pastoral goal of the church during these years was to re-Christianize the population. On the one hand, many people in various parts of the country had remained staunchly Catholic. On the other hand, many were alienated from the institutional church. Since there was a serious lack of knowledge about the teachings of the Catholic faith, the church put great stress on Catholic education in its own schools and tried to influence the educational efforts of state-sponsored schools. It was crucial to the church that the young be properly and effectively educated in their religious faith.

King Charles' reactionary rule provoked an uprising in Paris on July 27–29, 1830. Built-up resentment at the attempts to restore the old order led to some anti-clerical attacks. After Charles X fled to England, a new king, Louis Phillippe d'Orleans (1830–1848), was crowned. The challenge for loyal Catholics, during and after the Revolution, was always how to be authentically Catholic in the modern world. How was the institutional Catholic Church in France to be truly part of the one, holy, catholic or universal, and apostolic Church of Jesus Christ? The Revolution, and even subsequent events, had attempted to destroy or at least separate the church in France from the universal, pastoral responsibility of the pope. The reaction which these attempts provoked was "ultramontanism." The word connotes loyalty to the pope; literally it means "beyond the mountains," that is, a reference to Rome which lay beyond the Alps separating France from Italy.

The first "ultramontane" work in France of note was the book *Du pape* (1819) by a lay person, Joseph de Maistre (1753–1821). It re-emphasized and helped popularize the importance of the position and authority in the church of the bishop of Rome. This cause was greatly helped and then hurt by the writings of Felicite de Lamennais (1782–1854).

In 1816, Abbé (or Father) Hugues Lamennais, a prolific writer and apologist for Catholicism, wrote his *Essay on Indifference*. The work was very popular and brought him many followers. Later, after the 1830 revolution, he founded the journal *L'Avenir* (The Future).

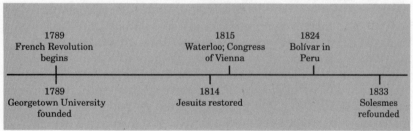

1789 French Revolution begins	1815 Waterloo; Congress of Vienna	1824 Bolívar in Peru	
1789 Georgetown University founded	1814 Jesuits restored		1833 Solesmes refounded

Lamennais tried to wed the liberal values of freedom of conscience, freedom of the press, universal suffrage, and separation of church and state with ultramontanism. The church was served by a universal pastor, the infallible bishop of Rome, who was free from all monarchical and national control. The wedding of liberal ideas with ultramontanism provoked a reaction on the part of bishops and, finally, the pope. Liberal Catholicism was condemned and Lamennais subsequently left the church. Much of what he advocated is taken for granted in modern societies.

Some of Lamennais' colleagues and associates pursued their objectives within the church. In 1833 a group of them began living according to the rule of St. Benedict as a community in the vacant monastery of Solesmes. This abbey, over time, played a key role in the liturgical renewal of the worship life of the Catholic Church. Henri Lacordaire (1802–1861), an associate of Lamennais, would play a key role in the rebirth of the Dominican Order in France and deeply influence the history of the Order of Preachers in the present century.

In February 1848, revolution broke out again in France. Various discontented factions of society coalesced to force the abdication of King Louis Phillipe, and a republic was proclaimed. Elections were held on Easter Sunday 1848. Seeing little social change, the poor and urban unemployed put up barricades in the streets of Paris during June of that year. By December 1848, Napoleon's nephew, Louis Napoleon (1808–1873), had become president of the republic. He soon dissolved the legislature, and by 1852 he had named himself emperor. During 1848, revolutionary attempts to change the status quo occurred as well in Italy, Germany, and Austria.

Italy

What is today modern Italy was for centuries a group of independent cities and kingdoms. Across the middle of the peninsula lay the

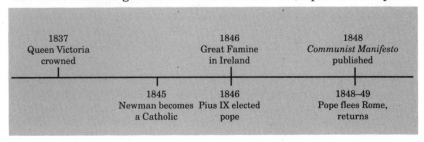

1837 Queen Victoria crowned		1846 Great Famine in Ireland		1848 Communist Manifesto published
	1845 Newman becomes a Catholic	1846 Pius IX elected pope		1848–49 Pope flees Rome, returns

Papal States, land given originally by Charlemagne to the pope. The idea behind such a patrimony was the desire to guarantee the sovereignty and independence of the pope as leader of the church. The Papal States were often conquered, and at times the pope had been held hostage to some political power. At other times, various domestic rulers and foreign nations were contenders for land in Italy north and south of the Papal States. The geographical position of the Papal States militated against any unification of the entire peninsula and, therefore, was an obstacle to a united Italy.

Pope Pius VI (1775–1799) had died in exile; Pope Pius VII (1800–1823) had been taken prisoner by Napoleon. When he returned to Rome in 1814, Pius VII worked to restore the importance and authority of the papacy. He was a holy and intelligent man who related well to the clergy of various nations, and was open to new ideas.

The pope's secretary of state, Cardinal Ercole Consalvi (1757–1824), a lay person ordained to the priesthood only in his later years, was an astute and pragmatic politician. Consalvi established concordats or written treaties with various governments promoting the interests of the church and Catholic people as well as the interests of the Papal States. He was convinced that the ideas of the Revolution in France would eventually triumph and that a total return to *l'ancien régime* was an illusion. Consalvi also promoted contact and diplomatic relations with non-Catholic countries, for example, England and Russia, in order to promote Catholic interests.

Pius VII died in 1823 and was succeeded by Pope Leo XII (1823–1829). This pope tried to steer the church through the reactionary efforts to re-establish the old order and the liberal attempts to modernize the church and society. His successor, Pius VIII (1829–1830), more or less continued the direction of his predecessor. He died in 1830, the year of the July revolution in France, after only twenty months as pope. At this critical moment in European history, Gregory XVI (1831–1846) was chosen bishop of Rome.

The Congress of Vienna had restored the Papal States, confiscated under Napoleon, to the control of the pope and given Austria a dominant position, especially in northern Italy. The administration of the papal territories was conservative and, at times, reactionary. For instance, under Pope Leo XII, Jewish people were required to live in the ghettos. Criticism from any quarter was discouraged. Those promoting Italian unification were outraged; those supporting the ideas born of the Enlightenment were merely confirmed in their view that the church was oppressive.

Pope Gregory XVI had been a monk, scholar, and theologian most of his life. He failed to grasp the thrust of currents moving in the political and social world around him. He opposed revolution, promoted the rights of the church vis-à-vis secular powers, supported missionary outreach to convert others to the church, and energetically defended religion against rationalism. This pope was pastoral and spiritual rather than political. Because he feared the liberal threat against the independence of the church, he kept a firm control of the Papal States. Revolts broke out in Bologna in 1831. There were other revolts in 1832 and then constantly after 1843. The move toward eventual Italian unification was under way.

The Catholic Church is always a multi-dimensional reality. While there was a conservative attitude toward change on the level of the curia (the bureaucracy which assists the pope in serving the universal Catholic community), there were creative efforts on the pastoral level in church life throughout Italy. For instance, in northern Italy, St. John Bosco, a young priest, saw the need to provide a way to educate poor young women and men. To that end, he established vocational schools, used printing presses, wrote religious books and pamphlets, and founded the worldwide Salesian Order of priests and sisters.

The *risorgimento* or nationalist movement toward a unified Italian nation involved radicals as well as moderates. The latter were Roman Catholics bent on remaining loyal to the church while also promoting freedom and representative government. This group took heart at the election of Giovanni Maria Mastai-Ferretti, Pope Pius IX (1846–1878), who became the longest reigning pontiff in history.

Revolution erupted in Italy as elsewhere in 1848. Pius IX refused to help in the battle against the established control of Austria. As a result, the *risorgimento* movement became increasingly anti-clerical. Threatened by radicals, the pope assumed a disguise and escaped to the Kingdom of Naples, where he resided for a year and a half. When he returned to Rome in September 1849, he was more than ever convinced of the dangers of liberalism to the church.

Notwithstanding the pope's position, the efforts toward Italian unification continued. Camillo Benso di Cavour, as prime minister of Piedmont-Sardinia (1852–1861), became a leader of a diplomatic approach, which eventually resulted in the establishment of the Kingdom of Italy by 1870 under King Victor Emmanuel. After the seizure of the Papal States, the king gave the pope three palaces, which would eventually become the territorial basis for Vatican City, an independent nation-state.

Another hero of the Italian campaign was Giuseppe Garibaldi (1807–1882), an ardent anti-clerical, who with his Red Shirts conquered southern Italy. Many of the leaders and people involved in unification efforts were Roman Catholics battling church leadership. This, of course, posed critical questions for the conscientious believer. This crisis continued on a political and social level until the Lateran Treaty of 1929. At the time, some saw the loss of the Papal States as a great threat to the independence and freedom of the pope as universal pastor. That thinking was conditioned by a medieval geopolitical world view. Providentially, the territorial loss freed the bishop of Rome from secular responsibility, giving the papal office increased moral prestige.

Germany and Austria

In 1815, Germany, like Italy, was not a nation-state, but a grouping of principalities and cities known as the German League. Protestantism dominated the northern area (Prussia); Catholicism was the religion of the south (Bavaria). In the aftermath of the French Revolution, lands, monasteries, churches, and institutions had been taken over by the state and, in effect, secularized. Universities were closed and the church, on an institutional level, was greatly weakened. In 1817, Friedrich Wilhelm III of Prussia (1797–1840) even attempted to unite the Lutheran and the Reformed Church (Calvinists), but this provoked too much upset among these congregations.

The Catholic "restoration" experience in southern Germany was aided by influential "circles." These were small communities of committed Catholics, sometimes ecumenical and at other times not, which met regularly to reflect on and deepen their Christian life. The Catholicism of these "circles" promoted an ultramontanism, giving greater recognition to the authority of the pope in church matters. This theological vision was promoted by their newspaper *Der Katholik*. King Ludwig I (1825–1848) established Munich as the great center for the revitalization of Catholicism. That city had been the German center of the Counter-Reformation in another century.

Romanticism, a reaction to the tenets of the Enlightenment, flourished at this time in Germany as well as across Europe. The movement emphasized mystery over reason, community over the individual, and tradition over progress. The church came to be seen primarily as an organic, developing community animated by the Holy Spirit and only secondarily as an organized institution. Catholic romanticism valued the pope as a uniting influence gathering all people into a church community. Such church unity was seen as contributing to the unification of Germany itself. The revolution of 1848, which spread across Europe, did not bring about German unification. However, it did not grant greater freedom for the church in the different German states, although conflicts continued to arise between church and state. These served only to move German Catholics more and more into the papal orbit. It became clearer that only a church, independent and protected from the state, could function properly.

Austria opposed the trend toward ultramontanism as long as it could. Under Emperor Joseph II (1765–1790) efforts were made to establish an independent, national Catholic Church (Josephinism). Those efforts were gradually eliminated through the influence of the Austrian foreign minister, Prince Klemens von Metternich (1773–1859).

England and Ireland

During the Reign of Terror in France, many priests and other religious personnel fled to exile in England. The Catholic Church in England had experienced great restrictions since the Reformation. For instance, Catholics were still not allowed as of 1815 to vote or hold office. England also continued its stranglehold on Catholic Ireland. It was only with the efforts of the Irish patriot Daniel O'Connell (1775–1847) and his Catholic Association that England agreed to pass the Catholic Emancipation Act in 1829. At the same time, as the number of Catholics in England grew, the Anglican Church weakened. Many felt that the Anglican community was desperately in need of reform. Over time, it had fractured into a number of other churches, for example, Methodists, Baptists, and Quakers. There were also different liturgical expressions in the community. The so-called high church resembled in many ways Roman Catholic experience; the low church favored the Reformed or Calvinist experience.

Reformers, many of them clerics and associated with Oxford University, joined together to form the Oxford Movement. Some of them, including the intellectual leader of this movement, John Henry

Newman (1801–1890), eventually converted to Roman Catholicism. Newman was an Anglican priest, a university pastor, a serious scholar and prolific writer. He gradually became convinced that the truth of faith and revelation required an authentic teaching authority, guided by the Holy Spirit. That authority could only be ultimately the bishops in union with the bishop of Rome. Some of Newman's works include his *Apologia Pro Vita Sua*, the *Grammar of Assent*, and his *Essay on the Development of Christian Doctrine*. Newman was received into the Roman Catholic Church on October 9, 1845. Later, in 1879, Pope Leo XIII named him a cardinal.

Another great challenge facing the Catholic Church in England at this time was the large wave of immigration from Ireland after the great famine (1846–1848). Most of these immigrants were poor working people forced to live in very harsh industrial areas of the country. The Catholic Church, therefore, in order to serve these poor, went to great lengths to increase its personnel and institutions throughout the country.

The population of Ireland in 1840 was more than eight million people. The economy was agrarian and the only industry was in northern Ireland, the province of Ulster. Daniel O'Connell organized the Irish to work for repeal of the 1800 Act of Union, in order to free the Irish from control and domination by England. Many clergy and some bishops supported the call for Irish independence. Pope Gregory XVI and his advisors in Rome, however, feared revolution and violence and requested the clergy to stay out of politics. That request did not stop clerical support for the repeal of the Act of Union. After O'Connell's death in 1847, other groups took up the cause of Irish independence. Throughout their struggle the Irish remained fiercely united both in their Roman Catholic faith and in their opposition to English occupation.

10

Christianity in England and America 1787-1865

The Industrial Revolution

The beginning of the nineteenth century in England saw major shifts in the way people earned their living. It was the time of the so-called industrial revolution. The population all over Europe had greatly increased toward the end of the previous century. Technological advances were made in industries, for example, the steam engine which contributed dramatically to increased production. Cities expanded or new ones were born. Capitalism as a economic system ran unchecked so that an urban working class, a proletariat, often living in sub-human conditions, exploited and unprotected, arose. The "factory" replaced the "field" as the governing metaphor for the cycle of life.

The Anglican or established Church of England failed to respond immediately to the new urban world. An evangelical or gospel-based renewal movement sought to pick up the pieces. This movement in England promoted not only evangelistic activity, but a strict morality as well.

Evangelical groups such as the Methodists became popular with the working, poorer classes. Their message was clear—salvation came by faith in the passion and death of Christ. The movement stressed the authority and inspiration of the bible. Very mobile, Methodist circuit riders preached in tents and emphasized personal experience. This form of religion had much to say by way of comfort to an alienated and oppressed people. The evangelism or gospel preaching of the Methodists as well as Calvinists and evangelical Anglicans attempted to effect change in the moral world of England. The wealthy were encouraged to be conscious of and caring to the poor in a spirit of *noblesse oblige*. The poor were urged to live clean, decent, respectable lives, notwithstanding their suffering. Frivolous forms of entertainment such as dancing, the theater, reading novels, and card playing were all discouraged. At times the evangelical movement strongly supported the temperance movement and prohibition. It also promoted strict observance of the sabbath and eventually worked toward the abolition of slavery.

The evangelicals of the nineteenth century were not unlike the Puritans of the sixteenth century. They eventually sought positions of power and influence whereby they might work to "convert" others. The evangelical movement gained control of Cambridge University, thus producing a number of "converted" graduates to go forth and save the world for Christ.

The question remained, however: How to convert the masses of working people? To this end, William and Catherine Booth in 1865 began their own Christian mission in London. Their Salvation Army tried to convert the heart of the individual before attempting to change social conditions. Booth opted for a military style in his missionary work with uniforms, corps, and citadels. With this commitment a new, just social order would be born.

The Second Awakening in America

The first "great awakening" in America had been made popular through the preaching of Jonathan Edwards. The "second awakening" occurred in the early nineteenth century and became very popular among Baptists and Methodists. The revival began in New England and spread to the mid-Atlantic states and, then, to the western frontier. Yale University in New Haven became a center of the movement for a time.

In New England, the "awakening" remained calm. People converted to the Lord Jesus, through whom salvation came. Personal commitment to gospel living marked such conversions. The result was a great concern for morality and especially combating the sin and illness of alcoholism through the establishment of temperance societies. Voluntary organizations of converted Christians sponsored a variety of causes (e.g., education for native Americans, foreign missionary activity, bible societies). The revival promoted *diakonia* or service to the poor and oppressed as well as to the handicapped. Reverend Thomas Gallaudet of Hartford devoted himself to educating the hearing- and speech-impaired.

The "second awakening" moved westward from New England to

Kentucky and Tennessee after they became states in 1792 and 1796, respectively. Characteristic of the frontier revivals were the tent or camp meeting and preaching by circuit riders. These camp meetings often took place in August or the early fall. Areas in the forest were cleared and people who had often traveled many miles would set up camp for however long the meeting lasted. With numbers of people, fervent preachers, children and animals, there was always a certain amount of chaos at the meetings. Religious enthusiasm at times manifested itself physically—falling or swooning, bodily spasms, dancing or laughing. Of course, some of what transpired provoked ridicule and abuse. Dwight Moody (1837–1899) brought the tactics of the "awakening" to cities after the Civil War. In 1886, he founded what would be called later the Moody Bible Institute in Chicago.

Moody was succeeded in his ministry by William Ashley (Billy) Sunday (1862–1935), a former baseball player. Given to such antics as smashing furniture or using other dramatic effects during his preaching, Sunday would unleash a barrage of words intended to move the hearer to be a "fighter" for God and not merely some "hog-jowled, weasel-eyed, sponge-columned, mushy-fisted, jelly-spined, pussy-footing, four-flushing, Charlotte-russe, Christian."

The "second great awakening" contributed to the expansion and vibrancy of a number of Christian denominations in America. The Baptist and Methodist churches benefited significantly. By 1855, the largest single denomination in America was the Methodists, with a million and one half members; the next largest denomination was the Baptists, with over a million faithful.

Roman Catholicism in the New Republic

The American Revolution, in the words of John Adams, took place "in the minds and hearts of the American people." It truly represented and produced a new way of thinking about the person and society. Equality, tolerance, individualism and independence were the values promoted by both the Declaration of Independence and the Constitution. American republicanism and democracy were the antithesis of *l'ancien régime*. Roman Catholics had experienced discrimination before the Revolution. Subsequently that changed, so that Catholics not only were accepted but, in fact, became politically active and involved. Bigotry against Roman Catholics, however, would return with a vengeance at a later date.

The peace treaty that ended the American Revolution was signed with England in 1783. The Roman Catholic Church in the United States then began formally organizing itself. John Carroll (1736–1815), a son of one of the leading Catholic families of Maryland, played a pivotal role in that process.

Born in the colonies, Carroll had been educated in Europe where he was ordained a Jesuit priest. With the suppression of the Society of Jesus in 1773, Carroll returned to Maryland to work as a diocesan priest. In 1784, the twenty to twenty-five ex-Jesuits working in America formed the "Select Body of Clergy" to regulate their affairs and administer their property. On June 9, 1784, Rome appointed John Carroll as superior of the mission in the United States. This was done with the encouragement of Benjamin Franklin. In 1790 the pope acceded to requests from priests in America to elect a bishop, and Carroll was chosen to be the first bishop of Baltimore.

One of the immediate problems faced by the fledgling church was the need for priests to minister to the scattered Catholic faithful. Carroll firmly believed that only a holy, well-educated, native-born clergy should serve God's people. To that end, he established the first Catholic college in 1789 at Georgetown and the first seminary at St. Mary's in Baltimore in 1791.

A special problem developed early in the church's experience in the United States. Perhaps the root issue was how to be American and how to be Roman Catholic. The Constitution clearly rejected the establishment of any single religion or denomination by establishing the principle of the separation between church and state. Independent Americans owed allegiance to no foreign ruler. Consequently, there was the pull toward a "national" church, given the American spirit of democracy and republicanism. On the parish level, this independence took the form of "trusteeism." According to that system, modeled on the polity of Presbyterians and Congregationalists, elected lay trustees would be in charge of and responsible for all the temporal realities of a given parish. At times, they would attempt to hire and fire pastors. Another, perhaps less lofty reason for trusteeism was the ethnic tension that arose at times between the pastor and the laity. For instance, Irish parishioners fought French clergy for control of the purse.

Carroll, given the need for priests, also encouraged the Sulpician Order to send priests to America. A number of them came from France to engage in seminary work, thus influencing the spirituality of future American priests. Jesuits also supplied teachers and missionaries from their headquarters at Georgetown. In 1806–1807, Father Edward Dominic Fenwick from Maryland brought the

Dominican Order from England to Kentucky. He later became the first bishop of Cincinnati, Ohio. Ursuline Sisters opened schools in New York and Boston. Elizabeth Ann Bayley Seton (1774–1821), the Episcopalian widow of a prominent New Yorker, became a Roman Catholic after her husband's death. She moved to Baltimore, where she began a school for girls and then another one at Emmitsburg, also in Maryland. Mother Seton went on to found the American Sisters of Charity. In September 1975 Pope Paul VI canonized, or declared, Elizabeth Ann Seton to be the first American-born saint.

In 1808 Pope Pius VII established four other dioceses in the United States: Boston, Bardstown in Kentucky, New York, and Philadelphia. There were then about seventy thousand Catholics in the United States, excluding the Louisiana territory. Carroll died in 1815 and was eventually succeeded by the Frenchman, Bishop Ambrose Maréchal. The church had grown quickly and there was a need to unify its organization. The First Provincial Council of Baltimore was convoked in October 1829. That meeting of bishops pointed out to Rome that in the United States there were already six seminaries and nine colleges, with three of them chartered universities. A number of religious houses for men were also flourishing, for example, those of the Dominicans, Jesuits, and Sulpicians. There were thirty-three monasteries and a number of different sisters' congregations as well as over two hundred thousand laity.

At Emmitsburg, Maryland, Mount St. Mary's College had been founded in 1808, following the 1789 establishment of Georgetown. Bishop John Hughes opened St. John's College at Fordham in New York City in 1841. Villanova began under the auspices of the Augustinians in 1842. Father Sorin and some Brothers of the Holy Cross began Notre Dame du Lac in South Bend in 1842 as well. Holy Cross College opened in Worcester, Massachusetts, in 1843 and St. Joseph's College in Philadelphia began in 1851.

Maryland and Kentucky were key areas for Catholic population and influence. That would quickly change, however, with the arrival of large numbers of Catholic immigrants from Europe. Then the Catholic experience would enter a new phase of expansion and geo- graphical shift. The growth in numbers, power, and influence would also unleash violent anti-Catholic prejudice. The first age of the Catholic Church in America came to an end at the First Plenary Council of Baltimore, which convened in 1852 under the presidency of Archbishop Kenrick. At that time there were six archbishops, twenty-six bishops, and one and a half million Catholics with fifteen hundred priests serving them. One of the recommendations of that meeting was that every Catholic church have a Catholic school. The dream of a Catholic school for every Catholic child never materialized. Nevertheless, the Catholic school system, dating in origin to this era, became a massive private school system unmatched anywhere in the church or in any other nation.

Church organization continued to grow and spread all through the first half of the century. Not only schools and parishes, but also hospitals and sanatoriums were established. Various religious orders native to the United States came into being, for example, the Paulist Fathers, founded by Isaac Hecker. Many new dioceses were established: St. Louis in 1826, Detroit in 1833, Nashville in 1837, Chicago and Milwaukee in 1843, Oregon City in 1846, and San Francisco in 1853.

The Immigrants

There were Irish immigrants in the colonies before the Revolutionary War. Four and one half million more emigrated to the United States in the century after 1820. During the 1830s two hundred thousand sailed from Ireland to America. Conditions in Ireland were dire with a growing population, scarce food, and ruthless landlords and taxes. With the "great famine" (1846–1848), the potato crop failed due to climate and a mysterious blight. An exodus began that brought seven hundred and eighty thousand Irish, mostly Catholics, to the United States. By 1860 one million six hundred thousand Irish had emigrated. The Irish suffered greatly, living in slums in major cities, working at back-breaking jobs for low pay, often without family or any support. Desirable employment often came with the condition "Irish Catholics need not apply."

Another sizable Catholic group to emigrate to America was the Germans. Between 1820 and 1920, more than five million arrived in the United States. About one million six hundred thousand were Roman Catholic. Italians, toward the end of the century, similarly set sail for America. About one million settled in the United States between 1880 and 1900; three million more arrived in the following twenty years. After 1880, more than two million Catholic Polish emigrated. Close to one million French Canadians, the vast majority being Roman Catholic, came across the border. Other national groups came in smaller numbers toward the end of the nineteenth century: Slovaks, Czechs or Bohemians, Lithuanians and Ukrainians.

At the time of the Mexican-American War (1846–1848), the United States annexed part of northern Mexico, adding about eighty thousand Catholics to the population. The number of Mexicans in the United States has grown dramatically so that presently there are more than three million, the majority of whom are Roman Catholics. Many are undocumented.

Because of immigration, the Catholic Church in America grew and expanded numerically, culturally, and geographically. It did not happen all at once, but it did happen relatively quickly in roughly three large waves of immigration. This growth challenged the church pastorally. Personnel were required to minister to the religious needs of these diverse people. Social institutions were needed to serve human needs. Catholic priests and sisters were recruited and educated in large numbers. Churches, schools, hospitals, and social service agencies were all built mostly from donations of money and other gifts from people who were of modest means or even poor. Immigration irrevocably changed the Catholic experience in America. It also provoked for a long time, and even into the present, religious intolerance and anti-Catholicism.

A number of motives coalesced during the first half of the nineteenth century, all of which contributed at times to a violent anti-Catholicism. Some of these factors were:

1) the rapid expansion of the Catholic Church through the immigration of a variety of different ethnic and national groups;
2) the Puritan heritage and English Protestant antipathy to Catholicism and "popery";
3) the Enlightenment's disdain for any authoritarian religion;
4) the threat that the Roman Catholic Church posed to the cultural hegemony of white, Anglo-Saxon, Protestantism (WASP);
5) the rise of poorer, urban, "foreign" lower classes which contributed to fear and the rise of "nativism."

At times, anti-Catholicism took a literary form. Newspapers featured articles and editorials warning of the danger of "popery" and "Romanism." Tracts and books castigated Catholic beliefs, whipped up fear against Catholics, and in general sought to discredit the Roman Church. Scurrilous items appeared, for example, Maria Monk's *Awful Disclosures of the Hotel Dieu Nunnery of Montreal* (1836). An influential anti-Catholic writer was Samuel F. B. Morse (1791–1872), the inventor of the telegraph.

Violence against Catholics broke out in Boston on August 11,

1834, when a mob burned down the Ursuline Convent, a girl's school in Charlestown. The perpetrators were tried, but acquitted. In 1844 riots broke out in Philadelphia, where two Catholic churches, thirty Irish homes, the diocesan seminary, and the Augustinian Friars' library were all burned down. Thirteen people were killed and more than fifty were wounded. As a young parish priest in Ellsworth, Maine, in 1854, Jesuit Father John Bapst, S.J., who later became the first president of Boston College, was tarred and feathered and ridden out of town on a rail.

In 1849 Charles Allen of New York formed the Order of the Star Spangled Banner. It was dedicated to preventing foreigners and Catholics from attaining political office. As a political organization, it was known as the "American Party," but because of its secretiveness it came to be called the "Know-Nothing Party." The Know-Nothing movement, for a time, garnered many votes for candidates to political office. It eventually faded away at the time of the Civil War. Nevertheless, it discouraged Catholic candidates from the political process. Abraham Lincoln had said on August 24, 1855:

> As a nation, we began by declaring that all men are created equal. We now practically read it "all men are created equal except Negroes." When the Know-Nothings obtain control, it will read: "all men are created equal except Negroes, foreigners, and Catholics." (Quoted from James Hennessey, S.J., *American Catholics*, New York: Oxford University Press, 1981, p. 126.)

Catholics and Slavery

By 1860 there were four and a half million black people in the United States, or fourteen percent of the nation's population. Three and a half million were slaves in the South. There were also slaves in the North. In 1775, slaves were twelve percent of the population of New Jersey and six percent of the population of Rhode Island. While slavery was institutionalized in America, there were also those who protested against it. Quakers in Philadelphia began the first anti-slavery association as early as 1775.

In the 1830s, abolitionism gained momentum. A variety of individuals were involved for different reasons. The revivalist movement of the "second great awakening" took on the anti-slavery cause, giving the crusade a religious and moral character. Harriet Beecher Stowe wrote her classic *Uncle Tom's Cabin*, which was an impassioned call for emancipation. The South saw in abolitionism a threat to its whole way of life and took on a defensive posture in support of slavery.

The Presbyterian Church divided along the sectional lines of North and South over the slavery issue. So, also, did the Methodist and the Baptist churches. Smaller denominations tended to reflect their geographical position. The Lutheran, Episcopal, and Roman Catholic churches remained undivided structurally, with their members on both sides of the issue. While Pope Gregory XVI, in 1839, condemned the slave trade, he did not condemn slavery itself.

In pre-Revolutionary days, the Roman Catholic Church had begun its presence in America in the south among the gentry. Many possessed slaves (e.g., the Carrolls, the Jesuits). Some did provide manumission or freedom for their slaves. Charles Carroll in 1797 attempted to pass a bill in the Maryland state senate that would have abolished slavery. He was unsuccessful in these attempts. Efforts, nevertheless, were made on the pastoral level to minister to the needs of slaves. Chapels and churches for blacks were founded; schools were established to teach them doctrine and offer basic education.

Bishops, clergy, and laity all took sides during the Civil War. There was no single Catholic position either on slavery or on the war itself. Priests served as chaplains to both the Union and Confederate armies. More than five hundred sisters served as nurses during the conflict, in which there were more than one million casualties with six hundred thousand killed. In general, a judgment can be rendered that the Catholic Church as an institution did not take a prophetic stance condemning slavery and its underlying racism. That kind of a stance awaited another period in history and a changed environment.

11

The Missions:
Eighteenth and
Nineteenth Centuries

The church of its very nature is missionary. To be a gospel community requires engagement with the world. Truth naturally seeks to be shared. Jesus, the way, the truth, and the life, and his teaching must be preached, as indicated in his command: "Go, therefore, teach all nations and baptize in the name of the Father and of the Son and of the Holy Spirit" (Mt 28:19). The missionary dimension of the gospel has been understood in different ways over the centuries. Sometimes missionaries baptized in a very heavy-handed way, and missionary work disguised cultural imperialism. There were other epochs, however, when the "good news" was communicated to the non-evangelized as truly a liberating, salvific message.

In the sixteenth century age of exploration, Spanish and Portuguese adventurers and missionaries roamed the known world. After the French Revolution and the Napoleonic era, the religious restoration in Europe overflowed to the rest of the world. Many new religious orders of women and men were founded in France to do overseas missionary work. The Congregation of the Sacred Hearts of Jesus and Mary (Picpus Fathers) was founded in 1805 to serve Oceania. In 1807 the Sisters of Saint Joseph of Cluny began ministry in Africa and Asia; in 1836 large areas in the South Seas were entrusted to the pastoral care of the Marists. The Jesuits were restored in 1814 to resume their role as missionaries throughout the world. The Congregation of the Holy Ghost did enormous service to blacks in both East and West Africa. During the nineteenth century, fifty-three male and two hundred female congregations were founded.

Lay women and men similarly contributed to the mission effort. Marie-Pauline Jaricot (1799–1862) established the Association for the Spreading of the Faith to pray for missionaries and raise funds for their work. Similar groups sprang up in Bavaria, the Rhineland, and Austria. A new era of mission work had begun. The exploits of this effort were often published in the *Annals of the Congregation of the Faith*, founded in 1823 to publish letters from bishops and missionaries. The periodical had a circulation of more than one hundred and fifty thousand by 1846 and was printed in several languages.

Pope Gregory XVI (1831–1846) had been intimately involved with mission work before becoming pontiff. The pope called for the establishment of local churches in the "mission" world with indigenous clergy and bishops. He promoted the opening of seminaries as well as an appreciation for local art and culture. Catholic missionary activity during the late eighteenth and nineteenth centuries was the work of Catholic bishops, clergy, religious and laity.

The Protestant mission effort was characterized by the proliferation of volunteer societies founded precisely to promote foreign mission work. For instance, in 1792 William Carey set up what would become the Baptist Missionary Society. The London Missionary Society (Methodists, Presbyterians, and Congregationalists), the Church Missionary Society (Evangelical Anglicans) and the British and Foreign Bible Society joined the effort as well. Similar groups came into being in Holland, Denmark, Germany, and the United States. These groups were voluntary and private, without any state support or even at times without official church support. The effort came from dedicated lay people concerned about the salvation of those in distant lands. Such people, many of whom were women, sailed from home to live in harsh conditions for the sake of Christ and the gospel.

Latin America

The vast continent of Central and South America had been colonized by Spain and Portugal in the sixteenth century. The colonial period lasted almost four hundred years. During that time, the Roman Catholic Church was deeply implanted through the establishment of churches, universities, hospitals, convents, monasteries, and orphanages. Religious orders and congregations attracted many candidates. Saints canonized by the Roman Catholic Church from this period include natives of Latin America such as St. Rose of Lima, St.

Martin de Porres, and St. John Masias, as well as saintly European missionaries such as St. Peter Claver and St. Louis Bertrand.

The mission effort was sponsored and often controlled by the state through the *Patronato Real*, whereby the Spanish court exercised control of the church. Church-state relations were complex. Missionaries often challenged government officials, particularly over the treatment of natives, while other members of the clergy fiercely supported the colonial regime.

Approximately eighty percent of the population of Latin America at the end of the eighteenth century was black, native, and mestizo (persons of mixed blood). For the most part they were dependent and second class citizens. Even in the church there had been discrimination, as manifested in the prohibition against ordaining natives to the priesthood. Creoles (whites of European heritage born in the new world) formed roughly fifteen percent of the population of sixteen million. Creole males were often anti-clerical, although Catholic. The church and clerics, however, were important to them inasmuch as they encouraged and supported the powerlessness and dependence of the masses.

Napoleon's conquest of Spain and Portugal aided the independence movement throughout Latin America. In 1808 Napoleon deposed King Ferdinand VII of Spain and replaced him with his brother Joseph Bonaparte (1808–1813). The Spanish colonies in Latin America remained faithful to Ferdinand, who was restored as king in 1814. The La Plata colonies (Argentina, Paraguay, and Uruguary) declared their independence beginning in 1816. José de San Martín liberated Chile in 1818; Simón Bolívar did the same, first for "greater Colombia" (Venezuela, Colombia, and Ecuador), and then later for Peru and Bolivia.

The Mexican independence movement was led by the Catholic priest, Father Miguel Hidalgo (1753–1811). On September 16, 1810, he declared independence, supported by a large army of Indians and mestizos. After Hidalgo was captured and executed in 1811, he was succeeded by a mestizo priest, José Maria Morelos, who was himself captured and executed in 1815.

Central America declared its independence from Mexico, of which it was a part, and later became Guatemala, El Salvador, Honduras, Nicaragua, and Costa Rica. The United States helped Panama to gain its independence from Colombia in 1903 and also aided the new nation in building the Panama Canal.

Napoleon invaded Portugal in 1807. The royal family fled to Brazil and lived in exile there until 1821. In 1822 Pedro, the son of the king of Portugal, declared independence for Brazil and named himself emperor. Instigated by the French Revolution, Haiti, after a rebellion against foreign control, declared its independence from France in 1804.

Clergy were on both sides of the nineteenth century movements for independence that freed the colonies in Latin America from their European rulers. Those bishops and priests born in Spain often supported the crown; native-born clergy or Creoles supported the independence movement. Many of the former returned to Europe with the coming of independence. Soon disputes arose between the church and the governments of the new republics, which were often led by anti-clerical Creole intellectuals and professionals, supported by the powerful Creole landowners. The new governments sought the right to name bishops, which the pope was unwilling to grant. Consequently, without bishops, there were few priests, and this profoundly affected the sacramental life of the Catholic Church. Because the religious orders were often suppressed by the governments of the new republics, the church faced a serious personnel shortage in the areas of pastoral care, education and the works of charity. The always contentious problem of church property and wealth also provoked conflict.

The issue, of course, in the post-independence era in Latin America was the relationship between church and state. What was the church's position in society? What was its role in temporal affairs? What kind of power should it exert over its members?

Liberals urged that religion be purely a private and personal affair. They were anti-clerical, sought to liberate land and the educational system from the church's control, condemned popular devotions as superstition, and opposed the idea of the public celebration of faith. Their ideas traced themselves in large part to the Enlightenment.

Conservatives opposed an "atheistic" state and promoted the established order. Often enough they supported the church to further their own agenda. Both liberals and conservatives came from the upper classes. Neither promoted the interests of the majority of the population who were poor and oppressed. Although Catholicism became the "official" religion of the new republics of South and Central America, the church often found itself engaged in conflict with the state.

Pastorally, the Catholic community served a variety of diverse peoples—Creoles, mestizos, natives and blacks. Counted among Catholic people were wealthy landowners, anti-clerical intellectuals, merchants, and service class people as well as masses of the poor and slaves. In the second half of the nineteenth century large numbers of European and Asian immigrants arrived in the southern hemisphere. These Catholics lived in urban areas, in the mountains and altiplanos, in desert or jungle areas. A major challenge for the church was the task of preaching and teaching an authentic, relevant gospel message to this diverse and geographically scattered population. Evangelization and catechesis (religious education) proved to be a daunting task for the church of Latin America in the nineteenth and twentieth centuries.

Africa

Portugal had been the chief colonizing power in Africa during the sixteenth century's "age of exploration." It had set up a series of trading posts along the western and then eastern coasts of the continent. Portugal provided missionaries for their traders, some of whom also ministered to indigenous peoples. The Roman Catholic Church thus got its second start in Africa. The strong presence of the church during the first six centuries of the Christian era in Africa had ended with Mohammed and the spread of Islam.

Interest in black Africa increased during the second half of the nineteenth century. A number of European countries sought African colonies both for territorial expansion and for the new economic and market possibilities which they offered.

Britain, France, the Netherlands, Belgium, Germany, and Italy all carved out their territory. Portugal ruled what was then Angola and Mozambique (Zimbabwe). The Dutch had expelled the Portuguese from what would be South Africa and had established its colony at the Cape of Good Hope (Capetown) in 1652. France took Senegal around the same time. Britain founded Sierra Leone for its freed slaves in 1799. Later, they took the Cape of Good Hope from the Dutch. France colonized Algeria, Germany took Namibia,

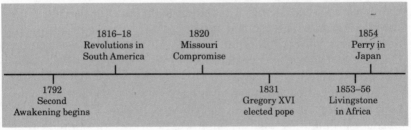

	1816–18 Revolutions in South America	1820 Missouri Compromise		1854 Perry in Japan
1792 Second Awakening begins			1831 Gregory XVI elected pope	1853–56 Livingstone in Africa

and Belgium conquered the Congo. The African colonial period continued until after World War II with different countries dominating different territory; for example, Egypt was first ruled by the French and later came under British control. England established a crown colony in Uganda and Kenya, while Germans ruled part of today's Tanzania and Italy ruled in Eritrea.

Christian missionaries accompanied colonization. Roman Catholic missionaries followed the steps of Catholic colonists; Protestants did the same with the colonizing efforts of Protestant nations. The caliber of these missionaries, who sought to convert the indigenous peoples of Africa to Christianity, was generally very high. Because human development of the new African converts was an integral part of the preaching of the gospel, missionary compounds included schools, dispensaries, and hospitals as well as churches.

White missionaries of the nineteenth century brought their European culture to Africa. For some, preaching the gospel meant preaching the superiority of white European values. Many missionaries, however, were acutely aware of the importance of respecting indigenous cultures. They challenged the abuses of colonizers. The concern for justice was preached in churches and taught in schools. A number of African nationalist leaders and subsequently leaders of the independence movement came out of this Christian formation. One of the first African church leaders was Samuel Crowther, the first black Anglican bishop in Africa, who sought to bring the message of the gospel to the area around the Niger River in West Africa.

Christianity in Africa followed the flag. Protestant missionaries went to Africa representing a variety of denominations. Most were evangelical and fiercely opposed to the slave trade. Thus was born the doctrine "Christianity, commerce, and civilization," which became a missionary strategy that meant simply that commerce would replace the slave trade. The missionaries believed that by promoting commerce, and the technology which it required, "civilization" would come to Africa.

The great champion of this missionary tactic was Dr. David

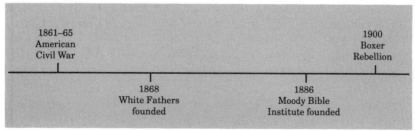

1861–65 American Civil War		1900 Boxer Rebellion
	1868 White Fathers founded	1886 Moody Bible Institute founded

Livingstone (1813–1873), who founded missions and explored great parts of the interior of Africa. During 1853–1856, he walked across Africa from west to east, exploring the Zambesi River, and he became the first European to view the Victoria Falls. He also walked across what is now South Africa, Botswana, Zambia, Mozambique, Malawi, Tanzania, and eastern Zaire and recorded these journeys. At one point, he disappeared for some time and was eventually found by the American journalist Henry Morton Stanley, who uttered the famous understatement, "Dr. Livingstone, I presume" when they met. The great explorer's heart was buried in Africa, while his body lies in Westminster Abbey.

Roman Catholic missionary efforts in Africa intensified through the labors of the new religious congregations that were established to implant the church there, for example, the Sisters of Saint Joseph of Cluny in 1819, the Holy Ghost Fathers in 1848, and the Society of African Missions in 1856. A major Catholic leader in Africa was Cardinal Lavigerie (1825–1892), the archbishop of Algiers and later Carthage. He founded the White Fathers (called that because of the white tunics they wore) in 1868. The following year the cardinal established the Congregation of the White Sisters. He encouraged his missionaries to inculturate, that is, move into the local culture as much as possible in order to present the gospel effectively and not as some foreign or western imposition. The cardinal believed that Africa needed African missionaries. Like Dr. Livingstone, he worked to end slavery.

Another significant Catholic figure in Africa was Charles de Foucauld (1858–1916). Foucauld began his career in France as a soldier, studying at the famous military academy of Saint-Cyr and then later at Saumur. He left the church as a young man, and during his student days led a rather dissipated life. After serving with bravery in the Sahara, he resigned his military commission. He had found the army, particularly living in France, too tame and so returned to Africa. There he experienced a religious conversion, and lived for two years in the desert disguised as a servant of a Jewish rabbi.

Foucauld returned to the church and joined the Trappists, a strict religious order of contemplative monks. Later he left them to become a solitary hermit living in the desert. He desired to be a missionary among the Muslim desert tribes, offering simply a witness of loving presence and care for others. It was his aim to live as a contemplative who by Christian charity would become a universal brother to all people. He always kept the Blessed Sacrament exposed in his small hut and spent hours there in adoration of the sacramental presence of Christ in the consecrated host. Brother Charles lived among the Tuareg tribes of the desert and eventually was murdered by a marauding band. His writings and accounts of his life later inspired the establishment of two religious congregations, the Little Brothers of Jesus and the Little Sisters of Jesus, groups who lived in absolute poverty and simplicity.

Asia

Christian missionary work in Asia faced enormous challenges: huge geographical distances, massive populations and deeply entrenched religio-cultural traditions, for example, Hindu, Buddhist, Islamic, Confucian, Shinto, and Taoist. Christianity had begun in Asia, but from the outset it had experienced greater success in the Mediterranean world. There were, however, Christian foundations in west and central Asia. During the thirteenth century, Dominican and Franciscan friars preached the gospel in east Asia. Unfortunately, the unsettled conditions of the fourteenth century ended their efforts. In the sixteenth century the work of missionaries, especially Franciscans and Jesuits, implanted the church in India, Japan, and China. Periodic persecutions in these countries almost wiped out the new missionary efforts begun in the age of exploration. The nineteenth century revival of missionary activity in both Protestant and Catholic churches brought renewed interest in Asia.

The evangelical revival in England had given birth to the Baptist Missionary Society. One of its leaders, William Carey (1761–1834), sailed for India where he began a remarkable career as an expatriate missionary. His work was prodigious and with the help of two other Baptists, Joshua Marshman and William Ward, Carey established a chain of mission stations near Bengal. He translated the New Testament into Bengali, published grammars and dictionaries, built schools, promoted agricultural advances, and led a campaign to outlaw "widow-burning" (sati was the custom whereby widows threw themselves on the funeral pyre of their husbands), which succeeded in 1829.

Given the English control of India, Protestant missionaries from the Anglican Church as well as the non-conforming English churches, such as the Baptists, established schools and institutions of higher learning. These churches also addressed social needs, as well as disseminating the word of God through various translations of the bible. Still, Christians remained but a small minority of the population, and Christianity was most successful among the poor, lower castes, for example, the untouchables. Hindu influence was at its weakest among the disenfranchised.

The Roman Catholic Church in India had deep roots. Some Catholics traced their ancestral faith back to Saint Thomas, the apostle, others to Saint Francis Xavier in the sixteenth century. In the nineteenth century, Roman Catholic missionaries ministered to Indian Catholics and to the Irish, who comprised nearly half of the British troops in India. They attempted some convert work, but that was directed mostly to Protestants.

Both Protestant and Roman Catholic missionaries faced the issue of whether to attempt to convert the elite castes or the lower castes, and how eventually to eliminate the entire system of castes. Candidates for priesthood from lower castes did not easily enter the seminary. Nevertheless, the rising consciousness of these lower classes called for just such priests. Higher or elite castes rarely converted to Christianity. Educated Hindus, however, did find the ethical teaching of Christ to be attractive and worthy of respect, although they did not generally feel compelled to surrender their Hindu religious and cultural identity. Parishes were divided over the issue of supporting the caste system or working to abolish it.

A question for both Protestant and Catholic missionaries was how they should view Hinduism. Was it wrong and erroneous? Was there some truth in it that, in fact, represented or contained authentic revelation? Was Hinduism to be understood as a kind of remote preparation for the gospel? These questions were faced by missionaries as they confronted Hinduism and the other traditional religions throughout Asia.

Christians in China were often persecuted, and the government in the first half of the nineteenth century opposed the entry of missionaries and traders into the country. A series of treaties with the European powers changed that situation, so that by 1900 there were nearly three thousand Protestant missionaries in the country, nearly one thousand Catholic priests, and a large number of nuns.

The Christian gospel made inroads among some people. Certainly, a portion of these were "rice Christians," that is, those who accepted baptism for some gain other than religious. The dependence of Christianity on foreign powers, however, alienated the vast majority of Chinese. This was most evident at times of national uprisings. Xenophobia provoked the 1900 Boxer Rebellion in Beijing, where a number of priests, bishops, religious, and thousands of Christians were massacred. European powers forced China to pay restitution for these losses.

By 1911 there were thousands of Protestant missionaries and churches in the country. An array of Catholic religious orders of men and women sponsored a variety of Catholic institutions, including schools, parishes, hospitals and orphanages. Chinese gradually assumed leadership positions in these various churches. The challenge Christianity always faced was just how to accommodate the gospel to Chinese culture.

Father Matteo Ricci, S.J. (1552–1610), had attempted to address those very issues for Catholics in the sixteenth century, and the "Chinese Rites" controversy ensued. The question arose again in the nineteenth century. While churches did make great gains in China, they remained always a minor presence in the vast population of that country.

Christianity was present in a unique way in Japan. In 1865 a group of "secret" Christians made contact with newly arrived Catholic missionaries in Nagasaki. These Christians, estimated to be between twenty thousand and one hundred thousand people, traced their roots to the preaching of Saint Francis Xavier and his Jesuit companions in the sixteenth century. Like the Chinese, the Japanese were fearful of the European influence of Christianity upon the native population. In fact, in 1597, twenty-six Christians, Japanese and foreign, had been martyred in Nagasaki. They were canonized and declared to be saints of the Roman Catholic Church in 1852. After the closing of Japan to all foreigners in the seventeenth century, the surviving Japanese Christians were without priests for two hundred years. These secret Christians had developed their own style and way of being of church. Unfortunately, with their discovery came government persecution.

Although Japan had been closed to foreigners since the seventeenth century, that changed in 1854 when an American, Captain Perry, forced the Japanese to sign trade agreements. This opened the country to missionary work as well. Japan sought to learn as much as it could from the west while maintaining its own culture. By the beginning of the next century, it had become a powerful nation, defeating China and Russia and annexing Korea.

Roman Catholic missionary orders established churches and schools, and Japanese assumed leadership roles in the church. Pope Leo XIII established the Japanese hierarchy in 1891. Protestant churches in Japan saw the establishment of small groups of Christians sharing the scriptures and rejecting western structures.

A leader of this movement was Uchimura Kanzo, who promoted a "churchless Christianity." These groups existed alongside traditional Protestant denominations. Once again at issue for both Catholics and Protestants was the question of how to be Christian and at the same time preserve cultural identity. How inculturate Christianity into the Japanese reality? How separate the person and teaching of Jesus Christ from its Western cultural expression?

In 1866 the fragile Korean Catholic Church numbered about twenty-five thousand members. During the first part of the century, both foreign and indigenous Korean clergy, bishops, and laity had often been persecuted. Many were executed and thus became the first martyrs of the Korean church. In 1876 Japan forced Korea to sign a trade agreement, thus opening the country as well to foreign missionaries. Methodists and Presbyterians arrived from the United States. Catholic and Protestant missionaries alike used Korean script to communicate their message. These churches often gave spiritual comfort to Korean people in times of oppression, especially during the years of Japanese domination. Christianity over time has become a significant, vibrant presence in Korea.

Churches followed the flag in other parts of Asia. In 1869 King Tu-Duc (1847–1882) ceded South Vietnam (Cochin-China) to France. By 1885 France occupied the entire country as well as Cambodia and Laos. Catholic presence was strong, therefore, in Indochina. The Philippine people remained heavily Roman Catholic even after independence from Spain in 1896 and during the American occupation.

Oceania

The English established the Anglican Church in Australia, originally a penal colony. Immigrants, especially from Ireland, brought the Roman Catholic Church, while the Scotch brought the Presbyterian Church. In general there existed a separation of church and state in both Australia and New Zealand. Irish Catholics, mirroring their experience in Ireland, resented any efforts by the English or Anglicans to rule them. The church supported the rights of Catholic immigrants, promoting their spiritual and human development. Irish Catholics soon became involved in both politics and labor movements in order to promote the rights of their people.

Indigenous people, that is, the aborigines in Australia and the Maoris of New Zealand, were often oppressed by colonizers or decimated by the diseases brought by the immigrants. Christian churches made efforts both to protect them and to convert them to Christianity. Missionaries preached the gospel in Polynesia as well as throughout the islands of Melanesia and Micronesia. Similarly, large numbers of Christians by the end of the nineteenth century could be found in Indonesia.

The Christian churches, Catholic and Protestant, had indeed expanded throughout the eighteenth and nineteenth centuries. Missionaries often accompanied either the imperialist colonizing efforts of nations or the commercial interests of traders. What they did in these areas to establish the church and preach the gospel varied often enough with the caliber of the missionary and the missionary's awareness of the distinction between the interests of the church and the interests of the nation. There still remained, however, areas of the world where people had as yet never heard of Christ or the gospel. Thus, Catholics and Protestants saw the missionary task as continuing.

FOR FURTHER READING AND REFERENCE

F. L. Cross and E. A. Livingstone, ed., *The Oxford Dictionary of the Christian Church*, 2nd ed. revised (Oxford: Oxford University Press, 1974).

James Hennessey, S.J., *American Catholics: A History of the Roman Catholic Community in the United States* (New York: Oxford University Press, 1981).

Hubert Jedin, ed., *History of the Church*, Vol. VII: *The Church Between Revolution and Restoration* (New York: Crossroad Publishing Company, 1981).

Richard P. McBrien, ed., *The Harper-Collins Encyclopedia of Catholicism* (Ligouri: Ligouri Publications, 1994).

Mark A. Noll, *A History of Christianity in the United States and Canada* (Grand Rapids: William B. Eerdmans Publishing Company, 1992).

12

The Reign of Pius IX 1846–1878

At the death of Pope Gregory XVI (1831–1846), the voting cardinals chose Giovanni Maria Mastai Ferretti, the cardinal bishop of Imola in Italy, as pope with the name Pius IX. He would become the longest reigning pontiff in the history of the church (1846–1878).

The Situation in Europe

Amidst the revolutions that had spread throughout Europe in 1848, Napoleon's nephew, Louis Napoleon (1808–1873), came to power. By 1852 he had declared himself Emperor Napoleon III. At first he sought an independent French church, naming bishops himself. Some years later, Napoleon would seek church support against liberal currents challenging his reign. The conservative clergy of France (the so-called ultramontanes) increasingly supported Rome and the pope against the more liberal bishops.

In Prussia, the 1848 revolution gained some independence for Catholics from Protestant government control, but this was of short duration. The Austrian tendency toward Josephinism, which lessened ties to Rome, was reversed in 1855 when the government signed a concordat or treaty with Rome, thereby strengthening relations. The newly liberated Catholic Church in England similarly reemphasized its connections to the Roman pontiff. Cardinal Nicholas Wiseman (1802–1865), and Cardinal Henry Manning (1808–1892), his successor as archbishop of Westminster, were both staunch ultramontanists. The church in Spain was also affected by the events of the times, and anticlerical violence resulted in the murder of priests and the confiscation of church property. Queen Isabella II came to power in 1844 and began to restore the church to a position of influence.

Europe experienced a major cultural shift during the first half of the nineteenth century. The Enlightenment and French Revolution challenged and changed the established order of things. "Liberalism" in the personal, political, economic and religious worlds to varying degrees replaced a medieval, feudalistic conception of the world. It promoted freedom, liberty, natural rights, parliamentary and constitutional governments, private property, rights of conscience, tolerance and the rule of law. The dark side of "liberalism" promoted the absolute autonomy of human reason versus revelation, nature versus the supernatural, individual freedom versus the common good, unlimited choice versus moral responsibility, rights versus duties. The church's experience of this dark side was anti-clericalism, loss of property, persecution, and a consistent effort to make religion irrelevant in the major areas of life. It was in this complex and volatile environment that Pius IX became pope.

Loss of the Papal States

The events of 1848 in Europe promoted the *risorgimento* or the movement to national unification in Italy. Initially Pius IX seemed to support the patriots. He initiated reforms in the administration of the Papal States and granted clemency to prisoners. However, he refused to participate in a revolt against the dominion of Catholic Austria which controlled northern Italy. The pope, valuing the independence that ruling the Papal States gave him, refused to surrender control of them. These moves won for him the fierce opposition and animosity of those working toward and fighting for Italian unification.

On November 15, 1848, a disillusioned radical assassinated the prime minister of the Papal States. Fearing an outbreak of revolution, Pius IX, in disguise, fled to Gaeta in the Kingdom of Naples, where he lived until 1850. He was restored to Rome only through the intervention of the French, a situation which caused serious resentment in Italian patriotic circles. The *risorgimento*, however, would not be stopped.

The king of Piedmont, Victor Emmanuel II, under Prime Minister Camillo Cavour (1810–1861), began to expand his territory. On September 20, 1870, his troops took control of the Papal States, thus ending the political, temporal power of the popes in Italy, which dated back to a gift from Charlemagne. Pius IX steadfastly refused to accept and recognize the new order of things. For him, the battle was between God and the church on one side against the revolution and Satan on the other. He saw himself not as a political power but as a custodian of the lands of the church. He believed that he did not have the right to give them away since they belonged ultimately to the Catholic people. The pope became a "prisoner of the Vatican," rejecting all contact with the new Italian government under the reign of King Victor Emmanuel.

Pope Pius IX, while resented by Italian patriots and "liberals," was nevertheless a truly popular leader among Catholics. His personality, hardships, and personal holiness won him many admirers. More and more did the person and office of the pope come to become revered and appreciated as central to Catholic life. It was a triumph for "ultramontanism" against nationalist or independence tendencies. Although Pius IX strengthened and renewed the church interiorly, his concern for the dangers of "liberalism" led him to isolate the church from the modern world.

Catholic Piety

While the pope had lost temporal power, he had in fact gained enormous influence and spiritual impact. Pius IX promoted devotion to Mary, the mother of God, throughout the Catholic world. In 1830, St. Catherine Labouré, a Sister of Charity in Paris, believed that she had experienced a series of apparitions of the Virgin Mary in which she had identified herself as the "Immaculate Conception," that is, that she, Mary, was free from original sin from the first moment of her conception. These apparitions gave rise to the Catholic practice of wearing the "miraculous medal" in honor of Mary. On December 8, 1854, Pius IX officially proclaimed the Immaculate Conception to be a dogma of faith for Roman Catholics.

On February 11, 1858, St. Bernadette Soubirous, a peasant girl in Lourdes, France, also experienced a vision of the Virgin Mary in which she again identified herself as the Immaculate Conception. Lourdes has since become one of the most popular sites of pilgrimage in the world, claiming a number of medically verified cures.

Devotion to Mary had been a constant in Catholic life from the earliest days of the church. Some of the great medieval cathedrals had been built in her honor, for example, Chartres and Notre Dame in Paris. The church believed that Mary was a symbol or an ideal for human possibilities because she had reached a perfection and completeness that all Christians were called to attain. She represented as well the "feminine" and "mother" in Christian spirituality.

Renewed Marian piety spread throughout the world under Pius IX. So did other devotions and practices that encouraged a warmer, more emotional and demonstrative spirituality. Pilgrimages came back into vogue, for example, in France to Lourdes, Chartres and LaSalette; in Spain to Santiago de Compostela and to the Benedictine monastery at Montserrat; in Italy to Assisi and Loreto.

A greater appreciation for the eucharist as a source of grace for the individual led to encouraging frequent reception of holy communion and first communion for children at a younger age. Perpetual adoration of the real presence of Christ in the blessed sacrament was promoted in parish churches. New attention was paid as well to the sufferings of Jesus Christ. Many embraced the devotion to the Sacred Heart of Jesus as a way of giving thanks for the suffering endured by Christ and making reparation for sin.

The Catholic ethos is always essentially sacramental. The piety and spirituality that developed in the church during the service of Pius IX as pope was tinged with romanticism, and at times certain abuses and a lack of taste were evident. Nevertheless, popular religiosity fed and deepened the spiritual lives of countless Roman Catholics.

Papal Authority and the First Vatican Council

Ever on guard, given his insights, graces, and limitations, Pius IX published in 1864 an encyclical (a letter written by the pope on some aspect of the church's teaching that he considers serious and important in content for Catholics), *Quanta Cura*, with its attached *Syllabus of Errors*. The latter was a list of propositions that the pope maintained a good Catholic could not affirm. The *Syllabus* was, in fact, a list of references to various other papal documents that treated the topics mentioned. Basically, the *Syllabus* rejected many of the tenets of liberalism, for example, rationalism, indifferentism, socialism, and the idea that the pope should reconcile the church with the tenets of liberalism. Thus the pope had drawn a line in the sand, putting the Catholic Church against the so-called modern world.

Pius IX had succeeded in promoting Catholic piety. He had centralized pastoral responsibility and authority in the Petrine office of the bishop of Rome. In his view, he had protected the people of God from very dangerous modern ideas detrimental to the life of the faith. He believed that he had indeed deepened the spiritual life of Catholics.

In a bold gesture to cement these moves, the pope convoked the twentieth ecumenical council in the history of the Roman Catholic Church. An ecumenical council, convoked and approved by the pope, is a worldwide meeting of the bishops, as the official teachers of the church, to consider serious church matters. Announced in 1867, the First Vatican Council met in 1869–1870. Of the one thousand active bishops throughout the world, about seven hundred participated, most of them European in nationality.

From the outset of the council, there was a movement to declare as dogma the infallibility of the pope and his primacy of jurisdiction. The ultramontanes saw such a declaration as merely confirming a long held belief of the church. More liberal Catholics feared such a declaration glorified the papacy at the expense of local bishops. One of the leaders of the opposition was the English layman, Lord Acton (1834–1902). Speaking about infallibility, Lord Acton stated that power corrupts, and absolute power corrupts absolutely.

Others opposed to such a declaration of infallibility included Bishop Dupanloup of Orleans, France (1802–1878) and the German theologian, Ignaz von Döllinger, of the University of Munich (1799–1890). Those promoting the declaration included Cardinal Manning of England, Father Beckx, superior general of the Jesuits, and the newspaper *Civiltà Cattolica*, as well as the French newspaper *L'Univers*.

Debate on the issue of declaring the infallibility of the pope and his primacy continued all during the 1870 spring session of the council. At one point Cardinal Guidi, a Dominican, proposed that the issue be the infallibility of the pope's doctrinal decisions, not a *carte blanche* infallibility. Guidi suggested that when the pope acted with other bishops and not independently of them, always respecting the tradition of the church, he taught infallibly. Pius IX was angered by the Dominican's suggestion and reminded him in public that "*La Tradizione Son' Io!*—I am the tradition!"

Believing that the church always taught by the guiding presence of the Holy Spirit, on July 18 the council formally declared that the pope teaches infallibly when he speaks *ex cathedra* (i.e., from the chair or papal throne, which is to suggest formally) in matters of faith and morals. The council then adjourned. The Franco-Prussian War broke out before the next session of the council could begin. In the absence of French protectors, the troops of Piedmont and King Victor Emmanuel marched on Rome and annexed it as part of the unified Kingdom of Italy.

Most accepted the teaching of the First Vatican Council. Some professors, such as Döllinger at the University of Munich and his followers, broke away in schism or separation from the Roman Catholic Church to form the "Old Catholic Church." Another negative reaction to the decisions of Vatican I occurred in Germany where Chancellor Otto von Bismarck (1815–1898) unleashed his *Kulturkampf*, that is, the struggle for civilization or the "battle for culture." Germanic, northern European culture pitted itself against Latin, southern Mediterranean culture.

Bismarck was the great instrument in building the German empire under Kaiser Wilhelm I (1797–1888). He sought to unify the various German principalities under the leadership of a Protestant Prussia, excluding Catholic Austria. While not particularly religious in the Protestant tradition, he thoroughly disliked what he judged to be cultic magic and priestly control within the Catholic Church. At the same time, he failed to really understand the church's teaching on papal primacy and infallibility. Thoroughly royalist, he nevertheless subscribed to liberal teaching about church-state relations.

In 1871 Bismark, the "Iron Chancellor," initiated a series of moves to restrict the freedom of the Catholic Church, which was a strong presence in Bavaria, the Rhineland, and occupied Poland. The *Kulturkampf* under the aegis of Bismarck:

1) eliminated the role of the Catholic Church in education;
2) expelled Jesuits and other religious orders from the empire;
3) punished preachers who were critical of the government;
4) limited the power of bishops through a series of "May laws" in 1873 and required candidates for the priesthood to pursue some of their education in German universities;
5) left dioceses without bishops and parishes without priests for long periods of time.

The whole effort attempted to loosen ties between German Catholics and the pope. It also promoted the prominence of the Protestant churches and Prussian power. The *Kulturkampf* took hold in strongly Protestant regions of Germany, but had a less serious effect in Austria, Switzerland, and Bavaria.

While the effort took its toll on the German Catholic Church, it was not of long duration. Pius IX had confronted Bismarck by condemning the "May laws" and the entire anti-Catholic movement. Bismarck had no room to negotiate and so held firm. The next pope, Leo XIII, attempted to ease the conflict, and by 1887 Bismarck's efforts to control the German church ended.

The American Churches After the Civil War

The events in Europe seemed far away to the American states
engaged in the Civil War. When that war was finally over, there
were approximately one million casualties with six hundred thousand dead. Catholics served in both the Confederate and the Union
armies, and Catholic bishops, priests, and religious were found supporting both sides of the conflict.

Occasionally there was a backlash against Catholics. For
instance, the conspirators involved in the assassination of President
Lincoln had met at the Washington boarding house of Mrs. Mary
Surratt, a Catholic. Although innocent, she was tried, convicted, and
hanged as an accomplice. Her son John was, in fact, involved, but he
escaped to join the army of the Papal States in Italy. Some suspected
a Catholic conspiracy since a Catholic medical doctor, Samuel A.
Mudd, ignorant of what had transpired at Ford's Theater, set John
Wilkes Booth's leg. Mudd was imprisoned for that act.

The Second Plenary Council met in Baltimore in 1866. President
Andrew Johnson attended the closing ceremonies, a recognition of
the importance of the four million American Catholics in the total
national population of thirty million. The Baltimore council treated
a variety of pastoral issues that the church was to face after the
Civil War, including the call for the establishment of religious communities and schools to especially serve the black community of
four million freed slaves. There already existed groups of black sisters, for example, Baltimore's Oblate Sisters of Providence, founded
in 1829, and New Orleans' Sisters of the Holy Family, founded in
1842. In 1891, the Josephite Community dedicated to ministry for
and with blacks was established. Other such groups followed: the
Society of the Divine Word, the Society of African Missions, et al.
White religious communities, unfortunately, did not often accept
black candidates until the twentieth century.

An exception was the Healy brothers, sons of an Irish Georgia
slave owner and his black slave wife. James Augustine Healy
became a priest and eventually the Catholic bishop of Portland,
Maine (1875–1900); his brother, Alexander Healy, taught in a seminary and then served as secretary to the bishop of Boston. Patrick
Healy, S.J., became president of Georgetown University
(1873–1882).

The Roman Catholic Church's ministry efforts to the black population in America were mixed. Some bishops, priests, and religious
did extraordinary service; others believed that their efforts should

be addressed to newly arrived Catholic immigrants. Catholic life and liturgy, at times, seemed to lack appeal to the black community. It often failed to take into consideration the uniqueness of black African culture.

The Protestant churches in America were often divided over the question of slavery at the time of the Civil War. The Presbyterian, Methodist, and Baptist churches split along sectional lines, that is, North and South. After the war and during Reconstruction, southern whites at times vented their anger on the freed black population. Ministers and churches at times abetted this anger. The Ku Klux Klan began as an organized effort to intimidate and frighten blacks. A second version of the KKK would later expand the object of its disdain to include not only blacks, but Catholics and Jews as well.

As soon as Reconstruction officially ended, southern whites moved to undo any gains made by blacks. The Supreme Court ruled in 1892 that "separate but equal" treatment of blacks was legal. There followed a series of laws that seriously discriminated against blacks in regard to education, accessibility to public facilities, and voting. Whereas slaves attended the churches of their master, freed blacks were encouraged to go elsewhere.

During and after Reconstruction a number of black Christian churches were established. The Colored Methodist Church began in 1870. However, the larger number of blacks who were Methodists joined the African Methodist Episcopal Church (AME, founded by Bishop Richard Allen in Philadelphia). The African Methodist Episcopal Zion Church had been organized under Bishop James Varick in New York City in 1821. Black Baptist churches and congregations, long in existence, eventually formed the National Baptist Convention in 1895. Black churches in general were very successful in evangelizing freed blacks, especially in the south.

The black Protestant churches became an important vehicle for black social and community life in America. They met and served the spiritual needs of an oppressed people and fostered the uniqueness of the African roots of black culture in the United States. These churches preached a Christianity that truly converted people to Christ and the gospel in their own idiom. Their "spirituals" and gospel music brilliantly exemplify and capture the soul of a unique Christian people. From these churches emerged generations of black community leaders and organizers, who in turn moved from the pulpit to the streets in efforts to free and liberate their people.

13

Leo XIII 1878–1903

The "modern" world began at the end of the eighteenth century when individuals and societies started to think of themselves as creative agents of their own destinies. The Roman Catholic Church found some of the tenets of "modernity" to be threatening or at least disturbing: individual rights could destroy the common good; freedom of conscience could challenge legitimate authority; empirical science could dismiss religion. The church's response to the modern age or to so-called liberalism was varied. Catholics in the fields of theology, philosophy, and other sciences, who attempted to dialogue with the modern world, often clashed with church officials. The dialectic between church and culture has always been a complicated process because for Catholics the very existence and understanding of faith and revelation are at stake. Just how complicated this could become can be seen in the twenty-five year papacy of Pope Leo XIII.

Gioacchino Pecci was born in central Italy on March 2, 1810. He studied with the Jesuits and was ordained a priest in 1837. That same year he was named a monsignor, and in January 1838 he became an apostolic delegate to Benevento in the Papal States and later to Perugia. In 1843, at just thirty-three years of age, he was ordained an archbishop and sent to Belgium as the nuncio (ambassador) of the pope. Pecci's bright diplomatic career, however, ended there after just three years when the internal politics of a liberal government caused his removal. He then became the archbishop of Perugia and remained there as pastor of that local church for the next thirty-two years. Pecci was elected pope at the death of Pope Pius IX in 1878, and took the name of Leo XIII.

The World of Leo XIII

Germany

Leo became universal pastor of the Roman Catholic community at a volatile time in western Europe. In Germany, Chancellor Otto von Bismarck had unleashed the *Kulturkampf*, his battle for culture. The new, modern state of Germany explicitly persecuted the Catholic Church in order to block the presence of the church and its leaders in the public life of the Reich. Various laws from 1871 onward limited church activity and expanded government control. Pope Pius IX had challenged Bismarck over the *Kulturkampf*. Eventually the chancellor and his supporters began to doubt the value of their strategy against the church but saw no face-saving way out. Pope Leo soon after his election contacted Kaiser Wilhelm I (1871–1878) and offered an escape from the impasse. Gradually over the next decade compromises were reached and the laws and rules of *Kulturkampf* ceased to be in effect so that in 1904, for example, the Jesuits were officially restored. The resolution of this problem did much to increase the prestige of the papacy and of Leo XIII personally.

Italy

The new government in Italy had not only annexed the Papal States but had also enacted a series of anti-Catholic laws; for example, religious orders were suppressed and their property confiscated, and religious instruction in schools was eliminated. Many Catholics followed the church's ruling which forbade them to participate in the government and to vote in elections. Pius IX had promulgated this ruling in his 1868 decree *Non Expedit* (It is not expedient). Leo desired a rapprochement with the Italian government, but he would not concede the state's right to the territories of the Papal States. The church systematically organized groups, clubs, associations, congresses, and movements within Italy which dedicated themselves to Catholic action on behalf of society. Many of these Catholic participants formed their own ghetto world and exerted a good deal of influence on public life. Other more liberal Catholics, without supporting the secular ruling class, believed that the gospel called them to change secular society from within. Therefore, they needed to be involved in the real world of politics and the media. The Catholic labor movement, the *Opera dei Congressi*, promoted a kind of Christian democracy. Pope Leo was often asked to support one or the other of these approaches by loyal and committed Catholics who sought a way to support the pope and Italy against the anti-clericals in power. The "Roman question," that is, the seizure of the Papal States, continued to be a troubling issue for the popes and for Catholic patriots until it was settled by the Lateran Treaty between the church and the Italian government in 1929.

France

Church-state relations in France deteriorated during the reign of Pope Leo. After 1867 there had been an increase in vocations to the priesthood and religious life, and the French government paid the salaries of many of these clerics and religious. Popular religiosity flourished, especially in rural areas. The church's apparent support of the conservative political regime of Napoleon III (1852–1870) antagonized liberal intellectuals, the press, the rising urban middle class, and the industrial workers moving to the cities.

In 1870–1871 the Franco-Prussian War ended the reign of Emperor Napoleon III and inaugurated the Third Republic. Republicans were children of the Enlightenment and for them Catholicism and all religions were obstacles to progress and the advance of science. Religion, they believed, was simply a personal persuasion and had no place in public life. Systematic secularization of national life became the republican agenda.

One of the obvious and first targets of "republicanization" was the Catholic schools run by religious orders. "Clericalism is the enemy" became the rallying cry of the liberals. The Jesuits, a religious society dedicated to educating the young, were expelled from France in 1880. Later, other religious groups were treated similarly and restrictions were placed on the public expression of religion. French Catholics and the Third Republic confronted each other. Pope Leo XIII, as in the case of Bismarck, sought a pragmatic solution that would allow the church to continue its spiritual mission without, of course, compromising on essentials. Such a course, how-

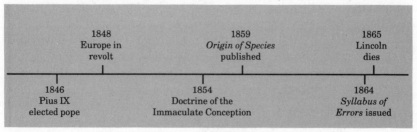

1848	1859	1865
Europe in revolt	*Origin of Species* published	Lincoln dies

1846	1854	1864
Pius IX elected pope	Doctrine of the Immaculate Conception	*Syllabus of Errors* issued

ever, was not particularly attractive to ardent, conservative, and generally royalist Catholics nor to secular anti-clericals.

Leo's policy for France was his *ralliement* (rallying). The pope sought a way of uniting Catholics and others to promote the good of society and protect the rights of the church. The symbol of Leo's policy was a toast made by Cardinal Lavigerie on November 12, 1890, to a group of visiting naval officers in Algeria calling for French Catholics to the "unconditional acceptance of the Republic."

At stake in the debate was the church's position vis-à-vis a modern state and world. Some Catholics, including those who were monarchists and royalists in sympathy, were intransigent, expecting the leadership of the church to support the traditional way. Other Catholics took the opposite position and clamored for the absolute separation of church and state. Leo sought a world that would freely shape itself and its institutions in terms of Christian insights. There were Catholics who followed Pope Leo's suggestion and supported the *ralliement* by forming groups, associations, newspapers, and political clubs which sought both influence and power. The pope's policies, however, lost favor in the heat of the "Dreyfus affair."

In 1894, when anti-Semitic propaganda was attributing the cause of Germany's success and the rise of the Third Republic in France to the Jewish people, a Jewish army captain, Alfred Dreyfus, was falsely accused of spying for Germany and found guilty of treason. As a result he was sent to Devil's Island in French Guiana. In 1898 new evidence surfaced that required a new trial for Captain Dreyfus. *La Croix*, a very popular newspaper owned by the Assumptionists, a Catholic religious order, took up an anti-Dreyfus position. Many conservative Catholics, aligned with or at least perceived to be part of the monarchist, anti-Republican movement *Action Française*, also chose to support the anti-Dreyfus side. Their position was opposed to Leo's *ralliement,* and the pope himself came to the defense of Dreyfus. Other Catholics, such as the writer Charles Péguy, were appalled at the support given to anti-Semitism

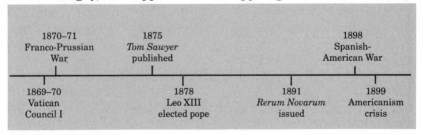

1870–71	1875		1898
Franco-Prussian War	*Tom Sawyer* published		Spanish-American War

1869–70	1878	1891	1899
Vatican Council I	Leo XIII elected pope	*Rerum Novarum* issued	Americanism crisis

by conservative Catholics. Péguy accused the church of being un-Catholic and France of living in mortal sin. When pro-Dreyfus politicians triumphed and the captain was pardoned, the church was made to pay for the stance of *Action Française*.

In 1902 Emile Combs, a former seminarian who had become fiercely anti-clerical, was elected French premier. New religious orders were allowed to be founded only with permission of the government, and fifty-four male religious congregations were abolished. Three thousand Catholic schools run by religious orders were closed. The affected women and men religious were forced to make their way on their own or leave France in exile. Practicing lay Catholics in government, the army, or schools were put under surveillance.

With the promulgation of the Law of Separation in 1905, the Napoleonic Concordat, which recognized the Catholic Church as the state religion, was abrogated. Church property was confiscated and given to private corporations or associations. The effect of this separation of church and state was very painful at the outset; for example, church personnel needed new sources of income to live on. In 1906 an association of "worker priests" was founded. These priests found work where they could, for example, in factories, and there sought to preach the gospel by their lives. In hindsight the benefit given to the church by the Law of Separation was the freedom to be a Christ-centered community, ministering to its own membership and the larger world without state interference.

The Revival of Thomism

St. Thomas Aquinas, the thirteenth century Dominican theologian, has bequeathed to the ages a vast body of writings containing a wonderfully coherent system of thought. Leaning on ancient Greek philosophers, such as Plato and Aristotle, and the Fathers of the church, especially St. Augustine, Aquinas offered an integrated, coherent, holistic world view. He articulated what it meant to be a human person, a human community, what human destiny consisted in, and how to achieve or realize that destiny. The human person was the image of God created to think and to love. In history the human person experienced the effects of original evil, understood as a tendency to fail in responding to God's call to move outside of oneself by loving and serving others. Nevertheless, sin never totally corrupted the human person. The grace made available through Jesus Christ healed and elevated human beings, thus enabling them to achieve their destiny by doing good to others through a virtuous life of service. Human destiny consisted in eternal salvation which was understood to be absolute happiness in union with God and all those saved by God's grace through Christ.

Aquinas attempted to harmonize faith and reason, science and religion, human thought and revelation. The apex of his work was his *Summa Theologica*. That opus has been compared to a Gothic cathedral in which each individual section had its own proper meaning but together with all other parts took on an even greater meaning. The *Summa Theologica* has been and is today truly one of the great intellectual masterpieces of history.

Pope Leo XIII deeply admired the thought of Thomas Aquinas. He was familiar with it through the work of his brother, a Jesuit, and a group of Italian scholars who promoted the revival of the study of Aquinas' philosophy. The pope saw in Thomism an articulated world view that was very much his own, and he sought to encourage an intellectual appreciation of the work of the "angelic doctor." In 1879 Leo published his encyclical letter *Aeterni Patris*, which urged the world's bishops to support the study of the works of St. Thomas. He himself applied the thought of Aquinas in a series of encyclical letters on social problems, human freedom, marriage and the family, education, and the study of sacred scripture. Leo XIII established the Roman Academy of St. Thomas (1879), and formed what would be called the "Leonine Commission" to produce and publish a critical edition of all the works of Aquinas. In 1880 he founded a center for the study of St. Thomas at the University of Louvain in Belgium, and in 1890 the theology faculty of the newly opened Catholic University of Fribourg, in Switzerland, was entrusted to the Dominicans.

Pope Leo's efforts on behalf of Thomism prompted a deeper appreciation for and renewed study of the history of medieval philosophy and theology. This resulted in an historical approach to Thomism which applied the insights of Aquinas to the modern era. Unfortunately, Leo's efforts also resulted in a static approach to St. Thomas' thought and a non-historical application of his doctrine. The latter approach would be found in manuals and textbooks used to educate seminarians for nearly one hundred years.

Pope Leo XIII was well aware of the signs of the times. The industrial revolution had transformed the world of work. Capitalism, urbanization, and poverty, with all their devastating effects on the person and family, had radically altered life and culture. Catholic associations and organizations had traditionally served the needs of the poor. In the second half of the nineteenth century, renewed initiatives were also made to address systems of oppression and to find ways to improve the lives of farmers, the middle class and industrial workers. Cooperatives, trade unions, youth groups, and specialized associations were supported by the church. These efforts prompted Karl Marx (1818–1883), the author of *The Communist Manifesto* and *Das Kapital*, to write to Friedrich Engels in 1869: "During this trip through Belgium, my sojourn in Aachen and the tour up the Rhine River, I have come to the conviction that we have to combat the clerics vigorously, especially in the Catholic areas…the scoundrels are flirting with the workers' question whenever it seems appropriate."

Leo addressed the social question in his encyclical letter *Rerum Novarum*, which he issued on May 15, 1891. He had been assisted in writing this letter by eminent Thomists, such as Cardinal Zigliara, a Dominican. Leo's social teaching represents gospel values presented within the framework of Aquinas' understanding of the social order. On the one hand, the pope rejected the inevitability of class warfare and attacked the socialism proposed by thinkers such as Karl Marx. On the other hand, however, the pope refused to support the greed and presuppositions of economic liberalism. *Rerum Novarum* taught:

1) There is great diversity between the enormous fortunes of a few and the terrible poverty of the masses.
2) Rich and poor, capital and labor, both have rights and duties.
3) There is a need for the state and law to protect the rights of the poor.
4) Laborers have a right to a just salary that will allow them to support themselves and their families.
5) Trade unions protect the legitimate rights of workers.
6) The right to private property is essential.
7) Workers should never resort to violence.
8) The wealthy should be charitable and concerned for the poor.
9) The wealthy should exhibit such charity and concern by giving to the poor what is superfluous after their own needs have been met.

In *Rerum Novarum*, the pope attempted to bring the church's teaching to bear on the newly developing social and economic worlds. Subsequent popes would continue to develop a social philosophy and theology, but often enough this Catholic social teaching has been opposed by many as either too radical or as too weak.

Biblical Studies

From the time of the Reformation, Catholics and Protestants both viewed scripture as the inspired word of God. However, their approach to the authority, meaning, and interpretation of texts of the bible differed. Protestants based their faith almost exclusively on the bible while Roman Catholics saw the bible and tradition as two distinct dimensions of the one source or font of revelation. Protestants allowed for personal, individual interpretation of scriptural passages; Catholics saw the books of the bible as the work of and for the community of the church. Protestants emphasized their reverence for the bible by placing it at the center of worship; Catholics celebrated both the word of God and the seven sacraments of the church's tradition in their liturgical life.

In the nineteenth century, both Catholics and Protestants were challenged in their belief in the truth of the bible as the inspired, revealed word of God. Modern intellectual achievements questioned the teaching of the bible. The industrial revolution had benefited from the advances made in the applied sciences, transportation, and communication. The theme of the age was "progress," and a greater appreciation developed for historical consciousness. It was thought that the past would lead always to a brighter future. New studies in geology and archaeology also showed that the history of the world traced back far longer than had been previously thought.

Charles Darwin published his famous book, *On the Origin of Species by Means of Natural Selection or the Preservation of Favored Races in the Struggle for Life* in 1859. "Natural selection" or "survival of the fittest" seemed to some to challenge the creation accounts found in Genesis. Darwin's theory of evolution meant that humans had evolved from apes and similar forms of life; this evolutionary advance had been at a great cost and involved the conquest of the stronger. Could a believing Christian accept evolution without rejecting the biblical account of creation? Darwin himself had become an agnostic over time. Nevertheless, when he died, he was buried in London's Westminster Abbey.

The question at hand, of course, was not only the truth of science but also the truth of religion. If one rejected the "two truth" theory, that is, that both religion and science were true in their own disparate fields, and also found unacceptable an inherent opposition between science and religion, then some accommodation had to be reached. Historical-biblical criticism, as a scholarly field of endeavor, took on great importance as a possible way of finding this accommodation. This field of study both examined ancient manuscripts to ascertain a correct text (textual or lower criticism) and also went beyond this to ask about the relationship of texts to each other (higher criticism): How were they written? By whom? For what purpose? Addressed to whom? Using what "forms" or literary genres?

Protestant Christian scholars, especially in Germany, became very prominent in the field of historical-biblical criticism. Julius Wellhausen (1844–1918) did pioneering work on the pentateuch (the first five books of the bible). Traditionally, Moses had been seen as their author. Wellhausen taught that a variety of sources from different historical eras fed into the final project which was the so-called pentateuch.

A major theme of biblical criticism was the search for the historical Jesus. Who was the person behind the New Testament's theological descriptions? H. S. Reimarus (1694–1768) tried to debunk the whole Jesus story. Jesus, for him, was a gentle Galilean teacher who confused his calling and was crucified. His followers put out a false story about a resurrection for their own gain. David Friedrich Strauss (1808–1874) published his famous *The Life of Jesus* (1835) in which he dismissed all miraculous and messianic material in the gospels as myth. Joseph Renan's *Life of Jesus* in France and J. R. Seeley's *Ecce Homo* in England did the same. F. C. Baur (1792–1860) used the historical method to determine authorship of biblical material. His conclusion was that only four of Paul's letters were authentic—Romans, Galatians, and 1 and 2 Corinthians.

Negative and subsequently discredited theories emerged at times. Nevertheless, a good deal of positive and valuable knowledge was gained about the bible and the early church through the use of the historical-critical method. Pope Leo XIII published his encyclical letter *Providentissimus Deus* on November 18, 1893. In that letter he approved the critical approach to biblical studies, although he warned of excessive reliance on a method and urged a balanced approach. In 1902 Leo established the Pontifical Biblical Commission. Its twofold function was to offer critical responses to questions that arose about the bible and to serve as a watchdog to protect orthodox Roman Catholic teaching.

The pope encouraged the Dominicans to establish the Ecole Biblique in Jerusalem. Named in honor of St. Stephen, the school opened in 1890 under the direction of Père Marie Joseph Lagrange, O.P. Father Lagrange professionalized the Roman Catholic approach to biblical studies, pursuing the historical-critical method, yet always respectful of the tradition of the church. His genius and ability as well as his scientific approach to the bible at times triggered controversy. Leo also encouraged the development of the Pontifical Biblical Institute under the direction of the Jesuits at their Roman university, the Gregorian. The Roman Catholic Church entered, if at a slower pace than Protestants, the field of modern biblical criticism under Pope Leo XIII.

Liberal Protestant Thought

The dialectic between the Catholic Church and the modern world was and is complex. A tension exists on a variety of levels—the cultural, political, economic, social, and psychological. Fundamentally, however, the conversation between church and world is always theological. The church, the people of God, must remain faithful to the truth of revelation. That truth is known and yet always remains to be known. The presence of the Holy Spirit in the church protects it against serious error or distortion. That belief of faith does not, however, excuse leaders like Leo XIII from struggling to live out their faith in new and challenging historical milieus.

Protestant Christianity, as well as Orthodoxy, similarly confronted modernity. "Pietism" and the evangelical revival characterized much of Protestantism in Europe and America during the eighteenth century. The nineteenth century saw the rise of liberal theology in different forms and in various countries.

The Victorian age in England was an era of proper manners and staid morality. It was also an age of religious doubt in which science and philosophy challenged the church. Darwin proposed his theory of evolution based on the premise of natural selection or "survival of the fittest." The theory was defended by the scientist T. H. Huxley, who coined the word *agnostic*. He simply did not know if there was a God or creator. Some believers reacted by vehemently denying evolution as being totally incompatible with the bible and declaring that the creation accounts in Genesis had to be interpreted literally. Other believers saw no necessary contradiction between belief and science, since the bible, for them, offered not a scientific account of the beginnings of the world but rather a religious account. The scriptures do not show "how the heavens go but how to go to heaven." A religious person could believe in a creator and accept a sophisticated nuanced theory of evolution that left room for creation.

In Germany there was a debate between philosophy and religion which resulted in a new liberal Protestant theology. Earlier,

Immanuel Kant (1724–1804) taught that speculative reason could not rationally prove the existence of God, the soul, or an afterlife. Religion, therefore, was based on the ethical sense which is innate to persons. God does exist as the judge of good and evil; the soul is a source of moral action; the afterlife is a reward or punishment for doing good or evil. Kant rejected rationalism and a cerebral religion. Religion, and Christianity in particular, was therefore about being and doing good.

In the nineteenth century, Friedrich Schleiermacher (1768–1834) offered a liberal theology which was rooted in his Moravian background, Kant's thought, the romantic movement of the day, and the historical-critical method applied to the bible. He attempted to show that religion was not a body of dogmas, teachings, and beliefs, not a form of rationalist thought nor even morals as Kant had said. It was not something in the mind or will. Rather, religion was rooted in "feeling" (*Gefuhl*) and affection. A person experiences a profound feeling of dependence on God and apprehends the infinite immediately and directly. Because beliefs and ethics derive from the contemplative awareness of God, theology's task is to reflect on this dependence. For Schleiermacher, the biblical accounts of creation, the existence of angels or the devil, original sin, etc., need reinterpretation in the light of "dependence." Science and religion need never conflict since it is always possible to readjust traditional thinking in light of scientific advances. In his chief works, *On Religion* (1799) and *The Doctrine of Faith* (1821), Schleiermacher taught that the differences between Protestants and Catholics were serious but that the differences among the Protestant churches were minimal.

Another contributor to Protestant liberal theology was Albrecht Ritschl (1822–1889), who was influenced both by the thought of Kant and by modern biblical criticism. For Ritschl, Christianity was about the central experience of Christ, that is, the historical Jesus. Religion, therefore, was very practical—it was about right living. The Christian woman or man had been justified and reconciled by Jesus and thus formed a fellowship which was the kingdom of God. Ritschl emphasized ethics and morality. At the same time, God's nature was love, and so punishment for sin and damnation were all but forgotten. Again, dogma and traditional beliefs were rejected in favor of what he believed to be the original New Testament understanding of Christianity, "the organization of humanity through action based on love."

Adolph von Harnack (1851–1930), a leading liberal church historian, attempted to spell out the essentials of Christianity in his classical work, published in 1900, *What Is Christianity? (Das Wesen des Christentums* or literally *The Essence of Christianity).* Present-day Christianity, for Harnack, was not simply an explicitation of what was original in the New Testament. Rather, it was an abandonment of the faith of the early church—teachings of Jesus were transposed into teachings about Jesus. He sought the "gospel in the gospel" which was not to be found in dogma nor morality nor in the institutional church. All of that was appendage. The essential message of Jesus was:

1) The kingdom of God, preached by Jesus, was the coming rule of God in the hearts of individuals.
2) God is a loving Father to the world and to individuals.
3) The human soul is of infinite value and so results in universal brotherhood/sisterhood.
4) Jesus only wanted people to keep his commandments, not to worship him or develop ritual.
5) Religion, then, is finally about love and mercy.

Harnack believed that this essence of the gospel had constantly been obscured or camouflaged by teachings, institutions, laws and customs.

Kant's critique of rationalism led him to conclude that morality was, in fact, the ground of religion. Søren Kierkegaard (1813–1855) taught that while reason could not prove the existence of God, a faith, nevertheless, could assert it. Christianity is a matter of faith—faith in God revealed in the person of Jesus Christ who is revealed in the word of God, the scriptures. Faith, for Kierkegaard, was not easy; it was very risky. For him, many played at Christianity. To be Christian was to shape all of existence in a relationship to Jesus Christ. This meant that true Christians struggled constantly to become conformed to Christ. Actual, real existence was the locus for Christianity, not some dogma, morality, or institution. To be Christian was to be a disciple, following Jesus in real life at all costs.

Liberal Protestantism in the nineteenth century sought to accommodate religion to the modern world. It can be characterized generally by the following:

1) an embrace of science and the scientific method—for example, biblical and historical criticism;
2) a de-emphasis of denominational differences;
3) a new appreciation for the imminence of God versus transcendence, the natural versus the supernatural, the humanity of Christ versus divinity, the Jesus of history versus the Christ of creeds, experience or religious consciousness versus reason;

4) ultimate authority in religious matters is personal experience
   and not the bible, creed, or some church authority;
5) ethical commitment to Jesus and the kingdom require social
   involvement to promote justice.

\

Americanism

The official Catholic approach to the modern world and to liberal
ideas was cautious. The pope and his advisors at times felt legitimately threatened by advocates of new thinking. Their concern was
always to protect and defend the truth of revelation and the magisterium (the teaching authority of the church). Liberal Protestants
in mainline churches (Lutherans, Calvinists, Anglicans, etc.) often
enthusiastically embraced new ideas and theories, accommodating
theology to modern science and philosophy. Thus, Pope Leo XIII
cautiously appraised the Catholic experience in the United States
as indeed novel and without precedent in Catholic history. The
pope's caution was seen in his condemnation of the errors of
"Americanism."

The Catholic Church in the United States had grown quickly and
numerically during the nineteenth century principally because of
immigration. Between 1821 and 1900, approximately sixteen million people arrived in the United States, many of them Catholics
from Germany, Ireland, Italy, Austria, and Slavic countries.
Catholic parishes ministered to the spiritual as well as the material
needs of their people. A key instrument meant to preserve the faith
of Catholics, often demeaned and under attack, was the Catholic
school system. No nation had ever developed such a large private
parochial network of schools, generally educating poor children or
those of modest means. By 1910 there were more than forty-eight
hundred Catholic primary schools in the country educating over one
and a half million students. These schools were funded by donations
from Catholic working people and staffed by women and men religious. The latter contributed their services in exchange for room
and board and with minimum other benefits.

The Irish influence in the American church was especially
strong. Many priests and bishops, who were born in Ireland or were
of Irish descent, came from working class families and never forgot
their roots. They ministered pastorally to their people in an incredible variety of ways, for example, through the administration of the
sacraments, preaching and teaching, and meeting material needs

by establishing cooperatives and credit unions and organizing athletic programs for youth.

One area of the church's social outreach in the United States raised suspicions in Rome. After 1878, the Knights of Labor, a trade union, was headed by a Catholic, Terence Powderly, and had a large Catholic membership. The Knights were blamed for the murder of a dozen policemen in Chicago's Haymarket Square and for other labor troubles. Some bishops forbade Catholics to join the organization; others condemned trade unions as a prelude to socialism or communism. Unions were seen as something of a surrender to liberal ideas. However, Cardinal Gibbons of Baltimore cautioned Rome against any blanket condemnation of the Knights. Working people, mostly Catholic, would have been shocked and disappointed by such a move. Catholics continued to participate in large numbers in the labor movement when the Knights were succeeded by the American Federation of Labor under the leadership of Samuel Gompers. For working people, trade unionism was not a socialist movement nor a communist ideology. Rather, it was an instrument for upward mobility.

At times ethnic diversity in America caused difficulties in the Catholic community. Toward the end of the nineteenth century, German and Italian Catholics arrived in the United States in large numbers. Irish clergy usually ministered to them, but there was a language and culture gap. Leo XIII urged the creation of "national" parishes to serve particular ethnic groups. This solution, while immediately adequate, challenged somewhat the "melting pot" approach of Catholic leaders such as the future Cardinal Gibbons who promoted a thoroughly American Roman Catholic Church.

James Gibbons (1834–1921), the archbishop of Baltimore, and Archbishop John Ireland (1838–1918) of St. Paul, Minnesota, were firm supporters of the American experience of separation of church and state and freedom of conscience. They promoted Catholic cultural assimilation and participation in the life of the nation. More conservative clerics like Archbishop Michael Corrigan (1839–1902) of New York and Bishop Bernard McQuaid (1823–1909) of Rochester, New York, feared the incursion of liberalism into the American church. These two perspectives or approaches on how to be Catholic and American had their defenders among Catholic leaders, professors, and journalists. The Hecker episode underlined the disagreement in the mind of the pope.

Isaac Hecker (1819–1888) was a contemplative, socially conscious young man when he became a convert to the Roman Catholic Church in 1844. Five years later, in Holland, he was ordained a priest in the Redemptorist Order (the Congregation of the Most Holy Redeemer), founded by Saint Alphonsus Liguori in 1732 to minister to the poor. On his return to the United States, Hecker worked in parish revival missions. He finally left the Redemptorists to found a congregation of priests who would minister not to Catholic immigrants but rather to non-Catholic Americans—the Congregation of Missionary Priests of Saint Paul the Apostle (the Paulists). In 1865, they founded *Catholic World*, the first Catholic monthly magazine in the United States.

Father Hecker saw the American experience of separation of church and state with its freedom and religious tolerance as an ideal climate for Catholicism. After his death in 1888, a protégé, Father Walter Elliott, authored a *Life of Father Hecker* filled with the founder's own thoughts and words. In 1897 a French edition of the book was published. Father Hecker's "Americanism" was much appreciated in more liberal French Catholic circles, especially among those who supported Pope Leo's *ralliement* policy in support of the Third Republic. Conservatives attacked Hecker, his ideas, and his supporters even though many did not really know what "Americanism" meant—if, in fact, such an "ism" existed.

On June 22, 1899, Leo XIII published an encyclical letter *Testem Benevolentiae* in which he condemned such notions as:

1) Catholic doctrine should be simplified to attract converts.
2) Church leaders should not pronounce authoritatively on matters of faith and morals.
3) Contemplative religious life has little value and religious vows are of questionable value.

Conservative bishops thanked the pope for his intervention. Gibbons and Ireland immediately agreed with the pope but denied that they or educated Catholics ever held the condemned propositions. The "Americanism" crisis soon passed. Nevertheless, some fundamental questions remained: What was the church's posture in the modern world? How could revelation be reconciled with modern thought, values and discoveries? In particular, given the unique experience of the United States, how can a church function in a democracy? How can one be loyal and devoted to the Roman Catholic Church and at the same time be an American patriot? The church would continue to struggle with these kinds of questions, and the next pope, Pius X, would similarly struggle with these issues and mightily defend the tradition.

14

European and American Christianity During the Pontificate of Pius X 1903–1914

The Life and Work of Pius X

Giuseppe Melchiorre Sarto was elected pope on August 4, 1903, to succeed Leo XIII (1878–1903). He chose to be called Pius X and thus aligned himself with the vision of Pius IX. Like his predecessors from antiquity, Pius X was chosen pope in an election by cardinals with the right to vote.

Preparation for the papacy is not planned. Sometimes the pope has an extensive diplomatic background, having represented the church in various foreign capitals. At other times he may come from the curia or bureaucracy which assists the pope in administering a worldwide church. Popes have had academic backgrounds and/or direct pastoral leadership experience. Pius X was a parish priest and pastor in northern Italy for seventeen years, then spiritual director for seminarians and a diocesan official, Bishop of Mantua (1884–1893), and, at the time of his election, patriarch/cardinal of Venice.

Given his temperament, ecclesiology (theology of the church), and lifelong experience in direct pastoral work, Pius X chose to focus his attention heavily on the internal life of the church. The reforms he instituted were intended to deepen the spiritual life of Catholics and to enhance the life of the entire community. His motto as pope was "To restore all things in Christ in order that Christ may be all in all." When he died the *London Times* wrote: "It is not an exaggeration to say that J. Sarto instituted more changes in the

administration of the Catholic Church than any of his predecessors
since the Council of Trent."

Reform Work

The Christian community shapes its life and mission always in
terms of the gospel of Jesus Christ. At the same time the community
is very much a human one with its bureaucracy and law. Pius X, at
the outset of his ministry, embarked on an effort to renew the
administrative and legal institutions of the church.

The "Roman curia," or central administrative offices of the church,
had multiplied over time, becoming very costly and in need of reorganization in order to make its service to the church more productive.
Since a realignment had not been done systematically for more than
three hundred years, the pope sought a restructuring of the curia.
The number of congregations (dicasteries or agencies), tribunals and
offices was reduced, duties and responsibilities were redistributed,
and lines of authority and accountability were clarified.

Any group or organization needs order and procedures in order to
accomplish its task. So, too, the church over the centuries compiled
its statutes and regulations in view of its mission to spread the
gospel to the ends of the earth. The church's body of laws is called
"canon law." From the twelfth century onward various attempts
such as the "Decretals of Gratian" (c. 1150) and the collection made
in 1234 by the Dominican canonist, St. Raymond of Penyafort
(1185–1275), sought to codify these various laws, regulations,
decrees and papal directives. By the twentieth century there was an
urgent pastoral need to reorganize and update church law. Within
two or three days of his election, Pope Pius X ordered a major review
and reform of canon law. Pietro Gasparri (1852–1934), an able
lawyer and indefatigable worker, was put in charge of the project.
Input from bishops and heads of religious orders was solicited. The
final version of the new *Codex Juris Canonici (Code of Canon Law)*
was finally published in 1917, three years after the death of Pope
Pius X. This collection of law for the Latin rite Church (Eastern rite
churches have their own body of law) would regulate church life for
the next half century.

Pius X has been called "the pope of the eucharist." The eucharist,
also called holy communion and the blessed sacrament, is central to
the worship life of most of the Christian churches. Roman Catholic
sacramental theology teaches that the eucharist is truly the body

and blood of Jesus Christ, who is really present under the appearances of bread and wine. Catholics believe that the sacramental presence of the Risen Lord in the consecrated bread and wine continues as long as these elements actually exist. Eastern Orthodox churches and some Protestant churches also share this theology of the eucharist. Pope Pius sought to give new prominence to the eucharist in the spiritual life of Roman Catholics by urging that:

1) Catholic people receive holy communion frequently. A person did not need to be holy before receiving the eucharist; rather holy communion promoted holiness of life.
2) Children, once they reached the age whereby they could discern the uniqueness of the eucharistic bread, ought to receive their first holy communion.
3) Catholics recognize that the only two requirements for frequent or daily reception of holy communion are the state of grace and the right intention.
4) A person did not need to go to confession for venial sins before receiving holy communion since the sacrament itself forgives all venial sins.

Through his efforts Pius worked to center Catholic liturgical and spiritual experience on the saving and sanctifying presence of Christ in the eucharist. To further encourage devotion to the blessed sacrament, he promoted national and international "eucharistic congresses," which were held in various parts of the world. These celebrations, which included special masses and processions of the blessed sacrament, helped to deepen Catholic devotion to the eucharist, contributed to a stronger belief in the real presence of Christ in the sacrament, and introduced a shift in terms of Catholic participation in the eucharist.

Pius X also called for the renewal of church music to enhance the celebration of the eucharist. In particular, he encouraged the use of authentic Gregorian chant, which the Benedictine monks of Solesmes in France had reintroduced. Thus the modern "liturgical movement" began to enter into the mainstream of church life. The pope called for the reform of the divine office or the breviary (a series of psalms, readings and prayers originally said by bishops, priests, deacons and cloistered nuns in the name of the whole church at certain times of the day). His goal was to enhance the worship or liturgical life of the whole Catholic community so that the faithful, as well as clerics and men and women religious, might grow spiritually by a greater participation in the official daily prayer of the church.

Believing that his program of "restoring all things in Christ" was dependent in great measure on the holiness and pastoral ministry of priests, Pius X was deeply committed to improving the formation and education of future priests. In a series of encyclical letters he encouraged priests to deepen their spiritual lives and to develop modern pastoral plans and practices based on good theology.

Pius X also believed in the crucial role that lay men and women had to play in the renewal of the church and the transformation of society. Hence he promoted the expansion of the role of the laity in the ministry and mission of the church. As the pope was committed to providing quality education for future priests, he was similarly concerned with encouraging better catechetical instruction for the religious education of lay people. He saw this as a field of endeavor in which trained lay persons could make their own special contribution.

The Challenge of Modernism

The leaders of the Catholic Church had struggled with the issue of modernization since the Enlightenment. How be the authentic witnesses to the person and teaching of Christ in an entirely new historical moment? How adapt to a new world culture without surrendering the truth received through revelation? Pope Pius IX (1846–1878) generally took a defensive posture toward modernity, concerned as he was to protect the rights of the church and to guard the faithful against error. Leo XIII (1878–1903) attempted to reestablish the Thomistic world view inherited from the middle ages as part of his strategy of engaging the modern world in a dialogue that would bring it to the truth. Pope Pius X (1903–1914) took a more combative stance against what he perceived as serious threats to the church's teaching that any conciliatory approach to the thought and culture of the modern world would entail. He set out to put an end to modernism.

In general, the term *modernism* was a trend or tendency at the beginning of the twentieth century which sought to update Catholic teaching and practice by trying to bring it more in line with contemporary thinking. Technically, however, the movement known as modernism, which was eventually formally condemned by Pius X, was a body of teaching which the pope saw as opposed to orthodox doctrine and practice and hence incompatible with the Catholic faith.

Germany

Modernism in its strict definition was not a major problem for the Catholic Church in Germany. However, there was a movement, "Reform Catholicism," which reacted against Rome's predilection for neo-scholasticism, promoted historical-critical research, leaned toward less centralization of church authority and, in general, opted for a more liberal posture.

France

A major figure in the modernist crisis in France was Alfred Loisy (1857–1940), a priest who taught scripture studies at the Institut Catholique in Paris. A brilliant scholar as well as a fine writer, Loisy attempted to apply the historical-critical method to the study of the bible. In 1902 he published a small book *L'Evangile et l'Eglise (The Gospel and the Church)*, which caused something of a sensation in church and intellectual circles. In his book, Loisy maintained that:

1) The gospels are not factual records of Jesus' ministry, but rather the record of the Easter faith of the early Christian communities in Jesus of Nazareth.
2) Jesus announced the coming of the kingdom but what actually developed was the institutional church.
3) The institutional church with its dogmas and sacraments is not found in the core message of the New Testament but is the result of teachings and practices that developed in early Christian communities under the guidance of the Holy Spirit.

In a subsequent book, Loisy would teach that Jesus' virginal birth, resurrection from the dead and divinity were doctrines believed by the early community of disciples but were not scientifically provable. He maintained that the true scholar must look at the texts of the bible simply as works of literature and not as the revealed word of God interpreted by the church.

Even Loisy's colleagues believed he had gone too far in embracing the new historical-critical method. His book was condemned and placed on the Index of Forbidden Books in 1903. Eventually Loisy left the church and gave up Christianity, declaring that he had lost faith in the divinity of Jesus Christ and the existence of a personal God.

England

In England, progressive Catholics looked to Friedrich Baron von Hügel (1852–1925). As an intellectual von Hügel endeavored to strike a balance between commitment to Christianity in the Catholic tradition and the best of honest, modern scholarship. At the same time he attempted to heal and reconcile those intellectual Catholics who were alienated from the church. Although his writings were never censured, von Hügel was a friend of many of the modernists both on the continent and in England.

George Tyrrell (1861–1909) was a convert to the Roman Catholic Church from Anglicanism in 1879 and was ordained a Jesuit priest in 1891. At first he taught in the Jesuit seminary at Stonehurst and then joined the staff of the religious magazine, *The Month*. Baron von Hugel introduced Tyrrell to the new historical-critical method in scripture and church history and to the thought of European intellectuals.

Father Tyrrell published a number of devotional books: *Nova et Vetera* (1897), *Hard Sayings* (1898), *External Religion, Its Use and Abuse* (1899). Some of these works and ideas were criticized by his Jesuit superiors in Rome. Gradually Tyrrell lost confidence in ecclesiastical authority and challenged traditional teachings of the church. After his expulsion from the Society of Jesus, he was excommunicated from the Catholic Church for his criticism of the declared dogmas or official teachings of the church. He died in 1909, after receiving absolution and the sacrament of the sick. However, since he had not been publicly reconciled to the church, he was not allowed burial in a Catholic cemetery. His friend, Father Bremond, who offered prayers at the grave in an Anglican cemetery at Storrington, was summarily punished by the local bishop and forbidden to exercise his functions as a priest. This suspension was later revoked.

Official Reaction

Modernism as a liberal tendency among some progressive Catholic intellectuals naturally provoked a reaction from conservatives. Suspicions, charges and accusations were indiscriminately made against any scholar advocating the use of the historical-critical method in biblical studies and systematic theology. Experts such as Father Joseph Lagrange, O.P. (1855–1938), founder of the Ecole Biblique in Jerusalem, came under criticism, notwithstanding his avowed efforts to reconcile new scholarship with official church teachings.

Modernism, strictly and technically defined, was officially condemned teaching that was erroneous and inimical to the true doctrines of the Catholic Church. After a series of warnings by Pius X and other church officials, the Holy Office (Congregation for the Doctrine of the Faith) in 1907 issued a decree, *Lamentabili*, which declared that a list of sixty-five theses or propositions about biblical inspiration, revelation, Christ, the nature of the church, dogma and the teaching authority of the church were erroneous. On September 8, 1907, the pope followed up with the encyclical *Pascendi Domini Gregis* condemning the body of thought, that is, modernism, which was based on agnosticism, immanentism and evolutionism. In 1910 the pope required clerics, pastors and seminary professors, among others, to take an oath against modernism. Pius X firmly believed that it was his responsibility as universal pastor to protect the faith and unity of the Catholic Church. He feared that the radical character of modernism could lead to a new division in the church comparable to that of the Protestant Reformation.

Many progressives in the church feared that the encyclical would deepen the alienation of the church from the modern world and its intellectual currents. At the same time, most had no difficulty in supporting what was condemned since they felt that only radical extremists were teaching such things.

Reactionary conservatives began a crusade to stamp out not only modernism but also any form of modern thinking that did not conform to their idea of "integral Catholicism." These "integralists" employed pamphlets, books, denunciations, secrecy, and vilification in the pursuit of their cause. Sometimes acting like secret police, prelates and others sought to extirpate even the hint of heresy or dissent against traditional teachings. Unfortunately, some excellent and loyal church scholars became victims of the witch hunt and were silenced or curtailed in their work by over-cautious superiors. These bible scholars and theologians were very devoted to the study of the revealed word of God and were totally respectful of the magisterium (teaching authority of the church). Still as scholars they felt that it was imperative to employ the insights of modern scientific methods in their work, not to undermine but to serve the faith development of the Christian community. The atmosphere of mistrust and fear created by "integral Catholicism" led to a fortress mentality which hindered the development of Catholic intellectual life.

Cautious and defensive, Pius X sought to serve the church he had

been called to lead in a time of intellectual and international fer-
ment. He initiated significant change and renewal within the
church while battling those things that he sincerely believed were
threatening its unity. Pius was a good, deeply spiritual pastor who
hoped "to restore all things in Christ in order that Christ may be all
in all." Deeply pained by the outbreak of the First World War, which
he had tried in vain to head off, Pope Pius X died on August 20,
1914. His profound spirituality and holiness were officially recognized when he was canonized a saint on May 29, 1954.

The Protestant World

Liberalism or modernism had begun to affect Protestant thought
early in the nineteenth century. Friedrich Schleiermacher
(1768–1835), the father of modern liberal theology, taught that
experience was the foundation and key for religion. Hence rationalists could have no real arguments to counter the belief systems proposed by the Christian churches.

The historical-critical method used by some nineteenth century
Protestant scholars in their study of the bible challenged many traditional beliefs, for example, Moses' authorship of the pentateuch.
There was no central teaching authority in most Protestant churches that would challenge new theories and conclusions which seemed
contrary to the traditional teachings of the Christian faith. Hence,
liberal Protestants had no difficulty in reconciling the findings of
biblical criticism with faith since the latter was rooted in experience
and not in creeds, ethics or the validation of a central teaching
authority. Liberal Protestantism sought to accommodate Christian
teaching to the modern world in order to revitalize Christianity. As
a trend it crossed denominational lines and downplayed differences
among churches. The movement highly esteemed science and the
scientific method and distrusted dogmatic certitude. Naturally, that
affected the way in which the Protestant world view thought of God,
Christ, church, and the human person. Thus the Unitarians, even
more radical than the liberals, thought that the doctrine of the
Trinity was at variance with the unity or oneness of God. They also
rejected other teachings of Christianity and eventually a wing of
Unitarianism severed all connection with Christianity, opting for a
kind of rationalistic, ethical humanism.

While liberalism or modernism strongly influenced some
Protestant thought and church life, it also provoked a reaction.

Conservatives reasserted traditional doctrine as well as confessional or denominational identity. Protestant fundamentalism rejected the liberal tendency in theology. This stance described conservative groups within churches as well as whole denominations. The chief characteristics of this protest were:

1) a strictly literal interpretation of the bible;
2) a rejection of the historical-critical method as applied to the bible and theology;
3) a clear, certain code of morality;
4) a deep appreciation for traditional teaching and values in a world of change and uncertainty;
5) a psychological security that they possessed the truth and hence were the elect or the "saved."

There were tensions within liberal thought itself. How preserve the essentials of Christianity while accommodating traditional beliefs to the discoveries of modern science? What was the objective essence of Christianity? Ernst Troeltsch (1865–1923), comparing religious traditions, concluded that Christianity could claim to be the truth about God only for Christians. Other religions, for example, Buddhism and Hinduism, could claim the same validity for their adherents. Believing that ethics needed continual readjustment to meet the issues of a constantly changing world, Troeltsch in his work *The Social Teachings of the Christian Churches and Groups* (1912) sought to show the relativity of the Church's social ethics throughout history.

Catholicism in Europe

France

Catholicism in France during the late nineteenth and early twentieth centuries experienced tumultuous changes. While some sectors of the population remained devout and loyal Catholics, many others left the church, simply did not practice their faith any longer, or even vehemently attacked the church. A number of bishops came to the conclusion that new pastoral efforts were needed to promote true religious conversion and that accommodation with modern, secular life was needed. Leo XIII had promoted a policy of *ralliement*, calling for a recognition of the Third Republic. This policy of reconciliation failed because many conservative Catholics preferred the monarchy and many republicans were wed to the idea of excluding the church and religion from all public life.

On December 9, 1905, a law separating church and state in France was passed. Church property was confiscated, even though provision was made that would allow some properties to remain in the hands of lay Catholics. Pope Pius X condemned the move and forbade Catholics to participate in any property association. The pope's firmness stymied the government's plan, forcing it to concede certain property (e.g., churches) to the clergy.

While the pope protested the law of separation, the French church, set free from government interference, although not its anti-clericalism, began to experience signs of renewed commitment. Certainly secularization contributed to a serious decline in the number of vocations to the priesthood and religious life and also promoted religious indifference among many of the French. But certain conservative groups, for example, *Action Française*, espoused a fervent Catholicism and attracted numbers, not always for religious reasons. Progressive renewal movements also came into being that sought to promote a modern, democratic and vital Catholicism.

Italy

The perduring issue for the church in Italy was the "Roman question," that is, the relationship of the Catholic Church to the unified Italian nation. That unification required the annexation of the Papal States, an action which a series of popes refused to condone. Moreover, there was the broader issue of how the church would adjust to the modern world and a secular state. While conservative forces were strong in the church, anti-clericalism often colored the posture of liberals. Laws had been enacted that were prejudicial to the interests of the church, for example, suppressing religious houses, nationalizing church property and curtailing Catholic influence in education.

Involved laity during the pontificate of Leo XIII had hoped that the prohibition on Catholic participation in Italian political life would be lifted. Since that did not happen, a movement of committed lay Catholics was born. The well-organized "Catholic Action" movement in Italy sought to promote religious faith and worked to realize a moral vision for society. One wing of this movement, more liberal and pragmatic, under the leadership of Father Romolo Murri encouraged direct political involvement. Murri founded a denominational Catholic political party, the *Lega democratica nazionale*, which was intended to be independent of the bishops. Murri espoused many liberal ideas, and eventually this movement was caught up in political modernism. Pius X included Murri's teaching in his condemnation of modernism, and the movement soon collapsed. The stage was set, however, for the re-entry of Catholics into Italian political and public life and the beginning of a Christian democracy. In 1911, inspired by the thought and the writing of the political philosopher Father Luigi Sturzo (1871–1959), a group of committed Catholics founded the Christian Democratic League, which was the beginning of the Italian People's Party.

Germany

The diplomatic approach of Pope Leo XIII to the *Kulturkampf* proved advantageous to the church when the anti-Catholic policy of Chancellor Bismarck gradually fell into disfavor. By allowing the chancellor to save face, the pope made it possible for many restrictive laws against Catholics to be repealed. The fifteen-year conflict between church and state had a positive side insofar as it unified Catholics in Germany and strengthened their allegiance to the pope.

Pius X sought good relations with the empire and appreciated its staunch defense of the existing order. Nevertheless, given the official bias toward Protestantism, real power in the empire and Prussia was never in Catholic hands. The Catholic Center Party prospered in the empire of Wilhelm II. But despite its acceptance and influence, the Center Party continued to stress civil rights for all as it had done during the epic of the *Kulturkampf*. While the party resisted right wing anti-Semitism, it did seek to prove Catholic patriotism by supporting ultra-nationalism. Another association of Catholic workers, peasants, members of the middle class and intellectuals—the *Volksverein fur Katholische Deutschland*—promoted democracy, and in 1914 it had over 850,000 members. As in France and Italy, the Catholic Church in Germany sought to come to terms with the political realities of a changing understanding of the state in the modern world.

The Empire

The Austro-Hungarian Empire under the Hapsburgs was unquestionably Roman Catholic, and Pius X saw Austria as the primary example of a Catholic country. For the pope this was exemplified in 1912 when Emperor Franz Joseph and his court, in full uniform,

publicly professed their faith by participating in the blessed sacrament procession at the eucharistic congress. While the Austrian part
of the empire was overwhelmingly Roman Catholic, the Hungarian
part had a significant number of Orthodox and Protestant
Christians as well as a sizable Jewish population (in 1900 there were
800,000 Jews). Liberal stirrings, however, for a more democratic
national experience often pitted peasants, bourgeoisie and the urban
working class against church leaders who controlled a great deal of
property and usually supported the status quo.

Iberia

While Spain had experienced anti-clerical regimes during the nineteenth century, the constitution of 1876 and the restored Bourbon
dynasty reasserted the rights and privileges of the church. The vast
majority of Spaniards had always remained loyal to the church, but
the clergy generally shunned innovation and new pastoral initiatives. Thus popular religion was often superstitious, routine and
devoid of good religious education.

In the early twentieth century, divisive issues began to surface as
progressive Catholics vied with conservative Catholics for control of
the government. Various groups (e.g., intellectuals and workers)
began to oppose church leaders and clergy for a variety of political,
economic and philosophical reasons. In 1909 a revolutionary leader,
Francisco Ferrer, was executed in the Catalan city of Barcelona. In
retaliation, one hundred and thirty-eight priests were murdered by
angry mobs, churches were sacked, and religious orders experienced government restrictions.

In 1911, after liberals forced a separation of church and state in
Portugal, there was an effort on the part of the anti-clerical leaders
of the new republic to secularize society and isolate the church from
any public role. The harassment and persecution of religious congregations was indicative of the stance of the new republic toward
the church.

The Slavs

The vast majority of the Russian people belonged to the Orthodox
Church. However, at the beginning of the twentieth century, there
were also about ten million Roman Catholics in Russia. Almost six
million were Polish, living in the Russian-dominated part of the former kingdom of Poland, while the rest were Lithuanians, White

Russians (Europeans as distinct from Asians), Ukrainians, Latvians and Germans.

The fortunes of Catholics changed with the whims of the czar and his advisors. Both Eastern rite Catholics and Latin rite Catholics were often restricted or controlled in their activity. Pope Leo XIII, through his overtures to the czars, Alexander II, Alexander III, and Nicholas II, temporarily won concessions for Catholics. By 1914, however, Catholics were once again being persecuted and the church was severely limited in its activity.

Polish and Lithuanian Catholics under the control of Russia, Austria or Prussia (the Polish-Lithuanian Empire had been dissolved at the Congress of Vienna in 1815) remained fiercely loyal Roman Catholics. They were often persecuted by secular rulers, while also being subjected to forced conversion and discrimination by the Orthodox Church.

The religious situation of other Slavic groups varied considerably from country to country as well as from region to region. In Galicia, Austria-Hungary ruled three and a half million Latin rite Polish Catholics and three million Ukrainian Catholics. The empire also ruled over 700,000 Orthodox and 350,000 Catholics in Bosnia-Herzegovina as well as Catholic Czechs and Slovaks in Bohemia, and Croatians, Slovenes and Serbs in other regions of the empire. Many of these Catholic people from diverse backgrounds found themselves threatened culturally and at times religiously. Drastic changes, however, would radically modify the world of eastern Europe later in the century.

Christianity in the United States

The Protestant Experience

The Protestant world in the United States from the Civil War to the First World War developed a variety of expressions in trying to respond to new religious needs. Finding themselves challenged by the new immigrants, the urban poor, and north-south regional divisions, white Anglo-Saxon Protestants developed new forms of evangelization and new denominations. A successful effort to serve the urban poor was through the founding of the YMCA and YWCA (Young Men's/Women's Christian Association) and evangelization was carried on through Sunday schools and revivals. New denominations, which sought more personal forms of religious experience, also came into being: the Salvation Army, the Holiness or

Pentecostal Churches, which became the Assemblies of God, and the Seventh-Day Adventists. Some liberal Protestants, concerned with the poor, promoted a movement called the "social gospel," which sought the evangelization of society and the transformation of its structures. The great proponent of the "social gospel" was the Baptist professor of church history, Walter Rauschenbusch (1861–1918). He and his followers questioned the morality of unchecked capitalism which, in their judgment, benefited the wealthy at the expense of the poor.

A unique new religious tradition that rose in the United States during the nineteenth century was Mormonism, founded by Joseph Smith (1805–1844) in 1830. Smith claimed that he had experienced a special revelation from an angel named Moroni who gave him the Book of Mormon, which supplemented the bible by presenting new revelations not contained in the current texts of the Hebrew and Christian scriptures. Smith was eventually hanged by an angry mob and was succeeded by Brigham Young (1801–1877), who led the Church of Jesus Christ of the Latter Day Saints (Mormons) to Utah. The church stressed communal living and the teachings of the Book of Mormon, and it allowed polygamy. Over time the religion has become more mainstream by placing great value on morality, hard work and missionary commitment.

Charles Russell (1852–1916), the founder of the Jehovah's Witnesses, rejected the doctrines of the Trinity and the divinity of Christ and taught the imminent end of the world, that is, in 1914. The Witnesses placed emphasis on the bible, missionary work, public example, and ardent evangelism, all with an eye toward the second coming of Christ. This was another instance in religious history of millennialism or Adventism, that is, a special focus on the approaching end of the world.

The Church of Christ, Scientist, was officially founded by Mary Baker Eddy (1821–1910) in Lynn, Massachusetts, in 1879. The major tenet of Christian Science was the conviction that sickness was a mental error. People could and would be healed not by doctors or drugs, but by the science that Jesus used to heal. Mrs. Eddy believed that she had discovered a secret meaning of scripture that would allow her to heal and to teach others to heal. Her publishing efforts, the most prominent of which were *Science & Health with Key to the Scriptures* and the daily newspaper, *The Christian Science Monitor*, were located at the mother church of Christian Science in Boston.

The Catholic Experience

Immigration to the United States from Europe occurred throughout the second half of the nineteenth century and the first half of the twentieth century. By the turn of the century, the Catholic Church in the United States had become truly a church of immigrants. In 1910 the number of Catholics had reached sixteen million out of a total population of ninety-two million. The Irish tended to stay on the east coast. Numbers of Italians and Poles also settled in the east (many Poles went to the coal fields of Pennsylvania) and others moved to the urban centers of the midwest, for example, Chicago, Detroit, and Milwaukee. The Germans generally went to the rich farmlands of the midwest.

The later arrivals often felt the discrimination of the dominant culture and at times that of their co-religionists as well. Especially during the dictatorship in Mexico of Porfirio Diaz (1876–1911), Mexicans moved to the southwest and California, where they comprised eighty percent of the migrant farm labor force. French-Canadian Catholics came to New England to work in the mills, while Portuguese, especially from the Azores, arrived there for the fishing industry. The largest Catholic groups were: Irish, German, Italian, Polish, French-Canadian and Mexican. These were joined by others, mostly from eastern Europe: Lithuanians, Czechs (Bohemians), Slovaks and Ukrainians.

As an urban, culturally and linguistically diverse church of the poor and working classes, the Catholic Church in the United States became the focus of life for most immigrants both religiously and socially. At the same time the church became the instrument for inculturation into the American way of life. Through its extensive parochial school system and other charitable agencies the church provided the means for upward mobility.

The American Catholic experience during this period of immigration (ca. 1880–1920) was different from that of Europe. Although the church in the United States was certainly one with the universal church in faith, morals and structure, it nevertheless manifested its own special identity. Given its unique development and history in the very original experiment in democracy which marked the United States, the American Catholic Church had unique characteristics:

1) Because of the separation clause in the Constitution, it did not fear government interference in church life or policy.
2) Being predominantly a church of the lower or poorer classes, it

felt the sting of bigotry and discrimination by those of the
dominant culture.

3) The church "took care of its own," that is, its ministry was
directed principally to its own membership.

4) Since it was not a dominant church, as in the Catholic countries of Europe, and found itself criticized or demeaned by outsiders, the church directed its concerns and energies to the
urgent religious and worldly needs of its own people, thus
becoming a ghetto within the larger society.

5) To meet the needs of the faithful, religiously and socially,
Catholics built an enormous network of parishes, schools and
charitable agencies across the nation.

6) Financing for these projects was purely voluntary and came
from the gifts of the ordinary faithful, who generously sacrificed
to build and maintain a vast number of church institutions.

7) Leadership in the church unquestionably remained in the
hands of bishops and priests who had no qualms about exercising their influence and authority over their congregations and
against any who would attack their people. While a more democratic form of church order had characterized the early phase of
the church in America, by the twentieth century the church was
less "congregational" and more "hierarchical" or "clerical."

8) The religious life of Catholics centered around rituals, that is,
mass and the sacraments, as well as devotions, for example,
novenas, processions, feasts, shrines, guilds and societies. This
spiritual lifestyle nourished personal piety and provided clear
identity for Catholics as a people and clearly distinguished
them from others.

In 1903 James Cardinal Gibbons, for forty-four years the archbishop
of Baltimore (1877–1921), became the first American to vote in a
papal election. After Pope Pius X removed the American church from
the jurisdiction of the Congregation of the Propagation of the Faith
five years later, the United States could no longer be considered missionary territory.

Immigrant Catholics continued to pour into the country in large
numbers until the outbreak of World War I (1914). Meanwhile sec-
ond-generation Catholics began their upward march in the professions, services, trades and church. Politics attracted the energies of
a number of Irish: the Tammany Hall political machine in New York
City produced Governor Alfred E. Smith, the Democratic candidate
for president of the United States in 1928. A weighty reason, if not

the only one, for his defeat was his Catholicism. In 1905 John F. Fitzgerald became Boston's third Irish mayor. In 1961 his grandson, John Fitzgerald Kennedy, became the first Catholic to be elected president of the United States. The Irish-Catholic presence in politics repeated itself across the country (e.g., Chicago, Kansas City and San Francisco).

The complex nature of the composition of the American church caused ethnic tensions to flare among Catholics over control of parishes and schools. German-Catholics protested the control exercised by Irish pastors and bishops. The large Polish population of Chicago similarly resented the Irish dominance in the church. Lithuanians objected to the Polish cultural flavor in individual parishes and schools. Italians felt misunderstood and without influence. Despite these difficulties and challenges, the church through its institutions became the most significant instrument in the assimilation process for immigrants as well as the chief religious and cultural guardian for millions of Catholics.

Since the days of Bishop John Carroll, Catholics had reflected on the question of Catholic identity in America. How could one be a Catholic and truly a patriotic American? Carroll had advocated embracing all that was good in the American experience: separation of church and state, democratic processes in the church, the use of English in the liturgy, religious liberty and ecumenism. Bishop John England, the bishop of Charleston, South Carolina (1820–1842), promoted a similar kind of Catholic inculturation into the American scene. For him the church was more the community of the Holy Spirit and less of a hierarchical institution. The church was the "body of Christ." England promoted lay participation in church activity and a more "congregationalist" model for parish life. Archbishop John Ireland of St. Paul, Minnesota, Bishop John Spalding of Peoria, and Cardinal Gibbons all supported the efforts to adapt the church to the modern age and the American experience. More conservative and traditional Catholics, fearing that such compromise with modernity would relativize the truth of Catholicism, reacted. The leaders of this group in the late nineteenth century were Archbishop Michael Corrigan of the Archdiocese of New York and Bishop Bernard McQuaid of the Diocese of Rochester, New York.

The controversy eventually led to the condemnation of "Americanism" by Pope Leo XIII. Still, Catholic thinkers and scholars in the United States continued to reflect on the implications of modern thought for Catholic theology. Some professors in seminaries employed the historical-critical method in biblical interpretation and church history. St. Joseph's Seminary in New York, which published the scholarly journal *The New York Review*, was a center for modern theological thought.

When Pope Pius X published his encyclical *Pascendi Domini Gregis,* which condemned modernism, in 1907, the effect of this action on Catholic intellectual life in the United States was palpable. *The New York Review* ceased publication. Professors were removed from seminaries, censorship was employed in theology schools, and intellectual speculation was curtailed. Modernism was in no way a serious crisis for the church in the United States. Its condemnation certainly put the breaks on scholarly inquiry and affected the more liberal theological wing in the church. However, the crisis did not directly effect the vast majority of Catholic women and men.

A certain pragmatism had always characterized American Catholics, who were a "can do" gospel people—they built churches, schools, orphanages and hospitals. They supported the poor at home and abroad and founded religious communities such as the Catholic Foreign Mission Society (Maryknoll) in 1911. Catholic people went to church, educated their children in the traditional faith, tried to live spiritual and moral lives and sought to improve their overall standard of living while pursuing the American dream. For them to be Catholic and to be American was simply an accepted fact.

FOR FURTHER READING AND REFERENCE

John Dillenberger and Claude Welch, *Protestant Christianity: Interpreted Through Its Development,* 2nd ed. (New York: Macmillan Publishing Company, 1988).

Jay P. Dolan, *The American Catholic Experience: A History from Colonial Times to the Present* (Garden City, New York: Image Books, 1985).

Hubert Jedin, ed., *History of the Church,* Vol. VIII: *The Church in the Age of Liberalism* (New York: Crossroad Publishing Company, 1981).

_____, *History of the Church,* Vol. IX: *The Church in the Industrial Age* (New York: Crossroad Publishing Company, 1981).

J.N.D. Kelly, *The Oxford Dictionary of the Popes* (New York: Oxford University Press, 1986).

Williston Walker et al., *A History of the Christian Church,* 4th ed. (New York: Charles Scribner's Sons, 1985).

15

European and American Christianity: World War I

On June 28, 1914, in the Bosnian capital of Sarajevo, Archduke Francis Ferdinand and his wife, Sophie, were assassinated by the Bosnian Serb, Gavrilo Princip. This event marked the beginning of a five-year period that would profoundly change the modern world. A month later on July 28, Austria-Hungary declared war against Serbia, and within a few days, on August 1, Germany declared war against Russia, and, on August 3, against France. On August 4, Great Britain declared war against Germany for invading Belgium. By the end of the month many of the European powers, as well as Japan, were at war. The United States would not enter the conflict until April 6, 1917, and the Bolshevik Revolution in November 1917 removed Russia from the war. When World War I officially ended by the signing of a peace treaty in the Hall of Mirrors at the palace of Versailles on June 28, 1919, a new map of Europe was created.

In the waning days of his papal ministry, Pope Pius X frequently warned against the widening conflict. However, as nationalism and imperialism ruled the day, Catholic people and associations were themselves caught up in these movements.

Just War Theory

Catholics and others have often struggled with the morality of war. Can violence be used to achieve justice? Can force and war be used legitimately by those professing a religion based on love? Roman Catholic moral theology traces the "just war theory" back to St. Augustine (354–430), through Thomas Aquinas, O.P. (1225–1274), Francisco de la Vittoria, O.P. (1485–1546), the "father of international law," and the Jesuit Francisco Suarez (1548–1617). The moral theory continues to evolve today, particularly in the face of nuclear weapons. In essence the theory suggested that one could take part in a defensive war morally if the following conditions were present:

1) it was declared by legitimate authority;
2) it was for a just cause;
3) it was fought as a last resort;
4) it did not involve the direct destruction of the innocent.

An aggressive war required careful examination of each of the above conditions and therefore was less easily morally justifiable.

Pacifism

Pacifism as a political and theological stance can be absolute (*all* war is immoral) or relative (*this* war is immoral). It has been part of the Christian tradition since the earliest days of the church. Christians in the imperial Roman forces sometimes resigned or were forbidden to re-enlist when the military were forced to participate in idolatrous worship. At the time of the Reformation there were Christian groups (e.g., Anabaptists, Mennonites, and some Baptists) who rejected absolutely the legitimacy of any war. Modern figures known for their advocacy of non-violence and rejection of war include the Hindu leader, Mahatma Gandhi, and the Southern Baptist minister, Dr. Martin Luther King.

Catholic pacifists have generally been relative, that is, against a particular war. Today some contend that, given nuclear arms, no war now can ever be morally justified. A German Dominican, F. Stratmann, has written persuasively for this position in *The Church and War* (1928) and *War and Christianity Today* (1956).

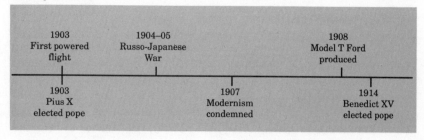

| 1903 | 1904–05 | 1908 |
| First powered flight | Russo-Japanese War | Model T Ford produced |

| 1903 | 1907 | 1914 |
| Pius X elected pope | Modernism condemned | Benedict XV elected pope |

Pope Benedict XV (1914–1922)

In seeking to be patriotic, Catholics in Germany and their Center Party increasingly supported the nationalist aspirations of the country. Church leaders and members in Austria-Hungary supported the Catholic monarchy as it sought to maintain order and expand its empire. While the unsettled "Roman question" kept Catholics in Italy by and large out of political life, nevertheless they rallied to the national aspirations of their country as it sought to establish an empire by invading Libya. French Catholics supported the army and consistently viewed Germany with suspicion. In this atmosphere pacifism was not the ordinary stance of European Christians, whether they were Catholics or Protestants. Catholics in fact viewed those who supported pacifism (often socialists, anarchists or Freemasons) as opponents of the church.

Although Pope Pius X spoke against the use of arms to settle international disputes and encouraged arbitration, few listened. After World War I erupted on June 28, 1914, Pius X, old and distraught, died suddenly on August 20. Cardinal Giacomo della Chiesa, who had been a papal diplomat and was archbishop of Bologna at the time of his election, was chosen to succeed him as Pope Benedict XV on September 3.

Pope Benedict faced enormous obstacles in his ministry as the sign of unity for the Catholic world. Two-thirds of Europe's Catholics were involved in the war; one hundred and twenty-four million on the side of the Allies, sixty-four million on the side of the Central Powers. He therefore immediately pursued three objectives as he began his papacy: 1) ensuring Vatican neutrality, 2) assisting victims of war and 3) establishing peace.

Papal Objectives

In an allocution on January 22, 1915, Benedict informed the world that as pope he would never condone injustice or the violation of

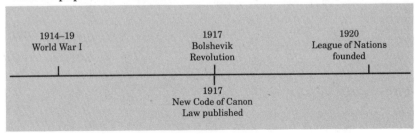

1914–19	1917	1920
World War I	Bolshevik Revolution	League of Nations founded

1917
New Code of Canon
Law published

human rights, and that he would continue to promote God's law for everyone everywhere. On the other hand, he believed that since the pope was ministerially responsible for women and men on both sides of the war, he must not take sides in a conflict which should in fact be settled reasonably and peacefully.

This neutrality was meant to free the pope to promote peace and to allow the Holy See to minister pastorally to the needs of victims, civilian and military, of the war. Sadly, Benedict was accused by each side of favoring the other. The Central Powers referred to him as "der franzosische Papst" (i.e., the French pope); the Allies called him "le Pape boche" (i.e., the German pope). Interestingly, in December 1921, the Turks erected a statue in Istanbul to honor Benedict as "the great pope of the world tragedy...the benefactor of all people irrespective of nationality or religion."

During World War I atrocities in the Mideast included deportations and massacres among the Armenian people, which took a toll of about one million lives. The pope intervened with the sultan, saving those who could be saved. Armenian orphans of this carnage were cared for at the Benedict XV Orphanage in Istanbul.

The pope established an international missing persons bureau at the Vatican to facilitate the reunion of prisoners of war and other refugees with their families. He persuaded Switzerland to accept soldiers ill with tuberculosis and promoted the exchange of prisoners of war, as well as the care of the sick and wounded in neutral countries. The funds for Benedict XV's efforts, which helped more than one hundred thousand people, came from special church collections and the Vatican's own resources.

While maintaining neutrality, Benedict tried to facilitate a peace process that would end the conflict. On August 1, 1917, he sent a seven-point peace plan to all the heads of the Allied and Central Powers. The plan called for:

1) freedom of the sea;
2) limitation of arms;
3) arbitration;
4) German withdrawal from France, independence for Belgium, England's return to Germany of its colonies;
5) reciprocal renunciation of war indemnities;
6) conciliation over rival territorial claims;
7) overall commitment to moral right and justice.

Austria was willing to accept the plan but France expressed

reluctance. Germany balked at a Vatican-sponsored peace plan and the United States rejected it. The pope's efforts had failed. When at last the war ended, the Vatican was excluded from both the Paris Peace Conference and the League of Nations at the behest of Italy. Nevertheless, a representative of the pope was present in Paris, making contacts with many diplomats. This activity became the basis for a wider role for the holy see in the postwar world of Europe. Vatican relations with France, which had been broken in 1905, were resumed in 1921. The canonization of St. Joan of Arc (1412–1431) by Pope Benedict on May 9, 1920, was a significant gesture toward the French people that proved helpful for the renewal of relations. Similarly a basis for the solution of the "Roman question" was laid in 1919 when the pope abolished the prohibition against Catholics participating in political life.

On May 23, 1920 Benedict issued an encyclical letter to the world, *Pacem Dei Munus*. In this letter he called for genuine peace and reconciliation among all peoples with no concern for indemnities, punishment or revenge. If Benedict's vision of peace had been accepted, perhaps World War II would not have happened. The pope died unexpectedly on January 22, 1922. During his pontificate the Vatican's presence as a moral force in the world had grown considerably.

American Catholics and the War

Speaking of the Spanish-American War (April–August 1898), Teddy Roosevelt said: "It was a little war, but it was the only one we had." The doctrine of the "manifest destiny" of the United States moved the country at the end of the nineteenth century to conquer much of what was left of Spain's empire. Cuba was set free and Puerto Rico and Guam were ceded to the United States, which also bought the Philippine Islands for twenty million dollars. President McKinley (1897–1901), a staunch Methodist, saw the war as a missionary crusade that would Christianize Filipinos. Since most Filipinos had been Roman Catholic since the sixteenth century, this perspective seemed to indicate prejudice against the Roman Church and Catholic Spain.

While many Catholics supported the war efforts and some Irish saw the liberation of Cuba as a reflection of their own fight for independence from England, others such as Bishop John Lancaster Spalding and Mayor Patrick Collins of Boston criticized American imperialism. A number of priests served as chaplains during the

war, and one, Father William D. McKinnon, is credited with broker-
ing the surrender of Manila. He subsequently set about organizing
relief programs for the Filipino people and has been honored for his
work by a statue in San Francisco's Golden Gate Park.

By 1910, out of a total population of ninety-two million in the
United States, there were at least sixteen million Roman Catholics,
mostly descendants of immigrants who had arrived since 1820. Anti-
Catholicism flourished in some areas, such as the south and rural
parts of the midwest. The Populist Party, for example, warned
against the threat of the power of the pope, the Jesuits and the
Knights of Columbus. The Knights, founded by Father Michael
McGivney at St. Mary's Church, New Haven, Connecticut, in 1882,
were and are today a fraternal benefit society of Catholic men. They
promote charity, unity, and loyalty to the church and patriotism to
the country. As a fraternal organization, the Knights over the years
have provided benefits for a variety of worthwhile projects, including
Catholic education, war relief and the particular needs of dioceses.

Many Catholic Americans supported the Allied cause during the
early years of World War I. However, German American Catholics
and Protestants backed the Central Powers as did some supporters
of Irish independence. England in 1916 had brutally put down the
"Easter Rebellion" in Dublin, which attempted to free Ireland, and
the leaders of the rebellion had been hanged.

When the United States entered the war (April 6, 1917), however, the Catholic community by and large joined the rest of the
nation in supporting the Allied cause. A million Catholics served in
the armed forces, as did more than fifteen hundred priest chaplains. The Knights of Columbus established service centers (more
than two hundred and fifty overseas and three hundred and sixty
stateside) with recreational facilities, chapels and offices to serve
the social and spiritual needs of people involved in the war. The
bishops established the National Catholic War Council (NCWC) to
coordinate Catholic efforts for social and political action. The council represented an institutional commitment on the part of the
church to social and political involvement, and it allowed the laity a
substantial role in this ministry.

On February 12, 1919, the administrative board of the NCWC
issued a social action policy statement, *The Bishops' Program of
Social Reconstruction*. The plan, written by Monsignor John A.
Ryan, was rooted in the theological understanding of social justice
presented by St. Thomas Aquinas and Leo XIII's famous encyclical
on justice, *Rerum Novarum*. Ryan had long been in the forefront of

American Catholic thinkers and writers on matters of social justice. His books, *Living Wage: Its Ethical and Economic Aspects* (1906) and *Distributive Justice* (1916), became classics. *The Bishops' Program of Social Reconstruction* called for:

1) minimum wage legislation;
2) unemployment, health and old-age insurance;
3) decent housing as well as vocational training for returning veterans;
4) control of the cost of living;
5) abolition of child labor;
6) equal pay for women doing the same work as men;
7) workers' share in management, not along a socialist model but by emphasizing cooperatives;
8) control of monopolies.

Critics blasted the document as "pro-labor" and "socialist."

After the war, the War Council would continue as the National Catholic Welfare Conference (today's United States Catholic Conference). Monsignor Ryan was named director of the Social Action Department of the NCWC in 1920 and remained there until his death in 1945.

In general the Allied cause was supported from the beginning by (Anglo-Saxon) Americans and found support among the clergy of the Presbyterian, Congregationalist, Methodist and Episcopal churches. When America entered the war, almost all Jews, Protestants and Catholics backed the decision. However, a minuscule number of pacifists, Quakers and Mennonites, dissented. Often they were severely criticized or ridiculed for their position, since many saw the war as a religious crusade against the unholy barbarians. Patriotism had become identified with religion.

Protestant churches also organized in an unprecedented way to meet the social and spiritual needs of people in time of war by forming a "Committee of One Hundred" to organize and accomplish tasks. Likewise, the Jewish Welfare Board and the Young Men's Hebrew Association did the same. The enormous effort by churches to minister to military personnel and civilians during the critical time of war, spiritually and socially, provided an opportunity for unparalleled inter-church cooperation.

16

Revolutions and War Again

The first half of the twentieth century was a tumultuous, historical period that offered particular challenges to the leaders of the Catholic Church and to millions of Catholics throughout the world. The First World War (1914–1919) posed moral dilemmas to Catholics and others about the justice and rightness of war and its conduct. It likewise called upon churches to act charitably and assist victims of war, both military and civilian. Nationalism and patriotism at times had undermined the gospel ethic of universal love and so called for both an individual and a collective examination of conscience.

Christianity in general and Catholicism in particular are not intended simply to be private personal matters or positions. The social, public nature of human life requires that a person's religious vision or world view influence and guide all aspects of life. Thus the church was inextricably involved in one way or another in the complex series of world events that marked the first half of the present century.

Ireland

Legitimate national aspirations for independence were always alive in Ireland, and at times insurrections, such as the abortive 1848 rebellion of the Young Irelanders, broke out. The rebellion occurred amidst the devastating famine (1845–1850) that drove half a million Irish to the grave and other millions to emigrate. Although the Irish bishops often found themselves opposed to extreme nationalism, many members of the Young Irelanders continued their efforts to liberate Ireland from British control by establishing a secret society, the Fenian Brotherhood, in 1858. While Charles Stewart

Parnell promoted "home rule" by obstructing the business in parliament (British), others agitated for land reform (the Land League).

On Easter Monday, 1916, the Fenian movement organized an armed rebellion under the leadership of Patrick Pearce and James Connolly, who declared the Irish Republic. After seizing Dublin's general post office, they occupied it for six days. England, engaged in the war in Europe, nevertheless, counterattacked. The efforts by British troops to restore order devastated much of the city. The executions and deportations of the rebels which followed inflamed anti-English feeling. The resulting popular support for the cause of Irish independence, gained by the brutality of the British response to the Easter Monday uprising, enabled Sinn Fein leaders in January 1919 to declare Ireland a republic. When England once more sent troops to crush the Irish, abetted by a cruel paramilitary force (the Black and Tans, called such because of the colors of their uniforms), the Irish Republican Army (I.R.A.) retaliated with guerrilla warfare.

The six counties of Ulster or Northern Ireland, where the majority of the population were Protestants, were given their own legislature, subordinate to England, in 1920. The twenty-six counties of the south became a British dominion in 1922. Civil war broke out, however, between the nationalists or republicans and those who accepted dominion status as expedient, for example, Michael Collins. The bishops condemned both violence and the republicans. Many clergy and Catholic laity, however, fiercely supported total independence. In 1932 the republican leader, Eamon De Valera (1882–1975), became head of the government, and in 1938 a referendum declared full independence from England. When Ireland became a recognized republic in 1949, the constitution gave special position to the Catholic Church while granting religious liberty to all religions.

Russia

Russian dead, wounded, missing, and prisoners during the first years of World War I, totaling nine million persons, were a significant cause of the widespread discontent with the ruling government and forced the abdication of Czar Nicholas II (1894–1917) in March 1917 and his eventual execution in 1918. Although a provisional socialist government under Alexander Kerenski (1881–1970) was established, popular uprisings among peasants, industrial workers and military destabilized the new socialist regime. A second revolution, the Bolshevik Revolution of October 24–25, 1917, under the leadership of Nicholas Lenin (1870–1924), then took control of the government. His principal assistants were Leon Trotsky (1879–1940) and Joseph Stalin (1879–1953). Through a period of civil war (Whites or Czarist supporters versus Reds or Bolshevik supporters), Communists maintained control and the Soviet Republic was in place by 1921 under the dictatorship of the Communist Party. After Lenin's death in 1924 a triumvirate ruled, but by 1929 all power resided in Joseph Stalin. The October revolution represented one of the most thoroughgoing political, economic, social revolutions in history. While communism in Russia lasted a little more than seventy years, its ideals came to dominate vast areas of the planet, for example, Eastern Europe, China, parts of Indochina and Africa, and at times Latin American countries, for example, Cuba. Communist parties also existed or flourished in a number of Western countries as well.

Communism was a world view with a concrete vision of the human person, community, destiny and way of acting. In a sense it was a secular religion. The philosophy behind it was based on the work of Karl Marx (1818–1883) and Friedrich Engels (1820–1895) as these were interpreted by Nicholas Lenin. Marxist-Leninism maintained the following:

1) all reality is material;
2) the human person is an economic animal;
3) dialectical materialism is the force guiding history (thesis versus antithesis results in a new synthesis);
4) history, then, is predictable and scientifically subject to control;
5) history, in fact, is the record of class struggles and warfare, that is, between those who owned the means of production (capital) and workers;
6) socialism is the inevitable culmination of this process in which workers finally will own the means of production;
7) the communist world may be inevitable but can only be realized through revolution which frees the proletariat from the oppression of the bourgeoisie;
8) communism will be the final triumph of socialism but requires in the meantime a "dictatorship" of the proletariat to ensure success and oppose capitalist attempts to block the revolution.

Inevitably communism required and justified totalitarianism and the abuse of human rights which accompanied it. It also meant the suppression of religion, since in the communist world view religion developed out of a particular historical epoch in order to support and justify oppressive regimes, for example, capitalism. Thus religion was "the opium of the people," a comfort to people in their oppression. As such it was counter-revolutionary and needed to be abolished; communism, therefore, fostered state-sponsored atheism.

The work of the great ninth century apostles to the Slavic people, St. Cyril and his brother, St. Methodius, and the missionaries they inspired bore fruit when St. Vladimir (979–1015) made Christianity the official religion of Russia. The "Cyrillic" alphabet of the Russian language traces its origins to St. Cyril. Russian Christians belonged to the Orthodox family of churches in the East that originated from Constantinople and shared with them a state of estrangement from the Latin West after 1054. While the largest Christian community in the Soviet Union was the official Russian Orthodox Church, there were also Latin Catholics, Eastern rite Catholics, mainline Protestant churches and some Pentecostal groups. When the U.S.S.R. extended its boundaries after World War II, great numbers of Catholics became a major presence, for example, Poles, Lithuanians, Czechs, Slovaks, Croatians, Slovenes and Hungarians.

The logic of tyranny and state sponsored atheism led to the suppression of the church; hence the Russian Orthodox Church was severely persecuted in the aftermath of the Bolshevik Revolution. Priests and bishops were put to death or exiled to Siberia. Churches were closed and property confiscated. Before 1917 there were five hundred churches in Moscow; by 1939 there were only seventeen. While persecution eased during World War II, it resumed again in the 1950s. In its activities the state-controlled Orthodox Church under communism was often perceived as acquiescing to Soviet policies.

Pius XI (1922–1939) had succeeded Benedict XV (1914–1922) on February 6, 1922. In the aftermath of the Bolshevik Revolution he challenged the Soviets, who had fiercely attacked the Roman Catholic Church, to allow the church its freedom to appoint bishops and instruct young people in the faith. He also ordered prayers to be said in Catholic churches throughout the world for the conversion of Russia. In encyclicals and other church documents Pius denounced atheistic communism and Bolshevik violence. The communists in turn viewed the Catholic Church as a major obstacle to implanting their world view everywhere. Bishops and priests, as leaders of the Catholic communities which they served, were severely attacked, imprisoned, executed or banished in Russia.

After World War II the boundaries of the Soviet Union greatly expanded as did the Soviet sphere of influence. The "iron curtain" separated most of Eastern Europe from the West. Religion of every kind suffered persecution—Judaism, Islam and Christianity.

Ukrainian Eastern rite Catholics were forced to live a secret church life or were required to abandon their tradition and become part of the Russian Orthodox Church. Cardinal Joseph Slipyji (1892–1984), metropolitan of the Ukrainian Catholic Church, was imprisoned for eighteen years. Other Ukrainian Church leaders met the same fate.

In Hungary many Catholic churches, schools, seminaries, and religious houses were closed or abandoned, and where they were allowed to remain open their operations were harassed. Church property was confiscated. Religious literature was taken from libraries and burned and new publications were forbidden. Cardinal Jozsef Mindszenty (1892–1974), archbishop of Esztergom, was accused of treason, arrested, tried and condemned to death in 1948. The bogus trial, in which a confession was extorted by torture and drugs, was watched by the world. In 1956 Hungarian freedom fighters freed Mindszenty, who later took refuge in the U.S. legation in Budapest, where he lived for fifteen years.

The communists took over the Czechoslovak People's Democratic Republic in 1948. Immediately the church came under attack. Schools, seminaries, religious orders and the Catholic press were suppressed. In 1949, after show trials, leading bishops were imprisoned, including Cardinal Josef Beran of Prague, who finally was exiled to Rome in 1965.

Communists established the state of Yugoslavia in 1946. The more than eighteen million people were chiefly Orthodox or Catholic with about two million Muslims living in Bosnia-Herzegovina. Persecution and state-sponsored atheism followed the establishment of the new communist country. Some Catholic priests were executed (about thirteen percent of the total), while many others were imprisoned, including Cardinal Aloysius Stepinac of Zagreb who was jailed for sixteen years.

During World War II Polish Catholics suffered terribly under both the Germans and the Russians. The Nazi authorities arrested and sent many bishops and priests to concentration camps. Among those who died was St. Maximilian Kolbe, who offered himself for death in place of a married man with a family. Church personnel held in concentration camps numbered: thirty-six hundred priests, three hundred and eighty clerics, three hundred and forty lay brothers, and eleven hundred sisters. Of that number nineteen hundred and ninety-six priests, one hundred and thirteen clerics and two hundred and thirty-eight sisters as well as untold numbers of lay persons died.

In 1945 a communist government was installed with Moscow's help. Again a familiar pattern of systematic persecution of the church began. Educational work with youth was curtailed and restrictions were put on all church activity. Many bishops and priests were imprisoned, including the primate cardinal, Stefan Wyszynski, who was freed in 1956 when Poland broke with a Stalinist mode of communism to go its own way. Still the church remained confined and restricted in a communist nation where ninety-seven percent of the citizens were, by and large, ardent, committed Roman Catholics.

On August 3, 1940, Russia annexed Lithuania, a largely Roman Catholic country, where the church soon became the object of persecution. The entire body of bishops and many priests were deported, leaving the Catholic community without the opportunity for sacramental life and other pastoral services. The church in Eastern Europe under communism became a "church of silence."

Italy

The unified Kingdom of Italy, formed in 1870, resulted in part from the annexation of the Papal States. With that event the pope lost all political territorial power. The government then confiscated almost all church property, dissolved religious orders, prohibited religious instruction in the schools, and in general promoted anti-religious and anti-clerical attitudes.

Notwithstanding hostility and efforts to limit its influence, the Catholic Church continued its mission. A number of new religious congregations for men and women were established to serve the concrete needs of diverse groups: youth, the sick, the infirm and the poor. St. John Bosco (1815–1888) founded the Salesian Order of priests, brothers and sisters to educate poor youngsters. St. Frances Cabrini (1850–1917) founded the Missionary Sisters of the Sacred Heart to work with the poor and Italian immigrants throughout the world. Mother Cabrini, who came to America in 1889, would become the first citizen of the United States to be canonized a saint. A number of other very holy women and men in Italy, such as Pope St. Pius

X and Maria Cristina of Savoy, the queen of Naples, also served the church courageously in difficult and changing times.

Because of the confiscation of the Papal States, the pope was left without the independence needed to be a universal pastor. Hence the strained relationship between church and state continued. Pope Benedict XV had sent signals to the Italian government that he would like to end the impasse and reach some solution for the "Roman question." Many faithful Catholic laity sought to be loyal to the church, but also hoped to be patriotic citizens of Italy. During World War I the state had ended much of its anti-Catholicism and the church had supported the cause of Italy. In 1919 a new political movement, the *Partito Nazionale Fascista*, under the leadership of Benito Mussolini (1883–1945), *Il Duce*, was formed, and in 1922 King Victor Emmanuel III named him prime minister. The history of Italy would be dominated by *Il Duce* until 1945.

The fascism of Mussolini was characterized by dictatorship, totalitarianism, the indiscriminate use of force and violence and the cult of personality. Machiavellianism became the way of doing business. In 1925 Mussolini proclaimed the Italian dictatorship; in 1935 he attacked Ethiopia; in 1936 he proclaimed the new Italian empire; in 1940 Italy entered World War II on the side of Germany. The regime employed secret police, a network of spies, secret trials and an army of bullies, the Black Shirts, to enforce cooperation. Eventually racism and anti-Semitism also became aspects of the ideology of fascism.

Many Catholic laity, as well as others, opposed Mussolini and suffered for their dissent. Father Luigi Sturzo of the Popular Party was exiled, while Catholic Action youth groups were attacked and beaten by Black Shirts. Still in its early years fascism was enthusiastically supported by the Italian people. The atheist, anti-clerical Mussolini saw that it was to his advantage to reach a settlement with the church over the "Roman question." On February 11, 1929, the Lateran Treaty was signed. The pope officially recognized the Italian nation and in return the government recognized the independence and sovereignty of the State of Vatican City.

Very soon this accommodation of the church to fascism dissolved. Mussolini, sometimes violently, moved against Catholic Action groups and their activities. The pope issued an encyclical *Non Abbiamo Bisogno* (*We Do Not Need*) in January 1931 in which he condemned fascist policies that were incompatible with church teaching. While earlier reactions of clergy and laity to Mussolini's fascism varied, with some in favor and others opposed, over time *Il*

Duce's radical positions unified Catholic opposition. Church leaders protested and opposition grew. Threats of an Allied invasion finally led to the dictator's downfall. He was arrested but then set free by German paratroopers. With the collapse of Germany, Mussolini sought to escape to Switzerland but was caught and executed by Italian partisans in 1945, along with his mistress Clara Petracci.

Spain

The problem of the "two Spains" is a metaphor for a number of interrelated questions. How can the church be authentic in the modern world? How does the church relate to modernity? How does the church preserve its tradition while modernizing? The radical liberalism of the Enlightenment preached secularism versus the sacred, freedom versus authority, the rights of the individual versus the community, progress versus tradition, the empirical versus the theological. The "two Spains" capture graphically this contest:

1) Catholic Spain with its saints, missionaries, art, literature, church organization, desire for stability and its commitment to monarchy.
2) Liberal Spain with its intellectuals, political movements, anti-clericalism, desire for change and its commitment to republicanism.

During the liberal regimes (1854–1856; 1873–1874) the church was persecuted, priests and religious were killed or exiled, and property was confiscated. This experience would then be followed by a period of peace and renewal. When Alfonso XIII assumed the throne in 1902, Spain had lost its overseas empire. With his consent General Miguel Primo de Rivera established a military government in 1923. During this period the church enjoyed relative peace. The king resigned in 1930 and on April 14, 1931, a republic was declared. After the former monarch went into exile, legislation was enacted which separated church and state, secularized education and nationalized church property. Discontent and violence precipitated constant changes in government until finally extreme liberals took control in 1936. In July of that year General Francisco Franco led a successful uprising and soon Spain was in the midst of a civil war.

The Spanish Civil War (1936–1939) pitted the Loyalists (socialists, liberals and communists) against the Nationalists. While Russians sent money and an international brigade from many countries fought on the side of the Loyalists, Italians and Germans supported Franco's Nationalists. Atrocities on both sides during the war were unparalleled. Almost seven thousand priests, sisters and brothers were killed by mutilation, fire and crucifixion, and twelve bishops were martyred, refusing to leave their posts in the Loyalists' (red) zone. Twenty thousand churches were destroyed. Bishops and international church leaders supported the nationalist cause, seeing it as a religious crusade against atheism and communism.

The Nationalists under Franco fought hard and long to defeat the Loyalists. Better supplied, they bombed even civilian targets. The great mural "Guernica" by Pablo Picasso reflects the horror of war as it destroyed that little town. At the end of the civil war in 1939, Franco was named chief of state, commander of the military, prime minister and head of the single party, the *Falange Española Tradicionalista*. During the Franco dictatorship the Catholic Church's position in the nation was officially recognized and restored.

Portugal

The nineteenth century liberal program in Portugal followed a common route: religious orders of men and women were suppressed and church property and goods were confiscated. In 1910 a republican revolution took even more drastic measures against the Catholic Church: priests and religious were imprisoned or exiled, lay committees were empowered to run church services, and religious instruction in elementary and secondary schools was prohibited.

The anti-religious attitude of the government finally caused a reaction on the part of church leaders as well as laity who began to defend the rights of the church. Intellectuals, such as Antonio de Oliveira Salazar (1889–1970), professor of economics at the University of Coimbra, took active roles in this new strategy. The ultimate result of this pro-active stance was a military revolution in 1926 which established a conservative dictatorship. Salazar became minister of finance in 1928 and prime minister in 1932. Relations with the church were completely restored under his dictatorship.

In 1917 three shepherd children believed that the Blessed Virgin Mary, who identified herself as Our Lady of the Rosary and called for personal conversion, had appeared to them six times between May 13 and October 13 at Fatima. As a result of the renewal of faith that resulted from the experience of the children and those who went there, Fatima became and still is a most popular Marian shrine. A statue of Mary as described by one of the children who is now a Carmelite nun, Sister Lucia, was sculpted by Father Thomas McGlynn, the noted Dominican artist, and adorns the facade of the basilica of Our Lady of Fatima.

Mexico

The same liberal-conservative conflicts that marked the Catholic countries of western Europe during the nineteenth century also occurred in the Catholic countries of Latin America that were former colonies of Spain and Portugal. In Mexico various liberal governments moved against the church, killing clergy and confiscating property. After Benito Juarez, president of Mexico (1857–1872), had expelled various bishops and the pope's representative from the country, conservatives rallied around Maximilian of Hapsburg (1832–1867), the brother of the Austrian emperor Francis Joseph I, and with French help took control of the country. However, the liberals, with assistance of the United States, regained control and executed Maximilian. When they had returned to power, Juarez and his general, Porfirio Díaz, closed monasteries, churches, schools and service agencies run by the church. Many religious orders of men and women were expelled. Church life, however, improved somewhat under the long presidency of Porfirio Díaz (1876-1911).

The anti-clerical current, however, continued to be present in Mexico waiting for a new opportunity to take power. Under Plutarco Calles (1924–1928) renewed persecution was directed against church personnel, and priests were no longer able to perform religious services. Some Catholics took up arms to defend their rights, for example, *Los Cristeros*, who wore crosses and went to battle with the rallying cry "Long live Christ the King." Between 1926 and 1929, seventy-eight priests, religious and lay persons were killed. Priests were forced to go into hiding, celebrating the sacraments and offering instruction to the faithful secretly. The church in Mexico had returned to the catacombs.

Notwithstanding great suffering, the vast majority of Mexican people remained loyal and committed Catholics. Very central to their piety and devotional life stood the figure of Our Lady of Guadalupe. Thousands of catechetical centers for religious instruction were established. Catholic organizations for workers (*campesinos*) as well as for middle class people and youth spread throughout the nation.

Persecution finally came to an end with the election of General
Manuel Avila Camacho (1940–1946).

Germany

The *Kulturkampf* charge that Catholics were not patriotic was put
to rest when German Catholics strongly supported their nation's
cause during World War I. The Treaty of Versailles in 1919, which
ended World War I, imposed severe penalties on Germany. The new
Weimar Republic faced insurmountable problems in the post-war
years. In October 1929 the crash of the New York Stock Market led
to serious unemployment, the reduction of trade and investment,
and a slackening in production. The repercussions of the crash were
felt everywhere, and by 1931 there was a world economic depression. The final result of the serious social and political unrest
caused by economic hardship in Germany was the victory of the
National Socialist Party (the Nazis) in the 1932 German parliamentary elections. Adolf Hitler (1889–1945) was appointed chancellor
on January 29, 1933.

Hitler's early career was not impressive. He had served in World
War I and was greatly disillusioned by Germany's defeat. After the
war the young Hitler became involved in politics. In 1925–1927 he
published his two-volume work *Mein Kampf*, which set out the central tenets of national socialism. They were:

1) the religion of Christianity eventually would be replaced by
   the religion of national socialism;
2) Hitler would be the absolute leader (*führer*) and the prophet of
   a new religion;
3) the Nordic race was supreme and the Aryans as the master
   race were entitled to rule all others;
4) Germans had a right to dominate the world and especially the
   subhuman races (i.e., the Jews and Negroes);
5) the state had the right to use any means to achieve its goals;
6) Germany needed living space (*lebensraum*) and thus was justified in territorial expansion.

In 1936 Hitler's troops moved into the demilitarized Rhineland;
in 1938 Austria was annexed; in 1939 Czechoslovakia and Poland
were invaded (Russia invaded eastern Poland and the Baltic
states). Denmark, Norway, Holland, Belgium and France were occupied in 1940. In an about-face, Hitler invaded Russia in 1941 and

then, after the Japanese attack on the United States at Pearl Harbor, declared war on the United States.

Bit by bit the Allies pushed Germany out of its conquered territory. The Allied forces landed in Normandy on D day, June 6, 1944. Earlier they had invaded Italy and Sicily, although their progress up the Italian peninsula was slow and costly. On March 9, 1945, Germany surrendered. As Russian troops approached Berlin, Hitler committed suicide in his bunker headquarters. By the end of the war over twelve million Allied military and more than five million of the Axis military had been killed. The number of civilian deaths and wounded as well as the missing was unimaginable. More than six million Jews were murdered in gas chambers and concentration camps as part of Hitler's "final solution."

Pius XI

Pope Pius XI, Achille Ratti (1922–1939), a scholar, librarian and diplomat, had become pope on February 6, 1922. During his seventeen years as universal pastor he worked constantly for a more peaceful, just world and for the expansion of Catholicism. Among his accomplishments were:

1) the encyclical (letter) *Quadragesimo Anno* (*Forty Years Later*) in 1931, which celebrated the anniversary of Pope Leo XIII's social letter, *Rerum Novarum*, and continued the social teaching of his predecessor;
2) promoting overseas missionary work and in particular emphasizing the need for inculturation, indigenous clergy and church leadership;
3) assisting Eastern Catholic churches by establishing special colleges in Rome to educate clergy and others in these rites, for example, Ukrainian, Ethiopian and Slovakian.

Pius XI resolved the "Roman question" through the Lateran Treaty in 1929. Seeing Bolshevik communism as the arch-enemy of humanity, he tried on the diplomatic level to protect the human rights of Catholics and others in Russia, but without much success. In 1937 the pope condemned atheistic communism before the world in his letter *Divini Redemptoris*.

Pius XI and his cardinal secretary of state, Eugenio Pacelli, tried to deal diplomatically with the Third Reich. At the urging of Germany, the Vatican entered into a concordat or treaty with Nazi

Germany in 1933. Unfortunately this move gave Hitler prestige and undercut Catholic opposition to his government. The hope was to legally protect the church with its programs, associations and ministries and to moderate Nazi policy by providing the church with a legal basis for opposing the dictatorship of Hitler.

Hitler, of course, flagrantly violated the treaty and rights of Catholics as well as others whenever it pleased him. Catholic Action groups were attacked by Hitler's police and Catholic schools were closed. Priests were persecuted and sent to concentration camps. The pope sent thirty-four notes of protest to the German government between 1934 and 1936, and through diplomatic channels the Vatican continued to challenge the basic principles of national socialism. On Palm Sunday, March 21, 1937, the encyclical letter *Mit brennender Sorge* was read in Catholic churches in Germany. In effect it taught that the racial ideas of the leader *(führer)* and totalitarianism stood in opposition to the Catholic faith. The letter let the world, and especially German Catholics, know clearly that the church was harassed and persecuted, and that it clearly opposed the doctrines of Nazism.

Pius XII

Cardinal Pacelli was elected Pope on March 2, 1939, the year that saw the invasion of Czechoslovakia and Poland. Austria had been annexed as part of greater Germany the previous year. As the world went to war again, a new pope continued the tradition of his immediate predecessors by pursuing neutrality, peace and humanitarian assistance.

Neutrality

Pius XII preferred to use the term *impartiality* to describe the posture of the Holy See during the war. It did not mean indifference but rather a continued commitment to moral right, truth and justice. The pope believed that the church should not take political sides but be truly a "mother" to all its children. The entry of Italy into the war in 1940 imposed restrictions that affected life in the Vatican, but still the holy see maintained impartiality. The pope was forced to hide important church documents in 1943 when German troops occupied the city of Rome. Police raided Vatican buildings to catch refugees who had been given asylum there. Until the Allied occupa-

tion in 1944, there was a genuine fear that Hitler intended to kid-
nap the pope.

Peace Efforts

Pope Pius XII, in a number of addresses, letters and homilies, elabo-
rated what might be called a theology of peace for the international
community. The pope attempted to be a voice of conscience to the bel-
ligerents at war and to the subsequent victors by exercising his
teaching and prophetic role as universal pastor. Although it is difficult to judge whether his moral leadership affected any outcome, the
prestige of the papacy was much more influential in 1945 than in
1919 when Benedict XV had been deliberately excluded from any
peace process and the League of Nations.

Papal Assistance

The needs of the victims of war were enormous and new ways had to
be found to meet these needs. Although Russia and Germany
refused their cooperation, the Vatican set up an information bureau
to trace missing persons and to facilitate communication. The
bureau received more than nine million inquiries and itself made
over eleven million inquiries. There was also an "Assistance
Commission" which dealt with charitable help to those in need, that
is, prisoners, internees, refugees, deportees, and the homeless as
well as the politically and racially persecuted.

Diplomatic efforts to ease the plight of the suffering were also
exerted with mixed success. The Vatican could influence the racial
policy of Italy toward Jews but had little influence in Germany.
Similarly it could do very little to assist the people in Russia, in
Russian-controlled Poland (two million people were deported) or in
German-occupied Poland. After 1941 the Vatican sought to lessen or
prevent the "deportation" of Jews, not then knowing of the genocide
in the concentration camps. However, it did begin to receive reports
of the extermination of the Jews by the spring of 1942. In March
1943 the Vatican received a report from a parish priest who had
learned that Jews were being gassed. The pope and Holy See continued through diplomatic channels to attempt whatever could be done
to help as many Jews as possible and to limit the horror. Pope Pius
XII spoke out at Christmas 1942, and again the following June,
always concerned lest he provoke even greater Nazi atrocities.

The Catholic Church in German-dominated territory found its

freedom restricted and often experienced severe persecution. This was especially true in Poland. Bishops were beaten, priests imprisoned, Catholic schools closed, sisters evicted from convents, and church property confiscated. Catholic Action associations were forbidden. Cardinal Adam Sapieha, the archbishop of Cracow (1925–1951), secretly educated candidates for the priesthood in his residence. One of these students was Karol Wojtyla, later Pope John Paul II. By the end of the war thirteen Polish bishops had been sent into exile or concentration camps at Soldau, Dachau, Auschwitz, Ravensbruck and Treblinka. Thousands of church personnel, priests, clerics, brothers and sisters were sent to concentration camps, where almost two thousand of them died.

Pius XII served as bishop of Rome for nearly twenty years (March 2, 1939, to October 9, 1958). During his papal ministry he wrote forty encyclicals and gave over one thousand major addresses. As pastor and teacher the pope:

1) constantly championed the rights and values of the human person and the family;

2) taught that the state always was to serve the good of the person and not the reverse;

3) condemned communism but distinguished between that system and the Russian people;

4) encouraged liturgical renewal, for example, revising the holy week celebrations.

In his encyclical *Divino Afflante Spiritu* (1943) Pius XII officially urged and approved the use of modern critical approaches to the study of the bible. The early fears of a scientific approach to the revealed word of God were dispelled, although caution and faithfulness to church teaching were expected of biblical scholars. In another encyclical that same year, *Mystici Corporis Christi*, the pope used St. Paul's metaphor of "the body of Christ" to describe the church. The Catholic Church was the "mystical body of Christ"—more of a "mystery" than a juridic enterprise. This understanding of the church was continued and expanded at the Second Vatican Council.

In 1950 Pope Pius XII exercised his papal infallibility by declaring it to be the belief of the Catholic Church that the Blessed Virgin Mary was assumed bodily into heaven after her death. That same year he issued another encyclical, *Humani Generis*, in which he reasserted certain Catholic theological positions that were then being debated or attacked by some modern thinkers. It was a defensive movement by the pope in the face of *la nouvelle theologie*, "the new theology." Some leading French figures in this movement were censured or restricted in their teaching and writings, for example, the Dominicans Chenu and Congar, and the Jesuits Daniélou and de Lubac. Many years later Congar, Daniélou and de Lubac would be named cardinals. When Pope Pius XII died in 1958, incredible changes were about to overtake the Roman Catholic Church.

17

The Jewish Story

The Judaeo-Christian tradition believes that God was present to the Jewish people in their history and through revealed words, electing them to be "the chosen people" who would communicate to humanity God's will to live in relationship with all women and men. The biblical history of the Jews recounts the conquest of their homeland in Palestine by the armies of Babylon, Persia, and Greece and then by Rome. While the Jews had known exile before, the sacking of the city of Jerusalem and the destruction of the temple by Emperor Vespasian and his son Titus in 70 C.E. occasioned the last great exile from their homeland, which became the central fact of their existence as a people in the post-biblical period.

Early Post-Biblical Period

The Greek word for "scattering" is *diaspora*. With the conquest of 70 C.E. and then again later (132–135) Jewish people had scattered to Babylon and other parts of Asia and the Roman empire. This meant that there was no longer a holy Jewish place (the temple) or sacrificial ritual. What would henceforth bind the people together would be the study of God's word. Commentaries with stories, proverbs, parables and personal sketches were made on the torah (the first five books of the bible) over and over again. Additional oral law (mishnah) was also compiled. All of this vast material was put together by scholars in two centers of Jewish study between 200 and 500 C.E., thus producing the Palestinian talmud and the Babylonian talmud. The word *talmud* literally means "study" or "learning." The bible and the talmud told Jewish people over the centuries what it meant to be Jewish and how to be Jewish.

It was as a Jew that Jesus of Nazareth began preaching: "The reign of God is at hand." The small Jewish community gathered around Jesus would quickly become the Christian movement. Although there were very substantial differences between Judaism and Christianity, both shared a great deal in common about God, the human person and the purpose of life.

The relationship between Jews and Christians was contentious from the beginning, as the books of the Christian scriptures indicate. In 80 C.E. Christian converts from Judaism were officially expelled from the synagogue by Jewish authorities meeting at Jamnia. Later some "fathers" of the church used harsh language in defending Christianity's beliefs and practices and in warning against the proselytizing efforts of the Jews.

Jewish-Christian relations, however, were critically shaped in the fourth century. Emperor Constantine was baptized on his death bed in 337 and within sixty years Christianity was the official religion of the Roman Empire. During the fourth century the "fathers" gathered in ecumenical councils to debate doctrines, formulate statements of belief and legislate the affairs of the new imperial church. Migrating populations or ethnic groups bided their time waiting for the right moment to cross the borders and enter the empire. Judaism in the Roman Empire was soon restricted in its movements and anti-Semitism flourished in some Christian circles. For example, in Spain the Council of Elvira (306) forbade Christians to marry Jews and discouraged fraternization. Within a century Jews lost their civil status and were barred from certain employment in the empire, for example, the military. The *Codex Theodosianus* (438 C.E.) refers in places to Jews as "a wicked sect," "a superstition," "a sacrilegious assembly." By the end of the fourth century Christian anti-Semitism was common enough—Jews were not only wrong, they were evil since they were guilty, in crucifying Christ, of deicide.

By the middle of the fifth century the Roman Empire in the west had collapsed before the onslaught of the new migrating peoples. Through intensive missionary efforts many of these new immigrants became Christian. Pope Gregory the Great (590–604) established the church's policy toward the Jews in the west. They were not to be persecuted and in fact had some civil rights, including the opportunity to appeal to the pope for justice. In the Byzantine Empire, however, Jews were not always tolerated. Emperor Heraclius (610–641) forbade the practice of Judaism and forced Jews to be baptized, even though such a practice was contrary to the teaching of the church.

Early Middle Ages

During the Merovingian (500–751) and Carolingian (751–987) eras, Jewish settlements were made throughout western Europe as well as in the east. While Jewish people experienced great suffering earlier in France and Spain, they were treated well by Charlemagne (768–814). His son, Louis the Pious (814–840), appointed Jews to positions of influence in the empire, appreciated their talents, and granted them legal equality, although such tolerance was opposed by individual church leaders. Jews lived in peace with their neighbors, dispersed as they were throughout the empire, and engaged in commerce and finance. This bright moment in Jewish history ended with the eventual collapse of the dynasty. Officially the policy was anti-Judaism (against what was viewed as theologically wrong or incorrect in the religion) rather than anti-Semitism (hatred of Jewish people simply because they were Jewish). Still, there were enemies and with time they would increase.

Jews in northern France and western Germany used the biblical name Ashkenaz and so European Jews would come to be called Ashkenazim. Jewish people whose cultural roots were in Spain and the Mediterranean world were called Sephardim. The Ashkenazic Jews were skilled in matters of finance. Many were also good scholars who pursued the study of the great talmuds—talmudic or rabbinic Judaism continued in the line of the early Pharisees. An eighth century splinter group, the Karaites, successors to the Sadducees, promoted individual interpretation of the torah over and against rabbinic authority.

Jewish theology, brought to Arabia by Jews who had fled there in 70 C.E., greatly influenced a young Arab, Muhammad (570–632 C.E.). In 622 the religious prophet fled Arab harassment in Mecca and went to Medina. By 732 the armies of Islam, which literally means surrender to Allah, held much of the Middle East, North Africa and Spain. Although their fortunes waxed and waned, depending upon individual rulers, Jews experienced Islamic rule as by and large tolerable. The "Covenant of Omar" laid out regulations for Jews and Christians in Muslim-controlled territory; for example, by the fourteenth century Jews wore yellow stars as badges of identification and Christians wore blue stars. Under Arab rule, however, Jewish cultural and intellectual life exploded, particularly in Spain.

In 711 the Muslim army conquered Toledo and thereby gained control of much of the Iberian Peninsula, which they called al-Andalus. Jews had been in Spain since Roman times and had often felt the sting of oppression. In 755 a member of the Umayyad family fled from Damascus to Spain and claimed the office of emir (commander) of Cordoba. By 929 Cordoba was a caliphate and became the center of enormous intellectual, cultural and artistic advancement. Jews fared well in the caliphate and were able to hold important political positions, establish *yeshivas* (academies for the study of the talmud) and maintain their identity through their rabbis, who provided teaching based on the talmud.

Jewish philosophers sought to interpret religion in the categories and concepts of their discipline, for example, Solomon ben Judah ibn Gabirol (1020–1050) or Avicebron. Spiritual classics and wonderful poetry that moved the Jewish soul were composed. One of the greatest figures in Judaism in this period was Moses ben Maimon (1135–1204), that is, Maimonides, who used Aristotle's philosophy to show that faith and reason were not in conflict.

Because of Muslim persecution, Maimonides and his family fled their native Córdoba for Morocco and then moved on to Cairo where he became a talented physician, leader of the Jewish community and prolific writer. He completed *Misheh Torah (Repetition of the Law)* in 1180, which had incredible influence on subsequent Jewish religious thought. Hundreds of commentaries have been written on it. Perhaps Maimonides most well known work was his *Guide for the Perplexed,* in which he sought to harmonize Aristotelian thought with the Hebrew bible. His prominence is summed up in the words "From Moses to Moses there was none like Moses." In his *Book of Knowledge* he laid out the thirteen basic tenets of Judaism:

1) God is the author and guide of everything that has been and will be created.
2) God is unity; there is none like unto his unity and he alone is our God.
3) God is not a body and he has no form whatsoever.
4) God is the first and the last.
5) We must pray to God alone and to no one else.
6) All the words of the prophets are true.
7) Moses is the chief of all prophets whose prophecy is true.
8) The torah that we possess is the same that was given to Moses.
9) The torah will never be changed and there will never be any other law of God.
10) God discerns the hearts of all people and knows all their thoughts and deeds.

11) God rewards those who keep his commandments and punishes
    those who transgress them.
12) The Messiah, though he delays, will come.
13) There will be a resurrection of the dead.

Later Middle Ages

The Crusades, beginning in 1096, had many goals: freeing
Jerusalem from the control of a weakened Islam, winning salvation
by dying for a holy cause, and gaining land, wealth and booty
through conquest, as well as fulfilling a desire for adventure.
Unfortunately the Jewish people were one of the first targets of the
crusaders. Many Jews in France and Germany were massacred or
were forcibly baptized during the First Crusade (1096–1099). The
same thing happened on a smaller scale during the Second Crusade
(1147–1149). St. Bernard of Clairvaux and other leaders intervened
on behalf of the Jewish people with some success, but many of the
Ashkenazim of Europe went to martyrdom to give glory to God (*kid-
dush ha-shem*) rather than commit idolatry.

When the Crusades opened new trade routes with the Orient, the
need for money and money lenders increased. Jewish people,
through their international contacts with other Jews of the diaspora, moved into the lending business. They did this not only because
so many other occupations were closed to them but also because,
unlike the Christians, they were not forbidden to make interest on a
loan (usury).

Jews were owned by lords and kings and came to be thought of as
pieces of property—the Germanic theory of *kammerknechtschaf* or
Jewish slavery. Certain church leaders abetted this political policy
for their own theological reasons. Thus the Jews, being squeezed
and taxed by lords and kings, needed money, just to be able to exist.
Authorities demanded more and more protection money which
could only be gotten through higher rates of interest on loans to the
poor and middle class. The rage of mobs against Jews during this
epoch not only was against unbelievers but also a way of canceling
debts. This caricature of the usurious Jew found its way into
English literature in Chaucer's *Prioress' Tale*, Shakespeare's
Shylock and Dickens' Fagin.

The Jews were first accused of the ritual murder of Christians
when the dead body of a boy was found in England on Good Friday
in 1141. The allegation was made that Jews killed Christians annu-

ally in mockery of the crucifixion and used the victim's blood in Jewish services. This story took hold and for centuries the "blood libel" has followed the Jews.

Throughout the Middle Ages there were constant attempts to limit contacts between Jews and Christians. The Fourth Lateran Council in 1215 reinforced this discriminatory treatment against Jews when it required that they wear distinctive attire. The "badge of shame" eventually took many forms, for example, the *Judenhut* (the Jewish hat) in Germany, the pointed hat in Poland, in England a piece of yellow taffeta, in Sicily a blue badge in the shape of the Greek letter "T." Jews were also ordered to live in special areas of cities and towns. By the sixteenth century these "ghettos," where Jews were compelled to live and where Christians were forbidden to dwell, were strictly monitored.

In 1347–1350, the bubonic plague, which probably spread through infected rats from ships docked in port, ravaged Europe and Asia. As people sought an explanation for this terrible disaster in which one-third of the population of Europe died, Jews became the scapegoat. Rumors spread rapidly that Jews had poisoned the waters in medieval cities, using a powder made of human hearts, lizards and consecrated hosts. People desperate for some explanation of this tragedy all too readily believed the libel and thousands of Jews were murdered in retaliation. Pope Clement VI (1342–1352), resident in Avignon, tried to protect the Jews but with little success.

Perhaps the only bright spot in the medieval world of the Jewish diaspora was the community of Jewish men and women in Rome. They were never expelled from the city and lived there peacefully among Christians. A principal reason for this situation was the tolerance and policies of the popes. Although Jews were not on the same level as Christians and at times experienced restrictions, nevertheless the popes at this time took care to respect their basic rights. Treatment of Jews in Italy, however, changed at the time of the Counter-Reformation. Under Pope Paul IV (1555–1559) the Roman ghetto was established, Jews could not own property, and they were forbidden to practice usury.

Although Jewish life and culture had prospered in Spain under the Muslim Umayyad dynasty, that changed under the Almohades. Many Jews, such as Moses Maimonides, left Spain, while others migrated to parts of Spain not under Muslim control (e.g., Castile, Aragon and Navarra). Treatment of Jews in these Christian kingdoms varied. After their marriage in 1469 the Catholic monarchs Ferdinand and

Isabella embarked upon the *reconquista* (reconquest) of Spain from the Muslims. They also committed themselves to battle all heresy, and to that end they established the Inquisition in 1480. These "inquisitions" (investigations) were meant to determine a person's Christian orthodoxy. Persons judged guilty of heresy were handed over to civil authorities for punishment since they were considered a threat to the fragile national unity. Of course a person could repent or in some cases convert and accept baptism. Many Jews did become *conversos* (converts). Some were sincere; others simulated conversion, often continuing to live their Jewish faith in secret. Many Jews were able in this way to lead very successful lives. As the fifteenth century progressed, however, great contempt developed for these secret Jews, called *marranos* (swine). They became the target of the Inquisition, and *marranos* all over Spain were eventually burned at the stake.

Encouraged by the grand inquisitor, the Dominican Tomás de Torquemada, on January 2, 1492, Ferdinand and Isabella issued a decree ordering the expulsion of all Jews from their kingdoms within thirty days. More than one hundred thousand refugees left Spain for Italy, the Ottoman Empire and Portugal. Leaving a land they had occupied for fifteen hundred years, these Sephardic exiles, speaking their Spanish dialect of Ladino, found Jewish communities in the Ottoman Empire in which they could begin a new life.

The spiritual and intellectual center for Jewry now became Safed in Galilee where a good deal of work and Jewish interest focused on *kabbalah*, a word meaning "revelation." The rabbinical Judaism of the torah was very rational, clear, and for all Jews. *Kabbalah* was a form of Jewish mysticism for the few which required its disciples to seek hidden wisdom. The principal teacher of this mysticism was Isaac Luria (1534–1572) whose parents had been expelled from Spain. Luria, "the Lion," was fascinated by the *Zohar*, the Jewish holy book of *kabbalah*. A key teaching was the possibility of union with God through a series of reincarnations. He taught the imminent coming of the Messiah and the responsibility of the Jewish people to hasten that coming.

Renaissance and Reformation

Money acquired in new trade and the banking industry financed the cultural awakening that was the Renaissance. The goal of the Italian Renaissance was to recapture the glories of ancient Rome so that once again that city would be the heart of the unified and universal church. Italian Jews contributed significantly to the Renaissance through the financial support they gave to the arts and by the gifts and talents which they as individuals brought to a variety of artistic endeavors.

In 1519 Martin Luther, dismayed by some of the fund-raising efforts used in the rebuilding of St. Peter's Basilica, challenged Catholic practices and launched what would become the Reformation. In the midst of bitter religious disagreements between Protestants and Catholics, Jews came under fire from both sides. Luther wrote scurrilous anti-Jewish pamphlets and Pope Paul IV in 1555 decreed that all Jews in papal territories had to live in ghettos. Seeking comfort in the midst of persecution from both Protestants and Catholics, some Jewish people turned to the mysticism of the Kabbalah while others joined Jewish messianic sects which claimed the imminent arrival of the promised Messiah.

In eastern Europe during the eighteenth century a new Jewish movement, Hasidism (from *Hasidim*, "the pious ones"), emphasized devotion to the traditional faith of Judaism expressed in the torah and also encouraged the mysticism of the *kabbalah*. The leader of the community was the holy man or perfectly righteous man, the *zaddik,* whose religious mission was to guide others to holiness by his example and teaching.

By the eighteenth century the Jewish diaspora was widespread on the European continent. Between three hundred thousand and four hundred thousand Jews lived in Germany. Holland had welcomed Jews with tolerance and from there some eventually moved back into England, from which they had been expelled in 1290. Thus Jews moved into the broader worlds of the Dutch and British Empires.

Large numbers of Ashkenazic Jews, speaking Yiddish (a combination of German and Hebrew), had left Germany for Poland in the late fifteenth century. In their Polish diaspora experience Jews developed integral communities in their ghettos, with their own courts entrusted to rabbis and councils. The *kahal* (elected administrative council) established *hadarim* (primary schools) and *yeshivahs* (talmudic academies), thereby creating a well-educated Polish Jewry. By the mid-seventeenth century the Jewish community in Poland was the largest in the world with more than five hundred thousand faithful. As always, however, they were resented by many. Pogroms (massacres or anti-Jewish riots), directed by Ukrainians and Eastern Orthodox cossacks beginning in 1648, may have destroyed between three hundred and seven hundred Jewish communities and taken between one hundred thousand and five hundred thousand Jewish lives.

Emancipation

The eighteenth century Enlightenment unleashed new ideas about freedom and equality. The early nineteenth century witnessed a number of political revolutions in France, Poland and the Austro-Hungarian Empire. The industrial revolution in England profoundly influenced the rise of capitalism throughout Europe. All these factors slowly fostered the emancipation of the Jewish people from legalized oppression. However, it goes without saying that granting basic human civic rights to Jews in the nations of Europe was not universally acceptable. For instance in Germany the philosopher Friedrich Schleiermacher (1768–1834) and the literary figure Johann Wolfgang von Goethe (1749–1832) were ardent anti-Semites. The emancipation movement posed hard questions for Jewish people. Who were they as a people? Could they be both Jewish and German, French, Italian or American? Jewish thinkers and leaders offered different responses. Moses Mendelssohn (1729–1786) was a leader of the assimilationist cause. He advocated a rapprochement between Jewish and modern thought, believing that the ideas of the Enlightenment could shape and contribute to Jewishness. In his view Jewish identity could change and accommodate itself to modernity. Mendelssohn's translation of the pentateuch and psalms into German became a kind of bridge to German literary and cultural life. However, his work was condemned by rabbis advocating only the use of Hebrew for Jews.

Mendelssohn and his followers sought to bring Judaism into the modern world. These "Reform" Jews built their own temples where they attempted to renew Jewish liturgy (e.g., by allowing women to sit with men in the synagogue). They also introduced instrumental music and replaced the strict use of Hebrew with the vernacular language. "Reform" Jews were opposed by "Orthodox" Jews (traditionalists), who rejected the work of Mendelssohn as well as his reforms and held on to the strict tradition. "Conservative" Jews, a third group within Judaism, attempted to steer a middle course, holding on to both the idea of renewal as well as the ancient rabbinic tradition.

With the partitions of Poland (1792, 1793, 1795) half the world's Jews, almost one million, came under the rule of Russia. They were forced to live in the Pale of Settlement, that is, newly acquired provincial territory. Eastern European Jews were often persecuted under the czars and they were forbidden entry into central or Muscovite Russia. Czar Nicholas I (1825–1855) conscripted young Jewish boys of twelve years of age into the army for as long as twenty-five years. Efforts were made to convert them to Eastern Orthodoxy while they were in the army. A Jewish woman was part of the extremist group that assassinated Czar Alexander II in 1881, and severe reprisals against all Jews followed. Throughout the 1880s and 1890s pogroms killed many Jews. Given intolerable living conditions, hundreds of thousands of Jews once again became refugees. While great numbers left Russia for the United States, others looked to Palestine as their homeland. They were helped in their dream of returning home by the Zionist movement.

Theodor Herzl (1860–1904) was a newspaper reporter at the time of the trial of Alfred Dreyfus in France. In 1894 Captain Dreyfus, a Jew, was found guilty of treason and sentenced to life in prison. Subsequently, after great debate all charges were dropped. However, *l'affaire Dreyfus* provoked anti-Semitism in some French circles and among some French Catholics. Nevertheless, a number of Catholics also supported and defended Dreyfus. Herzl left the trial convinced that the only deliverance from anti-Semitism was a political homeland for the Jews, and he was supported in this belief by Chaim Weizmann (1874–1952), who collaborated with Herzl. Most of the early settlers in Palestine were Russian Jews escaping czarist persecution.

Life in Palestine was hard since the land was difficult to farm and financial resources were scarce. Palestine, of course, was not a barren empty land. It was home to thousands of Arabs. The delegates to the first Zionist Congress in Basel in 1897 declared unequivocally that they sought an independent homeland in Palestine for Jewish people. While Herzl served as a powerful presence at the Congress, Weizmann worked to further the Zionist cause in England. The latter's efforts resulted in the Balfour Declaration of 1920 in which Britain approved a national homeland in Palestine for the Jewish people, while at the same time recognizing the civil rights of non-Jews there. Thus a major step had been taken toward the creation of the State of Israel. Still, as the dream of a Jewish homeland became a possibility, Jews in Poland, Romania, Hungary, Austria, Germany and Turkey continued to be viewed as foreigners and were oppressed. Anti-Zionism spread throughout the Near East and North Africa as well.

The Final Solution

In 1919 the National Socialist German Workers' (Nazi) Party was formed. In 1933 President von Hindenburg named Hitler, now head of the party and fervently anti-Semitic, as chancellor. Soon he was also the *führer* or leader of the nation. A Nazi slogan was *Juda verrecke!* (Jewry perish!) The terror that Jews lived in under the Nazis was unparalleled in history. Policies and laws separated Jews from contact with Aryans. Anti-Jewish riots occurred, properties were looted, and persons were wounded or killed. One such event was that of *krystallnacht*. At 1:20 A.M. on November 10, 1938, Germans attacked Jewish businesses and residences. The devastation and personal harm was incredible. Wherever the forces of Hitler were victorious, the ghetto was restored, as was the badge of shame. Thousands of Jews died as the fury of the Nazis against them increased, and many tried to flee.

The Nazis had been planning for the *endlosung* (the final solution of the Jewish problem) since 1938. Although it originally meant total expulsion, it soon came to mean total extermination. The genocide began in Russia, where German troops used machine guns to kill at least one million five hundred thousand Jewish men, women and children. Three million Polish Jews were either starved to death in their ghettos or sent to the gas chambers in concentration camps such as Auschwitz in southern Poland.

Not all occupied countries cooperated in the final solution. France, for instance, hid many of its Jewish citizens, especially children. Finland, Belgium and Holland refused to hand over any Jews. In rejecting the efforts of the Nazis, King Christian of Denmark threatened to wear the yellow badge himself if anything were done to the Jews. Countless women and men risked their lives and that of their families to save Jewish lives. Such heroes were the only lights in a vast night of evil—truly "righteous women and men."

The holocaust took six million lives—more than one-half of Europe's Jews and more than one-third of the world's Jewry. The profound evil of anti-Semitism came to its staggering but perhaps inevitable conclusion in genocide. The full horror of what happened was not known until after the war. Governments and churches have been criticized or defended for what they did or did not do to save the Jews. The debate sadly in some cases has fed once again either anti-Semitic passions or anti-Christian anger.

Israel

The Jewish population in Palestine in 1900 was seventy-eight thousand. In 1945 it had grown to five hundred thousand; in 1970 to two million five hundred thousand; in 1982 to three million three hundred thousand or twenty-five percent of all the world's Jews. After World War II European immigrants arrived in large numbers from Europe despite England's efforts to maintain a quota system. *Sabras*, that is, native-born Israelis, increased as well. On May 14, 1948 the Jewish National Council and the General Zionist Council proclaimed the new nation of Israel. For the first time since 70 C.E. Jews had a homeland. Russia and the United States immediately recognized the State of Israel.

The birth of the new nation, however, put the citizens of Israel in a state of war with their Arab neighbors that has continued on and off in the Middle East for the last forty years. Anti-Semitism sometimes takes the form today of anti-Zionism. Rightly or wrongly, Israeli political and military policies feed this mindset. War between Israel and the Arab nations broke out in 1956 and again in 1967. Recent developments, however, are a cause of hope for peace in the Middle East. President Anwar Sadat of Egypt in March 1979 signed a peace treaty with Israel. He was subsequently assassinated by Arab fundamentalists for his decision to make peace with Israel. Jordan and the Palestinian Liberation Organization signed peace treaties with Israel in 1994.

For many years the Vatican did not accord diplomatic recognition to the State of Israel. Such a posture, of course, rankled Israelis. The Holy See chose not to recognize the Jewish state officially because of the displacement of millions of Palestinians, many of whom were Christians. All Arabs would have felt betrayed by such a Vatican stance. Once Jews and Arabs, however, formally entered into a peace process, that is, the Israeli-PLO Peace Treaty, the Vatican moved quickly to establish diplomatic relations with the State of Israel in 1994.

The United States

The words on the Statue of Liberty were written by Jewish poet Emma Lazarus:

> Give me your tired, your poor,
> Your huddled masses yearning to breathe free,

The wretched refuse of your teeming shore.
Send them, the homeless, tempest-tossed, to me.
I lift my lamp beside the golden door.

There were some Jewish people in the United States during the Revolutionary era, and the oldest synagogue in the country is the Touro synagogue established in 1763 in Newport, Rhode Island. Large numbers, however, only came to the United States, especially from eastern Europe, in the nineteenth century. Like other immigrant groups they came to America to escape religious, ethnic, racial and economic prejudice and hardship. They came with a dream of a better life for themselves and their children.

By 1930 there were nearly five million Jews living in the United States. Many became very successful businesspeople, for example, the Gimbel Brothers and their chain of stores, Macy's and Abraham and Straus department stores and Levi Strauss (1829–1902), the manufacturer of blue denim pants, Levis. Most Jewish immigrants, as others, found themselves in poor, crowded neighborhoods such as New York's lower east side where life was hard. Many found employment in the sweat shops of the garment trade, working long hours for little pay in unhealthy conditions. In 1900 Jewish professionals assisted workers in establishing the International Ladies' Garment Workers' Union to better conditions. One such attorney was Louis Brandeis (1856–1941), who in 1916 was named the first Jewish justice on the United States Supreme Court.

The Jewish experience in the United States has been absolutely unique in their history. They have succeeded in all fields of activity—the arts and entertainment, the professions, business, the communication industry and science. Life for Jews in America, however, was not perfect. They were, like Catholics and African Americans, the target of discrimination. The Know-Nothings, the Ku Klux Klan, and other nativist groups actively promoted anti-Semitism in their programs and periodicals. Jews were often accused of being communists or playing political games for their own benefit. Leading Americans at times voiced strong criticism of Jewish power, for example, Henry Ford, Charles Lindbergh and the famed radio priest, Fr. Charles Coughlin.

Although outrageous anti-Semitism has not flourished in the United States, there is in some quarters a snide anti-Semitism. Jews are caricatured and criticized for their success, the policies of Israel, their powerful and influential lobby in Washington and their position in industries, such as the communications industry. This anti-Semitism is a kind of racism directed against Jewish people, simply because they are Jewish.

The Second Vatican Council

On October 8, 1965, the Second Vatican Council promulgated the *Declaration on the Relationship of the Church to Non–Christian Religions (Nostra Aetate)*, which is an official church teaching that highlights the Jewish origins of the Catholic faith. Recognizing that Jesus, Mary, the apostles and the earliest Christian were all Jewish, it states:

> Since Christians and Jews have such a common spiritual heritage, the sacred Council wishes to encourage and further mutual understanding and appreciation. This can be obtained, especially, by way of biblical and theological inquiry and through friendly discussions....Neither all Jews indiscriminately at that time, nor Jews today, can be charged with the crimes committed during his passion (Christ's)....Indeed, the Church reproves every form of persecution against whomever it may be directed. Remembering, then, her common heritage with the Jews and moved not by any political consideration, but solely by the religious motivation of Christian charity, she deplores all hatreds, persecutions, displays of anti-Semitism levelled at any time or from any source against the Jews.

The Catholic Church has sought to systematize interreligious dialogue with Jewish people by establishing international and national commissions. On October 22, 1974, Pope Paul VI inaugurated the Commission for Religious Relations with the Jews as part of the Secretariat for Promoting Christian Unity. Other Christian churches have taken similar actions. A new moment has arrived in the history of Christian-Jewish relations. The past cannot and should not be forgotten. The *shoah* (holocaust) must stand in history as a sign of the diabolical evil that human persons are capable of and where anti-Semitism or any racism can lead.

18

American Christianity 1920–1960

The Catholic Church in the United States

In the inter-war years the Catholic Church in the United States exhibited a new-found confidence. Catholics had served their country with great patriotism, and the church's institutions and leaders had aided and supported the war effort. The National Catholic Welfare Conference, set up during the war to coordinate assistance to those in need, became a permanent agency of the bishops. This was a time of growth and organizational expansion. By 1930 there were more than one hundred and sixty-three Catholic colleges and universities in the United States, and more than two thousand Catholic high schools. Powerful church leaders directed the fortunes of the Catholic community: Cardinals Dennis Dougherty, archbishop of Philadelphia (1918–1951), John Glennon, archbishop of St. Louis (1903–1946), Patrick J. Hayes, archbishop of New York (1918–1938), William O'Connell, archbishop of Boston (1907–1944), and George H. Mundelein, archbishop of Chicago (1915–1939).

Despite the new-found confidence and numerical growth of American Catholics, the Ku Klux Klan targeted them as well as African Americans and Jews, strongly indicating that Catholics were still not accepted in many quarters. Although his Catholicism probably cost him the election, Governor Alfred E. Smith, a Democrat, ran for president in 1928.

During the first half of the twentieth century, Catholicism as a world view was very much dominated by the thinking of St. Thomas Aquinas. From the Thomistic perspective the world was orderly, rational, meaningful and knowable. The human person was a moral agent responsible for self and the community. This was possible because God's grace empowered the person to overcome the incompleteness and egoism due to original sin. Christ saved and was the principal means whereby the rational creature returned to God, the creator. Everyone and everything had a place in this orderly and majestic vision, which profoundly influenced Catholic education in the United States.

Nowhere else had the church established such a remarkable and significant parochial school system. By 1959 some five and a half million students were in private schools, ninety percent of them Catholic. There were more than four million children in Catholic primary schools and two thousand four hundred and twenty-eight Catholic high schools teaching eight hundred thousand students. More than one hundred thousand young men and women studied in Catholic colleges. Jesuits dominated higher education with more than twenty-five colleges and universities across the country. Catholic education sought to produce intelligent Catholics and protect their faith, while also providing them with an opportunity for upward mobility. Poor children of immigrants were enabled to move up the ladder socially, economically and politically precisely because they were educated.

The backbone of the Catholic school system was most especially the women religious and men religious, priests and brothers, who staffed these educational institutions at all levels. There were more than one hundred and fifty-eight thousand sisters ministering in schools, hospitals and other agencies. Nine thousand brothers of various religious congregations were engaged in similar ministries. The sisters, brothers and priests in education contributed their services, generally receiving a very small amount of allowance in addition to room and board, but without health benefits, insurance and pension plans. Today this aging and retired work force of dedicated, generous ministers depends on the support provided by Catholics, often through special annual collections.

Early in the century teachers themselves often were modestly educated, but as professional standards demanded more education in the 1940s and 1950s, women and men religious spent summers gaining higher degrees in all disciplines. A movement, begun at Catholic University in Washington, D.C., and developed later at Providence College in Rhode Island and a host of other schools, allowed many women religious to be educated in theology, philosophy and sacred scripture. Schools of "theology for the laity" were also opened, for example, by Dominicans in New York, Boston and Chicago. The dedicated efforts of countless sisters, brothers, and priests helped to make American Catholics, as a group, the best educated Catholics in the universal church.

American Catholics, who were more pragmatic than speculative, attempted to live out their identity in all facets of human endeavor. There were groups of thinking, educated Catholics in all fields who read and discussed the Thomistic philosophers, Jacques Maritain and Etienne Gilson, as well as the literary figures, G. K. Chesterton, Paul Claudel, Graham Greene, François Mauriac, Evelyn Waugh and Georges Bernanos. Maisie Ward and Frank Sheed made many of these works available in the United States through their publishing house, Sheed and Ward, begun in 1933. The magazine *Commonweal*, begun as a Catholic journal in 1924, was a lay project, open and liberal on social issues. The vision provided by *Commonweal* helped the more liberal and intellectual brand of American Catholicism feed into and often coalesce with social Catholicism.

Catholic immigration slowed between the two world wars because of restrictions imposed by Congress in 1924. Some Irish and German Catholics moved into the middle class while eastern European and Mexican Catholics continued in the poorer or lower classes. After World War II large numbers of Catholics moved upward economically, and that has continued for most although not all groups. As many moved from "blue-collar" to "white-collar" professions, they also moved to the suburbs, where the church followed them with incredible building programs to serve the needs of parishioners.

The devotional life of Catholics, their popular religiosity, from the end of World War I through the 1960s, was a powerful force shaping Catholic identity. Devotion to Jesus in the eucharist flourished in parish life through benediction of the blessed sacrament, Corpus Christi processions and forty hours devotions, in which parish members would pray before the blessed sacrament. Veneration of Mary, the mother of God, through the rosary and novenas (e.g., to the Sorrowful Mother, Our Lady of the Miraculous Medal, Our Lady of Guadalupe and Our Lady of Perpetual Help), were popular. Father Daniel Lord, S.J., whose numerous books and pamphlets sold more

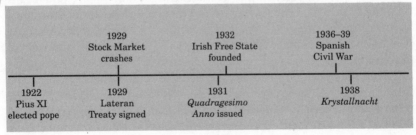

	1929 Stock Market crashes	1932 Irish Free State founded	1936–39 Spanish Civil War
1922 Pius XI elected pope	1929 Lateran Treaty signed	1931 *Quadragesimo Anno* issued	1938 *Krystallnacht*

than twenty-five million copies, stimulated Marian devotion among young people through the sodalities of the Blessed Virgin Mary.

The Catholic press developed as an educational tool for the local church. Diocesan newspapers brought Catholics the news, educated through special features, and connected the local to the universal church. *Our Sunday Visitor, The Catholic Register, The Brooklyn Tablet,* and the midwestern newspaper *The Wanderer,* as well as the magazines, *Commonweal* and *America,* were national publications. Radio stations carried a variety of Catholic programs, for example, *The Catholic Hour,* which featured Fulton J. Sheen, later bishop, television personality and Emmy winner.

Social Catholicism

The administrative committee of the National Catholic War Council had issued a statement, "The Bishops' Program for Social Reconstruction," in 1919. The document boldly presented the social teaching of the church in practical terms. After the economic turmoil of the Great Depression, Catholics worked for social reform in a variety of ways. The NCWC named Father John Ryan director of its social action department. He was assisted by a number of "labor priests" (e.g., Father Raymond McGowan), who taught Catholic social teaching in universities, summer schools and conferences. They influenced the shape of social legislation and lobbied for its passage. The great labor encyclicals, *Rerum Novarum* of Pope Leo XIII (1891) and *Quadragesimo Anno* of Pope Pius XI (1931), provided the foundation for their teaching. The concern for social justice, of course, was basic to the gospel of Jesus Christ. Justice for urban workers, many of them Catholic, was an obvious pastoral concern for the church. The Catholic Church attempted in a variety of ways to serve the needs of the poor and workers, whether urban or rural, through social and charitable service. At the same time, through the NCWC and its educational efforts the church moved to change the unjust systems through community organization and social action.

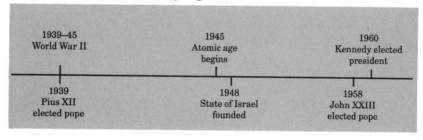

1939–45	1945	1960
World War II	Atomic age begins	Kennedy elected president
1939	1948	1958
Pius XII elected pope	State of Israel founded	John XXIII elected pope

One effort in this direction was the Association of Catholic Trade Unionists (ACTU) which was established in 1937 by some lay Catholics. They promoted labor unions through schools, newspapers and other educational tools. One very active member of the movement was Father Charles Rice of Pittsburgh, who held the radical belief that the whole economic system needed change. He promoted labor unions, walked on picket lines, agitated for better public housing for the poor by community organizations, and lectured and preached on behalf of social justice. Father Rice supported the Congress of Industrial Organizations (CIO), which claimed that many of its program came from the papal social encyclicals. The lay Catholic leaders of the CIO saw themselves called to social activism by vocation as Catholic lay persons, who would work alongside the clergy but would not be dominated by them.

Another example of Catholic social activism was the Catholic Worker movement. In May 1933, Dorothy Day (1897–1980), a convert to Catholicism, began selling her newspaper, *The Catholic Worker*, for a penny a copy. She sought to show that Catholics very much supported the aspirations of the labor movement. Dorothy Day looked to the French personalist philosopher, Emmanuel Mounier (1905–1950), and to Peter Maurin (1877–1949), a French peasant and philosopher who dreamed of a just social order for all. The movement of lay women and men which she began opened a number of hospices or "houses of hospitality" for the poor and unemployed and established a farming commune as well. Dorothy Day and her colleagues walked picket lines, opened soup kitchens, studied and prayed. Those who voluntarily joined the Catholic Worker movement lived very simple lifestyles, grounded in sacramental participation, frequent prayer and deep concern for social justice. Going back to the church's roots in the New Testament, they believed that if society were ever to change and if justice were ever to be achieved for all, then hearts must first be converted to the Lord.

Dorothy Day was a woman of holiness, intelligence, simplicity and toughness, who as a pacifist saw no just reason for war. That stance put her very much at odds with many, both within and outside the church, during World War II. Still, the Catholic Worker movement attracted many young, idealistic and serious Catholic women and men of social conscience.

Another prophetic figure in American Catholicism at this time was the Trappist monk, Thomas Merton (1915–1968). Bright and energetic, Merton did his studies in Europe and at Columbia University in literature. His journey or quest for meaning in life finally led him to join the Roman Catholic Church. In 1941 he entered the Trappist monastery of Our Lady of Gethsemane in Kentucky.

In 1948 Merton published *The Seven Storey Mountain,* an account of his spiritual journey. It became a national best seller and was translated into a number of languages. His spiritual quest resonated with many people searching for values and purpose in the modern world. Father Merton continued to write on spiritual topics and became one of the most influential authors of the day. In his work he sought to present the mystery of God to women and men in the contemporary world. At the same time he tried to connect religious commitment and contemplation with social responsibility. Among his more famous works were: *No Man Is an Island* (1955), *Seeds of Contemplation* (1965), *Conjectures of a Guilty Bystander* (1968) and *Faith and Violence* (1968). Merton died accidentally by electrocution while attending a conference on Eastern spirituality in Bangkok, Thailand.

World War II

Some Catholics such as Dorothy Day and those in the Catholic Worker movement opposed the involvement of the United States in World War II on the basis of pacifist principles, while Monsignor Fulton Sheen and Archbishop McNicholas of Cincinnati were isolationist in that they did not advocate intervention in a European war. Other Catholics, however, such as Governor Alfred Smith, Cardinal Mundelein and Monsignor John Ryan, supported America's participation in the war. A key ally of President Franklin D. Roosevelt was the archbishop of New York, Francis J. Spellman (1939–1967). After the attack on Pearl Harbor, December 7, 1941, Catholic leaders and laity by and large rallied to the cause in the name of patriotism.

Catholics served in all branches of service and made up twenty-five to thirty percent of the total military personnel. More than three thousand Catholic chaplains also served in the armed forces. The NCWC formed the War Relief Services Committee to coordinate the church's efforts to serve refugees, prisoners of war and displaced persons. The committee continued after the war as an arm of the American church to help the needy wherever necessary under the name Catholic Relief Services.

In 1939 President Roosevelt notified Pope Pius XII that he would appoint a special envoy to the Holy See. Myron Taylor was the president's choice. Although some Protestants and others objected on the grounds of separation of church and state, Taylor was not an official ambassador, so the appointment went through. Eventually the United States under President Ronald Reagan would establish formal diplomatic relations with the Vatican.

African Americans

In 1900 the majority of African Americans lived in the southern part of the United States. However, by 1960 half lived in the north, mostly in poor urban ghettos in New York, Philadelphia, Detroit, Washington, D.C., Chicago and Los Angeles. Most African Americans were Protestant. The Catholic presence in the south, with the exception of Louisiana, had not been strong. Certainly efforts had been made to minister to blacks, but they did not result in large numbers entering the Catholic Church. The Josephite Order of priests was founded in 1893 to minister to African Americans. Three groups of black sisters did the same: the Oblates of Providence (Baltimore), the Sisters of the Holy Family (New Orleans), and the Handmaids of the Most Pure Heart of Mary (New York). The Sisters of the Blessed Sacrament were white sisters working in black communities. The major concern of the American Catholic Church had of course been Catholic immigrants and not African Americans.

In 1940 there were three hundred thousand black Catholics; today there are more than three million. In the past the church, with few exceptions, acquiesced in systematic segregation. Blacks sat in special sections of the church; they received holy communion after white people. There were very few black priests. In 1943 the American Catholic bishops issued a pastoral letter calling for an end to racial discrimination and for a recognition of civil rights for African Americans.

One of the champions of interracial justice was the Jesuit priest John La Farge, S.J., son of the distinguished American painter, John La Farge. In 1936 this American Jesuit began promoting the cause of racial justice in the pages of *America* magazine, the influential Jesuit weekly. Father La Farge wrote, lectured, and founded the Catholic Interracial Council. By 1958 there were forty branches of the council across the country and it became the National Conference for Interracial Justice.

In 1954 the United States Supreme Court in "Oliver Brown et al. versus the Board of Education of Topeka" struck down the "separate but equal" clause that allowed segregated schools. A new moment in race relations thus began in the United States. Church leaders had earlier moved to end officially such segregation in Catholic schools.

Cardinal Spellman, arriving in New York as archbishop in 1939, insisted that schools in the Archdiocese of New York were for all children. In 1947 Cardinal Ritter desegregated the Catholic schools in St. Louis; Cardinal O'Boyle did the same in Washington, D.C., in 1956. New Orleans, under Archbishop Joseph Rommel, desegregated parochial schools in 1962 in spite of fierce opposition from some Catholic people. In 1958 the American bishops once again deplored racism of every kind. During the civil rights movement in the 1960s many American Catholics, clergy and laity, joined forces with other women and men to promote racial and social justice. They took to the streets in marches (e.g., in Selma, Alabama), sponsored prayer vigils, and preached and taught that racism was sinful on the individual and systemic level. Clearly persons, society and the churches were called to conversion. As the *Pastoral Constitution on the Church in the Modern World* of the Second Vatican Council, issued on December 7, 1965, stated:

> All men are endowed with a rational soul and are created in God's image; they have the same nature and origin, and being redeemed by Christ, they enjoy the same divine calling and destiny; there is here a basic equality between all men and it must be given even greater recognition....forms of social or cultural discrimination in basic personal rights on the grounds of sex, race, color, social conditions, language or religion, must be curbed and eradicated as incompatible with God's design...(n. 29).

Hispanics

Between 1920 and 1960 large numbers of Mexican and Puerto Rican people came to the United States. The latter were citizens whereas many of the former were undocumented aliens. Like other immigrant groups, they came with the hope of a better life. Most were Roman Catholics, who were poor, unskilled, and uneducated and spoke little English. By 1960 there were more than four million Mexicans living generally in the southwest and a million or more Puerto Ricans living predominantly in cities on the east coast.

Hispanics, like African Americans, felt the pain of discrimination and racism in American society. At times they also experienced it in the church. For instance in some parish churches they were required to sit only in the back or were sent to a special parish for the "non-Anglos." Pastors at first could not speak Spanish nor did they understand the Latino culture.

Nevertheless, pastoral efforts were made to educate Hispanic Catholics in the faith and practice of the church. Regular attendance at mass was encouraged. However, ministry to Hispanics and especially Mexicans in the southwest was difficult. There were not many priests, and parishes in rural areas were few and far between. Nevertheless, women and men religious served as missionaries, often at great cost and sacrifice. Lay catechists joined these religious in preaching and teaching the gospel. Resources for programs were scarce, but the church did the best it could to serve the needs of these people. Parishes celebrated the sacraments, educated adults and children, met the needs of the poor and comforted the sick and the dying. The local parish was often the center of life for people and neighborhoods as it had been for other national groups.

Archbishop Robert E. Lucey of San Antonio became a leading defender of the rights of Mexicans. Besides establishing a number of agencies in his archdiocese to serve the poor, he involved himself in the issues of health, housing and unionizing efforts for migrant farm laborers, who were among the most oppressed and marginal people in America. Individuals and families would travel for months at a time, following the crops to be picked. Often they were exploited by farmers and landowners as well as by their own crew chiefs. They lived in unsanitary camps without access to health care or education for their children.

The United Farm Workers Union was founded by Cesar Chavez to promote social justice for migrant workers. Chavez was a charismatic leader whose vision was deeply rooted in Catholic social teaching. A deeply spiritual man, he combined picket lines with hunger strikes, boycotts and prayer services. The red flag of the union was often accompanied by the banner of Our Lady of Guadalupe. Although Chavez eventually won recognition for his union and justice for migrant workers, the struggle continues.

The church in New York, under the leadership of Cardinal Spellman, developed a pastoral plan in 1953 to serve the Puerto Rican community. Many priests, sisters and lay ministers were routinely sent annually to Puerto Rico to learn the Spanish language and culture so that they could develop new pastoral approaches. These church ministers clearly saw the connection between the gospel and social justice, and so a number of parishes became centers of worship, education and community organizing. New York's Hispanic community continued to grow and diversify, welcoming Dominicans, Ecuadorians and people from most other Latin American countries.

Significant numbers of Cuban people came to the United States, especially Florida, beginning in 1959, when Fidel Castro, an ardent communist, came to power. Eighty-five percent of the Cuban people were baptized Roman Catholics and nearly one-third of all marriages were celebrated in the church. At first President Castro sought a rapprochement with the church, but that soon changed. The Cuban bishops, in 1960, issued a pastoral letter which, while supporting social justice and the redistribution of wealth, condemned communism. Castro struck back. Catholic schools were closed, Catholic publications were shut down and clergy were exiled. By the end of 1961 almost four thousand priests and sisters had fled the island; others were jailed. The Cuban constitution sought progressively to eliminate religion from the country. Practicing Catholics were denied employment and educational opportunities. The number of baptisms declined enormously over the next thirty years. Hundreds of thousands of Cubans went into exile in Spain, Venezuela and the United States. The largest Cuban exile community settled in Florida, where their numbers increased in 1980 as one hundred thousand more left Cuba via the beaches of Mariel. *Balseros* or "rafters" continue to attempt to make the passage across the Florida straits.

The church responded to the needs of these exiles through its parishes and social agencies. Many exiles had been professionals in Cuba. Nevertheless, poverty and discrimination stalked the Cuban community in its early days. However, Cuban refugees over the years have succeeded socially and economically as has no other Latin group.

Today after thirty years in power and the fall of communism, Fidel Castro seems to be modifying his relationship with the church. Under the leadership of Cardinal Jaime Ortega y Almino, the church in Cuba has begun a dialogue with the government. The Catholic community has moved from being a passive spectator to becoming the only active independent voice questioning the regime. Mass attendance has gone up by fifty percent and baptisms have increased sixfold since 1980. Weddings, first communions, funerals and catechism classes on the island seem to be increasing after a very stagnant period. In 1993 the Cuban bishops issued a pastoral letter calling for dialogue with all, including the present government as well as exiled groups. The letter criticized "the exclusionary and omnipresent character of the official ideology," that is, communism. In 1959 there were seven hundred priests, twenty-six hundred nuns and six million people, mostly Catholic, in Cuba. In 1994 there are eleven million people, two hundred and twenty priests and three hundred and thirty nuns. The problems in Cuba continue to grow, especially since the fall of communism in Europe.

Characteristics of American Catholicism 1920–1960

On January 25, 1959, Pope John XXIII convoked the Second Vatican Council, which formally opened in 1962. John F. Kennedy, a Roman Catholic, became president of the United States on January 1, 1961. The Catholic Church in the United States numbered about forty-four million in 1963. The universal church and the church in the United States had come a long way in the forty years since the end of World War I. American Catholicism in the era 1920–1960 was characterized by:

1) a solid identity based on a common creed, ritual, ethic and structure;
2) a loyalty to the pope and a deep patriotism toward the United States;
3) a generosity to the point of sacrifice in support of Catholic institutions (e.g., schools, hospitals, parishes, and missions);
4) a pragmatic commitment to the gospel which showed itself in the doing of good works and high levels of church participation;
5) the experience of freedom from government intervention due to the separation of church and state;
6) a confidence, notwithstanding the anti-Catholicism of some, that Catholics could and would succeed in all areas of American life;
7) a continuous growth through births and immigration as well as significant cultural and economic diversity.

The Protestant Experience

The early twentieth century saw the rise of the "social gospel" within American Protestantism. The social problems that arose from increasing urbanization and industrialization provoked concern among more liberal religious people. They believed that the gospel had something to say to the social order and, in fact, called for major adjustments in the way society organized itself. Walter Rauschenbusch (1861–1918) was one of the main promoters of this movement. His book, *Christianity and the Social Crisis*, clearly taught that ethics and the social order were requisites for true religion. The kingdom of God called for social justice, and the mission of the church was to work to bring about that kingdom.

Liberal Protestantism, with its efforts to modernize religion and the social gospel movement, however, involved relatively small numbers. The majority of Protestants in America were the "establishment." Methodists and Baptists were the largest denominations, followed by Presbyterians. The common Protestant vision stemmed from the Reformed theological tradition of Calvin. From his perspective the human person was seriously flawed by original sin, and salvation came from God through Christ as a gift. Some were predestined to salvation, others were not. The "saved" were blessed by God, often with material success. The human person was called to live a good clean life, work hard, pray, avoid frivolous entertainment and save money. Thus the "Protestant work ethic" fed into and formed the American dream.

Protestant church attendance waned after World War I and during the Great Depression. Socially active ministers had little influence in forming Christian consciences. People were frightened, insecure and bewildered. The Ku Klux Klan was revived and expanded the object of its hate to include not only African Americans but Catholics and Jews as well. By 1923 the KKK had more than three million members, and it had become an organization that sought to protect the white and Protestant character of American society.

The great Protestant crusade in America during this period was Prohibition. Temperance leagues had long been part of the Protestant experience. Preachers and churches mobilized in the early part of the twentieth century to prohibit the sale and manufacture of alcohol. They were successful in 1919 when the United States Congress passed the Eighteenth Amendment and then the Volstead Act to enforce Prohibition. The country was "dry" and presumably safe from the vices associated with alcohol. Prohibition lasted until the Eighteenth Amendment was repealed with the election of Franklin Delano Roosevelt as president.

While alcohol was seen as a moral threat, the theory of evolution was viewed by many Protestants as a doctrinal threat. In the small town of Dayton, Tennessee, John Scopes was indicted for teaching evolution, which was forbidden by Tennessee law. William Jennings Bryan acted on behalf of the prosecution, Clarence Darrow for the defense. The Tennessee supreme court finally rejected the trial's finding on a technicality. The battle of creationism versus evolutionism reflected the tension between tradition and modernity, faith and science, fundamentalism and liberalism. Conflicts broke out in various denominations; for example, the great Baptist preacher and author, Harry Emerson Fosdick (1878–1969), was forbidden to preach in New York's First Presbyterian Church. Partly as a result of this John D. Rockefeller built the interdenominational Riverside Church near Columbia University in New York. Fosdick was installed as pastor there in 1931.

The dominance of the Calvinist Protestant vision and ethic in American life lost its hold between the wars. America had changed—more urban, more industrial, more culturally diverse and more educated. During World War II Protestant churches collaborated across denominational lines to meet the concrete needs of a people at war and patriotically supported the Allied cause. Chaplains joined various military services, chapels were built on bases, and church agencies collected and distributed funds to the needy. The years following the war saw great social changes in the United States: the arrival of a certain affluence for many, the growth of suburbia, high mobility and the age of television. These social changes took place even during the long cold war with communism and the "police action" in Korea (1950–1953).

After World War II, religion in America entered a period of revival and growth. Church affiliation and attendance increased. In 1950 fifty-five percent of the population was affiliated with some denomination; in 1960 that number had increased to sixty-nine percent. One of the thrusts of this religious revival was to provide a kind of comfort and support to anxious people. Religion, with roots in modern psychology, attracted the faithful. Ronald Hubbard (b. 1911) with his book, *Dianetics: The Modern Science of Mental Health* (1950), founded the Church of Scientology, through which he claimed to make life better for its practitioners by the positive development of their personalities. Norman Vincent Peale in 1952 published his acclaimed *The Power of Positive Thinking*, which sold millions of copies. In 1955 Anne Morrow Lindbergh, the widow of the famed Charles Lindbergh, published a mystical meditation, *Gift from the Sea*.

Traditional Protestant revivalism took on a new life through the work of Billy Graham (b. 1918). Graham attended bible schools in North Carolina and Florida and was ordained a Baptist minister. A remarkably gifted preacher, he organized the Billy Graham Evangelistic Association in 1950. The crusades organized by the association have reached millions of people throughout the world directly and through television, radio, books and pamphlets.

Graham's message centered on the need to undergo conversion and to choose Christ as one's personal savior in order to experience a meaningful and happy life.

Evangelistic and fundamentalist Christianity had become a powerful force in American Christianity by the end of the 1950s. These religious conservatives opted for a literal understanding of scriptural passages, respect for authority, clean living and solid family life. They appealed to many who feared the growing secularism and liberalism of American culture and some American religion. Fundamentalists rejected much of what liberal theology and the social gospel movement preached and taught, opting for a traditional interpretation of doctrine and morality. There were those, however, who felt that it was possible to hold to the Christian tradition while at the same time benefiting from scientific discovery, seeking a more just society and evangelizing the modern world.

Protestant Neo-Orthodoxy

Theologians in Europe after World War I sought to retrieve for Protestantism the great Christian tradition which had been challenged, debated or rejected by liberal theology. A pastor in Switzerland, Karl Barth (1886–1968), published a commentary on St. Paul's epistle to the Romans in 1919. It was reprinted in a second edition in 1922. In that work Barth, as a pastor, strongly criticized liberal theology and preached the transcendence of God, whose word is revealed to us in scripture as a word of judgment. Human beings are sinful and need God's forgiveness. Barth believed that liberal Protestantism, by naively believing in the perfectibility of the human person, had diminished God and God's word and sought religious experience at the expense of faith in the "totally other." Beginning in 1932, Barth began a thirty-year project of writing and publishing the twelve volumes of his *Church Dogmatics*. This crowning work was his theology of God, Christ and human salvation based on the New Testament.

Inspired by Barth, Rudolf Bultmann (1884–1976) worked in the field of New Testament theology. Liberal exegetes and biblical scholars had tried to reach the "historical Jesus" in the text of the New Testament, contending that the rest was merely cultural accretion from early Christian interpretations. Bultmann taught that the New Testament contained the church's message about Jesus and this is precisely what Christian faith addressed. The words of Jesus, the scriptures, speak to us and challenge us—we do not judge them.

The New Testament must be demythologized and the myths found therein must be understood so that their religious message for human existence becomes clear.

Paul Tillich (1886–1965) began as a professor in Germany (1919–1933), but when he was forced to leave under Nazism, he emigrated to the United States, teaching first at Union Theological Seminary in New York City and then at the Divinity School of the University of Chicago. Tillich endeavored to correlate the gospel with the modern world and the existential situation of the human person. He authored a multi-volume *Systematic Theology*, which, although highly philosophical in its approach, maintained that revelation provided the word of life and ultimately answered questions raised by human reason.

Neo-orthodoxy in the United States was represented by the brothers Niebuhr. Reinhold (1892–1971) taught ethics at Union Theological Seminary in New York City and H. Richard (1894–1962) taught at the Divinity School of Yale University. At first Reinhold supported the social gospel movement, but then came to appreciate certain traditional teachings of Christianity, for example, original sin. He believed that an ethic for society could not be based on a utopian view of the world, which ignored evil and the effects of sin. All systems (e.g., labor unions, corporations, political parties, and governments) could be and were infected by pride and the desire for power. In 1932 he published his most popular book, *Moral Man and Immoral Society*. Richard Niebuhr concentrated his scholarly efforts on analyzing the relationship of Christianity to civilization. Using insights from religious sociologists (e.g., Max Weber), Richard sought to show that the churches were very much wrapped up in middle-class concerns and needed to distance themselves from the world to recapture their focus and mission. Among his more important works were *The Kingdom of God in America* (1937), *The Meaning of Revelation* (1941), and *Christ and Culture* (1951).

The neo-orthodox theological movement in Protestantism tried to reassert traditional understandings of God, scripture, creeds and tradition without totally rejecting the contributions gained from science, biblical criticism and historical studies. God, revelation, Christ, and sin were all realities for the church and its tradition. They were also relevant to the situation of the human person in the modern world.

19

The Eastern Orthodox Churches and Eastern Rite Catholics

At the death of Emperor Theodosius in 395 the Roman Empire was de facto divided into two—the Roman Empire in the west and the Byzantine Empire in the east (named after the original city of Byzantium, which was later called Constantinople and today is known as Istanbul in Turkey). The east was divided into large units called prefectures and into smaller administrative units called dioceses. These important civic centers became ecclesiastical centers as well. The early life of the church in the eastern empire (325–787) was dominated by the first seven ecumenical or worldwide councils:

1) The Council of Nicaea I (325) condemned Arianism and taught that Christ was "true God from true God," "begotten not made, one in essence with the Father." It declared that Rome, Alexandria and Antioch were the three great dioceses or patriarchates of Christianity.
2) The Council of Constantinople I (381) affirmed that the Holy Spirit was God "who proceeds from the Father, who with the Father and the Son together is worshiped and glorified." Constantinople was made second in honor after Rome as a patriarchate.
3) The Council of Ephesus (431) battled Nestorius, who seemed to teach that in Christ two persons coexisted in the same body, endangering the unity of the person of Christ. Nestorius refused to call Mary the mother of God (*theotokos*).
4) The Council of Chalcedon (451) taught that in Christ there was but one person with two natures, that is, human and divine, versus the Monophysites, who held for one person with one nature, that is, divine, thus endangering Christ's true human identity. It also numbered Jerusalem among the great patriarchates.

5) The Council of Constantinople II (553) explained how the two natures, that is, divine and human, in Christ existed in a single divine person.

6) The Council of Constantinople III (680–681) defined the integrity of Christ's human nature against the Monothelites, who claimed that there was but one will in Christ, that is, divine, and not two, that is, divine and human.

7) The Council of Nicaea II (787) protected the legitimacy of venerating icons as sacred symbols of holy persons against the puritan attack of the iconoclasts or image smashers.

By the end of the eighth century the church had clarified its doctrine about the Trinity and Christ and established its creeds—the Nicene and the Nicene-Constantinopolitan. It had designed a church order or structure that gave special recognition to the pentarchy, the five patriarchates of Rome, Constantinople, Alexandria, Antioch and Jerusalem. Sacramental actions, rites and objects, such as icons, had their appropriate place in the liturgical life of the community. The first major division of the Christian church had also occurred with the "Oriental Orthodox churches" declaring independence from Rome and Constantinople.

The first separation within the Orthodox (literally meaning "right worship" and by extension "right thinking") churches occurred in the fifth and sixth centuries because of different christological theologies. The Nestorian churches of Persia and the Monophysite churches of Armenia, Syria (the Jacobite Church), Egypt (the Coptic church) and Ethiopia separated themselves from the Latin and Greek churches of Rome and Constantinople. Nestorian missionaries brought Christianity to parts of the Arab world and Asia. Over the centuries various groups of Nestorians have reunited with Rome, for example, the Nestorian church of Cyprus (1445) and of Malabar in India (1599). The Eastern Syrian patriarch and Pope John Paul II signed an agreement in 1994 on the nature of Christ, a major step toward reunion. The Monophysite churches today number about fifteen million: Armenia with one million six hundred thousand, Syria with one hundred and thirty thousand, the Coptic Church of Egypt with almost three million, the Ethiopian church with nine million and India with one hundred and seventy-five thousand.

The Great Schism between the church in the West and in the East had a number of causes and developed over hundreds of years. Theological, political, social, linguistic and economic factors contributed to church separation and division. The Latin-speaking church in the west and the Greek-speaking church in the east were divided over the pope's claim to universal, jurisdictional authority and the theological understanding of *Filioque*, that is, that the Holy Spirit "proceeds from the Father and the Son," a phrase added to the Nicene-Constantinopolitan Creed by the Western church. These disagreements involving patriarchs, popes, emperors, and councils led to misunderstanding, contention, compromise, and temporary reconciliation, but finally to separation.

The Orthodox or Byzantine Church of Constantinople was aggressively missionary. During the ninth century the monks Sts. Cyril and Methodius set out to convert the Slavic peoples living outside the boundaries of the Byzantine Empire. The two brothers invented a Slavonic alphabet and set about translating the bible and liturgical texts into the Slavonic vernacular. They worked in Moravia (the Czech Republic) and their disciples moved into Bulgaria, Serbia and Russia. Around 917 a Bulgarian patriarchate was established, and in 1346 another one in Serbia. In 988 the Russian ruler Vladimir of Kiev (980–1015) converted to Christianity and married the sister of the Byzantine emperor. Orthodox Christianity became the state religion of Russia until the Bolshevik Revolution in 1917.

In 1453 Byzantium was attacked by the Islamic Turks. After seven weeks of intense battle the Greek Christians succumbed. On May 29, both Greek and Latin, Byzantine and Roman Catholics united in prayer in the great church of Hagia Sophia. After receiving holy communion the emperor himself joined the battle and was killed. Hagia Sophia or the Church of Holy Wisdom became a mosque. The Patriarchate of Moscow, formed in 1589, assumed great importance in the Orthodox world in the years after the collapse of Constantinople in 1453. Officially, however, Moscow never replaced Constantinople as the "ecumenical patriarchy."

The Orthodox Church today is structured as follows:

Patriarchates:
Constantinople—1,500,000
Alexandria—3,000,000
Antioch—300,000
Jerusalem—150,000
Bulgaria—6,500,000
Serbia—7,000,000
Russia—55,000,000
Rumania—16,000,000

Catholicate:
Georgia—2,000,000

Autocephalous Churches:
Cyprus—350,000
Sinai—100
Greece—8,000,000
Poland—400,000
Albania—300,000
The Czech Republic—50,000

Autonomous Churches:
Finland—60,000
Estonia—100,000
Latvia—185,000
Hungary—40,000
China—20,000
Japan—35,000
Macedonia—175,000
Three Russian churches exist outside of Russia as well as the Ukrainian and Ruthenian churches.

Characteristics of Orthodoxy

The Orthodox Christian experience has more in common with Roman Catholicism than with other Christian churches. Doctrine, sacramental life and liturgy as well as a magisterial church authority are features in the life of both churches, even if not always understood in the same way. Orthodoxy places great emphasis on the following:

1) Tradition—It is the faith that has been handed down from one generation to the next beginning with Christ and the apostles. Faith is consistent and changeless, found in the bible, the creeds, the councils, the fathers, the canons, holy books and icons. Faith is a great gift received from the past to be preserved and handed on to future generations. Tradition, unlike traditions, is the living presence of the Holy Spirit in the life of the church.

2) Liturgy—Eucharist is the highest moment in the life of the Christian community because the triune God is made present to human persons in a mysterious sacramental way. The risen

Lord is present through the Holy Spirit in the offering of bread and wine. The eucharist is one of three moments of Christian initiation; baptism, chrismation (confirmation) and eucharist are all received together even in the case of infants. The great celebrations of the liturgical year and the seven sacraments are the starting point for theology as well as a primary place for catechetical instruction—*lex orandi, lex credendi* (the experience of praying guides the experience of believing).

3) Mary—In the Orthodox tradition saints are revered since the living and the dead are all part of "the communion of saints." The most exalted of all saints is Mary, the mother of God (*theotokos*), the ever-virgin (*aeiparthenos*), the all-holy (*panagia*). Mary is the first of those called to resurrection, and as mother of the God-Man Jesus Christ she plays a special intercessory role in God's plan for humankind. Mary is venerated, praised and shown great devotion but never worshiped as though she were a goddess.

4) Church Order—Government in the Orthodox Church is basically left up to each local church. The pentarchy or body of the patriarchs of Rome, Constantinople, Alexandria, Antioch and Jerusalem, holds a precedence of honor over others. Many Orthodox concede a primacy of honor to the patriarch of Rome, that is, the pope, who is the first among equals. They do not, however, concede to the patriarch of Rome universal jurisdictional authority. The more recent patriarchates, Bulgaria, Serbia, Russia and Rumania, as well as the autocephalous churches have developed from the ancient patriarchates but now are independent. The former are governed by their own patriarchs and the latter are governed by an archbishop or metropolitan. Autonomous churches are still somehow linked to a mother church and are not yet fully independent. There are three major orders in the Orthodox Church—bishops, priests and deacons—as well as two minor orders, subdeacon and reader. Priests who wish to marry must do so before ordination. Bishops are chosen from among monastic celibate clergy.

The Diaspora

Orthodox Christians, like all peoples, have moved throughout the world bringing with them their culture, language and religion. In the nineteenth century the Greek Orthodox established an exarchate or diocese in London; by the mid-twentieth century there were also dioceses in Paris, Bonn and Vienna. At the same time the Russian Orthodox established centers in Munich and Paris as well as a number of monasteries. Before World War I most Orthodox émigrés were poor. However, after the Bolshevik Revolution in 1917 waves of Russian exiles, many of them members of the nobility and wealthy merchants, also left for western Europe and the Americas.

Russian immigrants to the United States brought with them their religion and often their own regional divisions and animosities as well. The various Russian Orthodox communities in the United States were divided for most of the first part of the twentieth century. In 1970 they were reunited as an autocephalous church, known as the Orthodox Church in America. Their seminary, St. Vladimir in New York, claimed as faculty the celebrated Orthodox theologians and ecumenical pioneers John Meyendorff and Alexander Schmemann.

Greek immigration to America began in the 1890s. By 1940 more than five hundred thousand had arrived in the United States. The ecumenical patriarch of Constantinople established the Diocese of North and South America to organize church structures and pastoral life. Metropolitan Athenagoras, later ecumenical patriarch, did admirably as the first bishop of the new diocese. He was succeeded by Archbishop Michael (1950–1958) and then by Archbishop Iakovos (b. 1959). A major seminary was established in Brookline, Massachusetts, a theological journal was published, and a liberal arts college was founded. Today the Greek Orthodox Church in the United States numbers more than one million five hundred thousand faithful.

A major pastoral challenge to the Greek and to all Orthodox churches has been how to maintain commitment and identity to religion in the face of secularism and to the Orthodox cultural heritage in the face of the Americanization of younger generations. Some leaders advocate inculturation, for example, English in the liturgy, new translations of liturgical texts and aggressive evangelization among youth. Others seek to preserve the tradition, language and customs of their past without any adaptation to modern culture.

Ecumenism

Orthodox Christians believe that they are the "one, holy, catholic and apostolic church." Christians in the final analysis must believe and share the same faith. A variety of rites or liturgical styles has always been part of the Orthodox experience, that is, Alexandrian, Antiochene, Armenian, Chaldean and Byzantine. Unity does not require uniformity; nevertheless, "one faith" must be the goal of all ecumenical activity. Until that is realized, participation in the sacramental life of other churches is prohibited. For example, receiving eucharist in a non-Orthodox church is not permitted. Catholics, on the other hand, are allowed by their church with permission and in case of necessity to receive sacraments in an Orthodox church. That is because both share the same faith and theological understanding of sacraments.

Among Christian communities Catholicism and Eastern Orthodoxy have the most in common. Theological differences persist, however, and these can be overcome only through the Holy Spirit, dialogue, openness to the truth, humility and patience. The great hurts of the past that both churches inflicted on each other must be forgiven and healed. Such forgiveness ought to be done not only on an official level or among leaders. A true sense of community must also reach the level of the faithful in both churches. A new moment has begun in interchurch relations. Pope Paul VI and the ecumenical patriarch Athenagoras met three times: 1) 1964 in Jerusalem; 2) 1967 in Constantinople; 3) 1967 in Rome. Pope John Paul II has met with Patriarchs Dimitrios and Bartholomew. On December 6, 1965, the mutual condemnations and excommunications of the year 1054 were removed by the Vatican Council in Rome and the Holy Synod in Constantinople. The Roman Catholic Secretariat for Promoting Christian Unity (now the Pontifical Council for Promoting Christian Unity) established a special section for dialogue with the Orthodox churches. In 1980 both churches set up a joint international theological commission to study such issues as the "Filioque" and the Petrine ministry of the pope. The joint commission has published a number of theological documents which have treated such topics as the mystery of the Holy Trinity, the eucharist, the sacraments, the sacrament of order and the question of apostolic succession.

With the collapse of communism in Eastern Europe a thorny question has arisen. The Catholic Church legitimately seeks to minister to its faithful in Eastern Europe. At the same time the Orthodox Church claims much of this area as its own and resents any efforts by Catholics to re-establish, renew or begin a church presence. The Vatican recently published guidelines for apostolic activity by Catholics in Eastern Europe and especially in the

Commonwealth of Independent States, formerly the Soviet Union. If these guidelines are followed by Catholics and if Orthodox are truly understanding, the newly developing situation in Eastern Europe ought not to be an obstacle to church reunion.

Eastern Rite Catholics

After 1054, except for the Maronites, there were no organized Catholic Eastern churches, that is, Eastern churches in communion with the bishop of Rome. Political, cultural, economic and theological differences had led to division and church separation. The horrendous conduct of crusaders, pillaging Orthodox churches in their conquest of Constantinople in 1204, deepened resentment. In 1198 the Armenians in Syria reunited with Rome. In 1596 the Union of Brest-Litovsk reunited large numbers of Ukrainians and White Russians to Rome, the basis of today's Ukrainian Catholic Church. While Rome has viewed these partial reunions as a hopeful sign, the Orthodox have strongly resented these reunions. Their claim has been that they were simply the result of political or economic pressure. While the latter is true to some extent, there is, nevertheless, good cause to believe that there were truly religious factors present in such reunions. Rome hopes that Eastern rite churches can be bridges toward ultimate church reunion with the Orthodox.

During the twentieth century many eastern Europeans emigrated to North America—more than three million Orthodox and more than one million Eastern rite Catholic people, most of whom were of the Byzantine rite, such as Slavs from the old Austro-Hungarian Empire and Ukrainians from Galicia or the western Ukraine. Many settled in the coal mining regions of Pennsylvania. At first these Slavic Catholics of the Byzantine rite were subject to Latin rite bishops, who often enough did not understand their rites and customs. For instance, lest scandal be given to Protestants, Latin bishops in America forbade Eastern rite priests to be married. Given the lack of hospitality, many of these Slavs joined the Russian Orthodox Church. In 1907 the pope appointed the first Byzantine rite bishop in the United States, Soter Ortynsky. Soon after, a Ukrainian and a Ruthenian hierarchy were established with geographical dioceses. The former were located in Philadelphia, Pennsylvania, Stamford, Connecticut, and Chicago, Illinois. Ruthenian dioceses were established in Pittsburgh, Pennsylvania, and Passaic, New Jersey.

Eastern Catholics in America today, like the Orthodox, are challenged pastorally. Intermarriage often leads persons into the Latin rite as does the ready accessibility of a Latin rite parish. Younger generations no longer know the languages of Europe nor the liturgy and traditions of their ancestors. The use of English in worship and catechetics is increasingly employed for the sake of effective evangelization.

The Search for Reunion Today

The relations between the Eastern Orthodox Church and Eastern Catholic churches have always been somewhat tenuous. The Orthodox did not approve of Eastern Catholic reunion with Rome. They felt that it was largely the result of political or economic pressure brought to bear by Roman Catholic rulers in whose territory Eastern rite Catholics lived. Orthodox many times still harbor a grudge against what they view to be forced reunion. Eastern rite churches, on the other hand, feel resentment at times toward the Orthodox. While both churches suffered under the state-sponsored atheism of the Russian communist regime in the Soviet Union, Eastern rite Catholics in the 1940s, especially in the western Ukraine, were suppressed by the state or forced to join the Orthodox Church. Some of these Catholics went underground to practice their faith secretly; others pretended to join the Russian Orthodox Church. Often church property was confiscated by the government or turned over to the Orthodox Church. Now with the collapse of communism, animosity, concern and tension exist at least between some Eastern rite Catholics and the Russian Orthodox Church. This poses a problem for church reunion and is a major challenge to ecumenical efforts.

At a recent meeting of the joint international commission for the theological dialogue between the Roman Catholic Church and the Orthodox Church held in Lebanon June 17–24, 1993, a document was issued entitled "Uniatism, Method of Union of the Past and the Present Search for Full Communion." The document calls for unity between the church of the East and the church of the West, but clearly indicates that the type of union achieved in the past is neither a method nor a model for the unity Christian churches seek today. The statement calls for respect between both churches as well as freedom of conscience and dialogue, and excludes all types of efforts on the part of Eastern or Western Catholics to convert others at the expense of the Orthodox Church. It is hoped that when such documents in fact become operative, the proper environment will be established in which church reunion can be attained.

FOR FURTHER READING AND REFERENCE

Sydney E. Ahlstrom, *A Religious History of the American People*, Vol. 2 (Garden City, New York: Image Books, 1975).

Roger Aubert et al., *The Christian Centuries*, Vol. 5: *The Church in a Secularised Society* (Mahwah, New Jersey: Paulist Press, 1978).

Abba Eban, *Heritage: Civilization and the Jews* (New York: Summit Books, 1984).

Edward H. Flannery, *The Anguish of the Jews* (Mahwah, New Jersey: Paulist Press, 1985).

Hubert Jedin, ed., *History of the Church*, Vol. X: *The Church in the Modern Age* (New York: Crossroad Publishing Company, 1981).

John Meyendorff, *The Orthodox Church: Its Past and Its Role in the World Today* (Crestwood, New York: St. Vladimir's Seminary Press, 1981).

New Catholic Encyclopedia, "Eastern Churches," and "Orthodox Churches," by G. A. Maloney (New York: McGraw Hill, 1967).

Kyle M. Yates, Jr., ed., *The Religious World* (New York: Macmillan Publishing Company, 1988).

20

Modern Movements of Renewal

The period from 1920 to 1960 witnessed efforts on a number of different fronts to renew the life of the Catholic community. These efforts or movements were triggered by the need and desire to minister pastorally to God's people in an effective way. Both in Europe and America, church scholars, pastoral agents and committed lay women and men set out to imbue Catholic experience with a new enthusiasm.

The Liturgical Movement

The liturgy is the public worship offered to God by the church. Baptized Christians participate in the priesthood of Jesus Christ and are thus empowered to offer praise, thanksgiving, petition and worship to God the Father through the risen Lord Jesus in the Holy Spirit. The primary liturgical acts of the people of God, the body of Christ, are the sacraments and most especially the celebration of the eucharist. The eucharist or mass is the highest form of praise and thanksgiving since it re-enacts the sacrifice of Christ on Calvary. It is a mystical meal through which the faithful commune or unite with the risen Lord Jesus in thanksgiving to the Father. Liturgy is the public worship of the community, not simply the private prayer of an individual.

The liturgical movement was an attempt, clearly successful, to renew the worship life of the Catholic community. The Council of Trent (1545–1563) had set down standards for liturgy which remained in effect for more than four hundred years. For instance, the eucharist or mass was celebrated in Latin; the priest presided with his back to the people; people prayed individually and silently. The French Benedictines of the monastery of Solesmes under Abbot Prosper Gueranger (1805–1875) had studied and promoted the use of Gregorian chant. Continuing that initiative, Pope Saint Pius X in 1903 had called for a reform of church music. In 1905 he called for frequent reception of the eucharist and the reception of first holy communion at the age of discretion (usually about seven years of age). The pope sought to involve the active participation of all the faithful, priests and laity, in the liturgical rites and worship of the community.

The Benedictine priest-monk, Father Lambert Beauduin (1873–1960), who had been a worker-priest before becoming a monk, inaugurated the modern liturgical movement in Belgium. Pastorally zealous, Beauduin experienced personally the depth of religious ignorance among people that he believed was occasioned by ignorance of the liturgy. At a congress held at Mechelin (Malines), Belgium, in 1909, he insisted that people be given vernacular translations of the mass and vespers.

In Germany the Abbey of Maria Laach became the center for liturgical renewal from 1918 onward. There the first "community mass" or "dialogue mass" was celebrated in which the laity recited together the responses to the prayers of the priest. Father Romano Guardini promoted congregational participation among various youth groups, where it was enthusiastically received. Young women and men, Catholics by birth and choice, found the liturgy to be an experience of community, mystery, praise, thanksgiving and deep prayer. Guardini furthered development of an authentic, meaningful and pastoral liturgy in his work and scholarship. His popular book, *Der Herr (The Lord)*, in 1937 also promoted the reading of scripture as well as Christian involvement in the world. Pius Parsch (1884–1954) brought the mass in the vernacular to the ordinary faithful by publishing the liturgical texts for Sundays (more than twenty-five million were sold down to 1930) and through books of instruction, for example, *The Church's Year of Grace*, first published in 1932, which went through fourteen editions up to 1958. These books and pocket editions of texts helped to bring the renewal movement to the parish level. Similar efforts took place in France.

In the United States the Benedictines made St. John's Abbey in Minnesota a center for the American liturgical movement. There Father Virgil Michel founded the review *Orate Fratres* (since 1951 it has been called *Worship* magazine). After his death in 1938 Father Godfrey Diekmann became editor. The Liturgical Press provided abundant material to parishes throughout the country.

In 1947 Pope Pius XII published his encyclical, *Mediator Dei*. It was in effect a call to renew the worship life of the church seen as

the mystical body of Christ. The pope urged all members to participate actively in liturgy and especially in the "great prayer," the
eucharist. In 1951 he revised the rites of the Easter vigil (Holy
Saturday), and then in 1955 all the celebrations of Holy Week. In
1953 the rules of fasting before receiving holy communion were
modified. Previously no food or water could be taken after midnight
before the reception of communion. That was changed to abstention
from food and drink (water and medicine not included) for at least
one hour before communion. In 1957 evening mass was permitted.

These efforts at renewals of the liturgy paved the way for *The
Constitution on the Sacred Liturgy* promulgated by the Second
Vatican Council on December 4, 1963. The constitution
Sacrosanctum Concilium taught that the liturgy, as the public worship of God, was the ultimate goal of all church activity as well as
the source of that activity. Therefore, Christian people should
actively participate and be effectively nourished by the public
prayer life of the community. For this to happen the liturgy needed
to be renewed. The constitution states:

> In the restoration and promotion of the sacred liturgy the full and
> active participation by all the people is the aim to be considered
> before all else, for it is the primary and indispensable source from
> which the faithful are to derive the true Christian spirit...(n. 14).

> In order that the Christian people may more certainly derive an
> abundance of graces from the sacred liturgy, holy mother Church
> desires to undertake with great care a general restoration of the
> liturgy itself. For the liturgy is made up of unchangeable ele-
> ments divinely instituted, and of elements subject to change.
> These latter not only may be changed but ought to be changed
> with the passage of time, if they have suffered from the intrusion
> of anything out of harmony with the inner nature of the liturgy or
> have become less suitable...(n. 21).

The Ecumenical Movement

The word *ecumenical* comes from the Greek *oikumene* meaning
"universal" or "worldwide." As a movement it denotes the process
whereby Christian churches attempt to overcome differences and
move toward unity. Throughout the centuries there have been
efforts to reunite various Christian churches. The twentieth century movement, however, is a concern of Catholic, Orthodox and

Protestant churches, and has produced institutions to foster unity, for example, the World Council of Churches and the Vatican's Pontifical Council for Promoting Christian Unity.

In 1910 at the World Mission Conference held in Edinburgh, Scotland, Protestant missionaries shared their unhappiness at the scandal of division within Christianity and its harmful effects for the missionary effort. The International Missionary Council was formed to promote collaboration among missionary groups and societies. In 1925 the Life and Work Conference at Stockholm brought together different Protestant representatives whose goal was to form a movement that would foster cooperation among Christians in international political, social and economic life. They claimed that "service unites, but doctrine divides." Others, however, felt that doctrine was the ultimate point of division and that Christians needed to dialogue among themselves about what they believed. Thus the Faith and Order movement began officially in 1927 at Lausanne. These three organizations—the International Mission Council, the Life and Work Conference and the Faith and Order Conference—came together to form the World Council of Churches.

Meeting for the first time at Amsterdam in 1948, members of the World Council of Churches stated clearly that they all acknowledged Jesus Christ as Lord and Savior. They were not forming some super church but rather a community of autonomous churches. One hundred and forty-seven churches from forty-seven countries were represented. The majority of the Orthodox churches did not initially belong, nor did the Catholic Church. At the third plenary meeting in 1961 at New Delhi, the Orthodox patriarchs did become members. An official Catholic delegation also participated in the meeting. By the time of the fifth plenary meeting in Nairobi, Kenya, in 1975, two hundred and seventy-one churches had become members of the World Council.

The movement toward unity among non-Catholic Christian churches has progressed during the present century. Generally it has been realized that compromise on doctrine and identity would be a false unity. One effect of this has been the movement toward greater unity within denominations themselves, exemplified in the formation of world associations by Anglicans, Baptists, Lutherans, Methodists, Presbyterians, Congregationalists and Disciples of Christ. The ecumenical patriarch, Athenagoras I (1886–1972), promoted Pan-Orthodox conferences, for example, in 1961 at Rhodes. Some churches have indeed united: Anglicans, Congregationalists, Methodists and Presbyterians became the Church of South India in

1949, while, in the United States, Congregationalists and Reformed became the United Church of Christ.

Catholic participation in the ecumenical movement took place on popular, scholarly and official levels. Interchurch cooperation had occurred, especially in the United States, during both world wars. In religiously pluralist societies people of differing faiths easily mixed. In other nations (e.g., Germany), the limited number of church groups found common ground under the Nazi threat.

Scholarship contributed to new understandings about the origins of church divisions and the factors that continue to divide the churches. The Catholic scholar Joseph Lortz (1887–1975), in his *Reformation in Deutschland* (1939), gave credit to the religious motives of the Reformation and pointed out the Catholic faults and guilt for the split. In Germany Max Joseph Metzger in 1938 founded *Una Sancta*, a brotherhood dedicated to serious intellectual study and prayer for church unity.

In France Yves Congar, O.P. (1904–1995), became a leader in the ecumenical movement. His book, *Chrétiens désunis* (translated into English as *Divided Christendom* in 1939), became very influential and laid the theological foundation for Catholic ecumenism. The Belgian priest Lambert Beauduin, O.S.B., founded a priory at Amay (later moved to Chevetogne) as a meeting place for ecumenical dialogue. In 1926 he began the publication *Irénikon,* a Catholic journal dedicated to ecumenism. Father Paul Couturier (1881–1953) promoted and spread the World Octave of Prayer for the unity of Christians, January 18–25. During this week Christians everywhere were encouraged to pray for church unity.

The official response of the Catholic Church to the ecumenical movement was one of prudent support. Pope Benedict XV had refused an invitation to send representatives to the first Faith and Order conference in 1919. Pius XI often reached out to the Orthodox, established the Pontifical Oriental Institute, urged the study of Orthodox theology and liturgy, and, with Benedict XV, forbade efforts to Latinize the peoples of the Orthodox churches.

In 1949 the Holy Office (today the Congregation for the Doctrine of the Faith) issued an instruction which officially encouraged Catholic participation in the ecumenical movement and called for greater interest and support from Catholic bishops, pastors, priests and laity. Pope John XXIII established the Secretariat for Promoting Christian Unity (June 5, 1960) under the leadership first of Cardinal Augustine Bea and then Cardinal Johannes Willebrands. Both were serious theologians and greatly involved in the Catholic ecumenical

movement. On November 21, 1964, the Second Vatican Council promulgated a decree on ecumenism, *Unitatis Redintegratio*. It stated:

> The restoration of unity among all Christians is one of the princi-
> pal concerns of the Second Vatican Council. Christ the Lord
> founded one Church and one Church only (n. 1).

The document went on to teach:

1) True unity consists in unity of faith (doctrine), worship (liturgy) and order (structure).
2) Division was not the will of Christ.
3) Christian churches already share much in common.
4) Other Christian churches are, therefore, in communion with
   the Catholic Church to varying degrees.
5) It is in the Catholic Church alone that the fullness of the
   means of salvation are obtained (n. 3).
6) Nevertheless, the Catholic Church's membership needs daily
   purification and renewal to truly witness to Christ (n. 4).
7) Special bonds of unity exist between the Orthodox and the
   Catholic Churches which both possess true sacraments, above
   all the eucharist and the priesthood by apostolic succession, and
   thereby they are still joined in a very close relationship (n. 15).
8) Christians, to overcome separation, must have a spirit of
   mutual forgiveness, honesty and patience.

Since the council, the Catholic Church has been profoundly committed to the cause of church reunion. Christians are brothers and
sisters in Christ but only partial communion exists. In a variety of
ways—prayer, personal contacts, national and international meetings, joint studies—the Catholic Church today is in contact with
other Christian Churches. Through the Pontifical Council for
Promoting Christian Unity ecumenical dialogue goes forward.

Catholic Action

The church is a community of persons baptized into Jesus Christ
and gathered together in the Holy Spirit. Its mission is to worship
God, proclaim the gospel and serve. This community constantly
examines its action to see that what it does is effective. The liturgical movement, especially in its modern form, sought to renew the
worship life of the church. Its goal was to promote an informed,

vital, spiritual participation for all people in the eucharist and the prayer life of the community. On another front the ecumenical movement sparked both interchurch cooperation, mutual respect and new theological insights about God, Christ, the Spirit, church, sacraments and morality. This period—1930 through 1960—was an exciting moment for Catholic Action as well.

From the 1930s onward pastoral ministers attempted in a new way to bring the gospel to bear on the problems of the modern world. They sought to reach women and men in their daily lives— with their burdens, sufferings, joys and hopes. Ministers included laity, who were called to participate in the apostolate of the hierarchy by reason of the priesthood of the faithful.

Catholic Action took a variety of forms. At times it was realized through general service and programs at the parish or diocesan level. It was also actualized in specialized movements such as *Jeunesse Oeuvrière Chrétienne* (JOC) and *Jeunesse Etudiante Chrétienne* (JEC). These organizations, founded by Father Joseph Cardyn (later a cardinal) in Belgium in 1924–1925, spread throughout the world after 1945. Father Cardyn sought to minister to young people by enabling them to come to terms with their Christian commitment in the situations in which they found themselves, whether it was in the world of work and industry or the world of studies. Small groups of young people would meet on a regular basis to 1) see, 2) judge and 3) act. In group discussions they reviewed their lives, examining the concrete situation in which they found themselves (see). They then judged what needed to be done to change that situation to conform it to the demands of the gospel (judge). Finally they acted on their insights, and with the grace of Christ they sought to change the often sinful economic and social situations in which they found themselves (act).

In Italy Catholic Action was highly organized and under the control of the bishops. Before the Lateran Treaty of 1929, lay Catholics organized to promote the rights of Catholics and support each other in a hostile environment. Later many of the leaders of Catholic Action became members of the Christian Democratic Party and held important offices in post-war Italy.

Catholic Action, which came later to be called the lay apostolate, deeply respected the proper vocation of the Catholic woman or man in the world. As part of the mystical body of Christ, the baptized and confirmed were called to witness publicly to Christ and the gospel. The peer ministry movement *Cursillo de Cristianidad* began in Spain in 1949. This "little course in Christianity" begins with a three day retreat conducted by teams of lay men and women, as well as priests, brothers and sisters. Generally it becomes a profound experience of conversion that is to continue on the "fourth day," that is, for the rest of life. This is helped by regular meetings (*Ultrega*) to review life in small group sharing. The Cursillo movement has spawned a number of similar kinds of events for youth in high school, as well as university students. By 1977 there were over two and one-half million Cursillistas.

A number of lay movements addressed the needs of families and the apostolate to families. Patrick and Patricia Crowley played key roles in the development of the Christian Family Movement (CFM), which began in Chicago in 1947. Five or six couples, usually from the same parish, would meet in homes for discussion and action in family, political, and economic and social life. At their meetings these couples reflected on scripture, analyzed their situations and planned action, following the model of the JOC (i.e., see, judge, act). The goal was to fulfill their Christian vocation as laity by bringing the gospel to bear on the reality of the world. CFM today is active in a variety of countries.

The Cana Conference is a retreat movement for married couples begun in St. Louis, Missouri, in 1944 by Father Edward Dowling (1898–1960). Couples meet in an informal atmosphere with the retreat director to reflect on the reality, problems and spirituality of marriage. The hope is that marriage and family life will improve and develop through a more explicit spirituality designed for lay married people. The Cana Conference also developed the Pre-Cana Conference, designed to inform and instruct engaged couples before they marry.

In Spain Father Gabriel Calvo founded Marriage Encounter (*Encuentro Conjugal*) to help married couples "rediscover" or "meet again." In a weekend retreat couples explore their lives and their relationships as husband and wife and examine God's presence in their marriage. A key for a happy and holy marriage is open communication, which the movement fosters during the retreat and after. Marriage Encounter has become worldwide since its beginning in 1953.

The Legion of Mary was an earlier lay apostolic movement developed in Dublin, Ireland, in 1921. This highly organized movement emphasized personal spiritual development that would then lead to action on behalf of the gospel. Members attended weekly meetings to share prayer, scriptural readings, and guidance from the director. At least two hours of apostolic activity per week were expected. By the mid-1960s there were more than a million members throughout the world. In many parishes the Legion of Mary came to be the key evangelizing unit, nourishing the faith and spirituality of its members and bringing the gospel to others.

In 1947 Pope Pius XII gave official church approval to secular institutes. These were communities whose members as individuals or in small groups tried to lead a life of deep holiness in the midst of the world through their secular calling. One of the most influential of such communities is *Opus Dei* (the Work of God) founded in Madrid in 1928 by Monsignor José María Escrivá de Balaguer (1902–1975), who was beatified by Pope John Paul II. Opus Dei was officially approved as a secular institute in 1947, and in 1982 it became the Personal Prelature of the Holy Cross and Opus Dei. Well-educated professional lay women and men, as well as the priest members of Opus Dei, work to transform the world by witnessing to the gospel in a variety of ways and occupations after receiving training in Opus Dei centers and residences. By 1990 there were more than seventy thousand members throughout the world. The Prelature also sponsors universities in Pamplona and Rome. Opus Dei has not been without its critics. Some suggest that its operation is too secretive or aimed at infiltrating political and economic centers of power. Others charge that its theology is too conservative. Whatever the criticisms, Opus Dei continues to be the most successful secular institute, and it truly develops a profound spirituality in women and men lay apostles.

The *Schonstatt Werk* is a movement which began in Germany in 1914. Lay women and men, priests, sisters and brothers, dedicated to bringing Christ to the world of everyday work, with special devotion to Mary, form its various branches. Schonstatt communities are found today in South Africa, Chile, Argentina, Brazil, the United States, Australia and India. Clerical members of Schonstatt have assumed important posts in local churches and the Roman curia, as have members of Opus Dei.

In 1943, during World War II, Chiara Lubich (b. 1920) began a spiritual movement in Trent, Italy, where young people came together to form communities and to reflect on the scriptures. They did so because Jesus said: "Where two or three are gathered together in my name, I am there in their midst" (Mt 18:20). Members tried to find "communion" with Jesus in every situation of life. The *Focolari* or "little communities of life" include single women and men, as well as families, dedicated to following Christ in a variety of lifestyles and occupations. Priests and religious of other orders have also associated themselves with the movement, which includes youth groups, parish communities, and ecumenical associations and sponsors schools of common life in many countries.

Another effort to meet people's hunger for authentic community, exercise the apostolate and reach out to non-believers or non-practicing Catholics is the "Neo-Catechumenate" begun in Madrid in 1962. Today the movement has communities in Europe, North and South America, Africa and Asia. The Neo-Catechumenate introduces a candidate to the experience of community life, scripture and eucharist. Instruction in the faith or catechesis moves through different phases, thus introducing a person to the fullness or renewal of Christian life over a period of time. At the end of a two year period the catechumens renew their baptismal promises and assume their Christian responsibility in the world as committed mature Catholics. The Neo-Catechumenate foreshadowed the formal and official re-establishment of the catechumenate in 1972 with the promulgation of the *Rite of Christian Initiation of Adults* (RCIA) in the Catholic Church. The latter had been called for by the Second Vatican Council. Through the RCIA a person seeking baptism enters a process of conversion, instruction and service as a preparation for becoming a Catholic.

The *Comunione e Liberazione* (Community and Liberation) movement in Italy promotes the experience of Christian community and the lay apostolate among youth and young adults. Through the experience of friendship, prayer and reflection, young lay women and men personally appropriate the faith in which they were baptized. By seeing Christ as the center of all personal, social, cultural and political life, the movement seeks to form and motivate young Catholics in assuming their vocation to transform that world in which they live and work.

Catholic Action or the lay apostolate in the twentieth century has evolved practically and theologically. Women and men, married and single, young and old, individuals and families, have come to assume their proper place in the ministry and mission of the church. All the baptized and confirmed share in the priesthood of Christ through their call to worship, proclaim the gospel and serve others in union with their pastors. The diverse experiences of many movements, groups and communities have made significant contributions toward the new understanding of church which was officially promoted at the Second Vatican Council. Since that council (1962–1965) there has been an explosion of lay ministries in the church as well as a continuing theological reflection which seeks an ever deeper understanding of the vocation of the Catholic lay woman and man in today's world.

A Pastoral Experiment

Ever since the Enlightenment, sectors of western Europe have been alienated from the church. Many intellectuals and large numbers of working class people either renounced the church or simply drifted away. Traditional Catholic countries faced the phenomenon of disengagement or de-Christianization. Values and truths formerly accepted without question were doubted or rejected. The reality of God receded from daily existence. Personal experience became the criterion for what was right or wrong, and there were no moral absolutes. Religious practice, when it occurred, was often cultural or nostalgic. Church personnel and pastoral ministers, especially in France, felt impelled to do things differently to win back those, such as the working class, who no longer practiced their faith.

In 1943 Fathers Henri Godin (1906–1944) and Yvan Daniel issued a document entitled *La France, pays de mission? (Is France a Mission Country?)*. Their thesis was that the parish church and pastoral agents could not simply go along as usual if they hoped to penetrate and serve the world of the French worker. The archbishop of Paris, Cardinal Emmanuel Célestin Suhard (1874–1949), agreed and formed the *Mission de Paris*, a group of priests who would be missionaries to workers and the poor, serving them in non-traditional ways and living in the same conditions as they did. Through this initiative the cardinal hoped to break down the wall between the church and the modern world. A developing Catholic intellectual life provided theological and philosophical reasons for a new pastoral approach, for example, the Dominican M.-D. Chenu, Jacques Maritain, Emmanuel Mounier, the review *Vie Intellectuelle*, the Jesuit and Dominican theological schools and the editorial house Du Cerf.

The priest-worker was a priest who worked all day at a secular job, which was not distinguishable from that of any other worker, and who often was not known to be a priest. During World War II when French youth had been deported by the Nazis to work in German factories, bishops asked young priests to go and secretly minister to the needs of these French workers. Nearly all of the priests were discovered and either sent home or to prison. But they also experienced the alienation of workers from the church and how effective ministers could be as witnesses to the gospel if they inserted themselves into the world of the workers by laboring, living and struggling with them. Eventually about one hundred priests became workers in France. While living alone or in small communities, they supported themselves on what they earned. It was expected that as laborers they would join the trade union or political parties, some of which were Marxist and communist. Their pastoral experiment of living in solidarity with the working class lasted roughly ten years, but eventually it was halted by pressure from the Vatican in 1954.

The priest-worker movement frightened some church authorities in Rome. The fundamental issue once again was the relationship of the church to the modern world: how to remain faithful to Christ and the gospel and at the same time effectively evangelize the modern world? Rome saw pastoral experiments such as the priest-worker movement as too radical and essentially incompatible with the office of priest. The Vatican also criticized and rejected the theological premises behind such pastoral initiatives. The Holy Office under Cardinal Giuseppe Pizzardo moved to halt the new thinking. The involvement of priests in the working world was modified and eventually turned over to secular institutes.

The Dominicans in France, leaders in new thinking and pastoral activity, were hit hard. Fathers Chenu, Congar and Feret, brilliant theologians, were forbidden to teach. The director of the publishing house Du Cerf was exiled, and its review *L'Actualité* was halted. Three Dominican provincials were removed from office by the master of the order, Father Emmanuel Suarez. The master acted out of fear that Rome would suppress the Dominican Order in France. Fathers Regamey and Couturier, active in modern ecclesiastical art and architecture, were to be supervised closely.

The tactics of Vatican officials at the time often seemed heavy-handed and unjust, and their policies myopic. However, much of the theological thinking and many pastoral theories of the Dominicans were later endorsed by the Second Vatican Council. Father Chenu, reflecting on this period, said: "People later congratulated me on my obedience in those difficult times....I would prefer that it was my faith that was involved....To obey—one abases oneself easily, a passive virtue. But I had faith, faith in the church." Father Ives Congar, later to be named a cardinal in his old age, would say: "Acquiring a knowledge of history is the surest way of acquiring confidence in the church. History teaches that nothing is new and that the church has survived sadder and more difficult situations. History is a school of wisdom and of limitless patience."

The Missionary Movement

Catholic missionary activity expanded during the twentieth century and took different directions as a series of papal encyclicals gave official church direction to mission policy. Pope Leo XIII (1878–1903), in six such letters, taught that the entire church, clergy and laity, were responsible for missionary work. He called for an indigenous clergy and hierarchy in missionary territories. Pope Benedict XV (1914–1922), in his encyclical *Maximum Illud*, strongly promoted the formation of local clergy. The presence of European missionaries was to be temporary, and they were not to promote the interests and prestige of their own native countries in any way. Pius XI (1922–1939) followed his predecessor in encouraging the development of a truly indigenous church that was not a foreign import. He personally ordained a number of Chinese, Indian and Japanese bishops. Pius XII (1939–1958) wrote ten missionary-related letters and ordained the first African bishop in 1939. The Second Vatican Council took up the theme of the church's missionary task in its *Decree on the Church's Missionary Activity (Ad Gentes)*, promulgated December 7, 1965.

Presently there are almost a billion Catholics in the world. By the year 2000 there will be an estimated one hundred and sixty million Catholics in the fifty-nine countries of Africa (18.7%); two hundred and seventy-eight million Catholics in the thirty-six countries of Europe (51.6%); five hundred and thirty-three million Catholics in the forty-six countries of Latin America (85.9%); one hundred and two million Roman Catholics in five North American countries (34.7%); ten million Roman Catholics in the twenty-eight countries of Oceania (30.6%); one hundred and four million Catholics in the thirty-six countries of south Asia (4.6%); four million seven hundred thousand Catholics in the eight countries of east Asia (0.3%); three million eight hundred thousand Catholics in west Asia in countries formerly of the Soviet Union (1.2%).

Missionary priests, brothers and sisters serve the church in all of these areas. In modern times most Catholic missionaries came from Europe, although in the twentieth century they have been joined by large numbers of North Americans. The Catholic Foreign Mission Society of America (CFMSA) (Maryknoll priests, brothers and sisters) is a group dedicated exclusively to overseas mission work, as is the Quebec Foreign Mission Society (QFMS). More than one-third of today's missionaries are indigenous to the country (e.g., seventy-two percent of Catholic priests in India are Indian). Very few of the leaders of newly created archdioceses and dioceses within local churches are foreign-born. African, Asian and Latin American representation in the college of cardinals and the Roman curia is at an all time high. Large numbers of lay women and men have also become a major force in today's missionary movement.

Preparation of missionaries, especially since the Second Vatican Council, has become more sophisticated and subtle. The foreign missionary is engaged in a transcultural project to preach the gospel of Christ. Such a person must respect, appreciate and know the host culture. Missionary work, in the ecclesiology of the Second Vatican Council, understands the promotion of social justice and service to the poor and oppressed as part of the essential mission of the church and not just pre-evangelization. The missionary attempts to inculturate the gospel in liturgy, formation, education and pastoral practices on every level. Western European or North American culture is but one cultural expression of the gospel. Of course, inculturation must preserve the gospel of Christ and the tradition of the church.

The theology of mission today does not see its goal only as saving souls. God's universal will for the salvation of all makes grace available to all humankind—to religious and non-religious people everywhere. The Catholic missionary seeks to witness to the one savior, Jesus Christ, and to establish the church, the community of believers, as a witness to the fullness of salvation available through Christ. The missionary task is always the responsibility of the community, and thus the distinction between a sending and a receiving church gives way or at least is only a temporary moment. Mission extends to the not yet Christian as well as to the no longer Christian. Hence the evangelizing missionary task is no longer conceived of solely in geographical terms.

New Thinking

St. Anselm had defined theology as *fides quaerens intellectum*, faith seeking understanding. The way to accomplish the theological task, therefore, was to correlate faith and revelation with human experience. By the mid-twentieth century, theologians were in a position to employ the latest scientific techniques and discoveries in their effort to understand faith, for example, the historical-critical method, textual criticism, sociology of religion, and anthropology. Each of the various movements in the church (i.e., the biblical, liturgical, ecumenical, pastoral and missionary movements) happening almost concomitantly contributed to new ways of understanding faith, which brought significant insights to all the other movements. What clearly characterized the new theology was its return to sources, that is, the bible and the Fathers of the church, as well as its pastoral concerns for the modern world. Many scholars worked in a variety of theological fields such as dogmatic, moral, kerygmatic, liturgical, biblical and pastoral theology. Outstanding theologians, who were active between 1930 and 1960, unknowingly set the stage for the Second Vatican Council.

Romano Guardini (1885–1968), ordained a priest in 1910, was born in Italy but lived and worked in Germany his whole life. As a theologian he sought to "pray while thinking and think while praying." Guardini was a professional theologian who both studied the relationship of the church to the modern world and involved himself in pastoral life with students. He was a leader in the liturgical movement and wrote on the church, not only as an institution but also as a community of the baptized. Many of his writings addressed issues of literature, mysticism, prayer, conscience and the essence of Christianity. His book, *Der Herr (The Lord)*, had a great influence on deepening a Christ-centered spirituality.

Karl Rahner, S.J. (1904–1984), was a German Jesuit who taught both in Austria and in Germany. His body of work is prolific and has been translated into a variety of languages. Rahner attempted to use the phenomenology of Martin Heidegger and the Thomism of Joseph Maréchal in the service of a theology that sought to address the real questions of the modern world. His books treat many topics, such as spirituality, Mary, priesthood, sacraments and death, but he wrote especially about the presence of God's grace in the world and ecclesiology. Rahner's most important works include *Handbook of Pastoral Theology*, the theological encyclopedia *Sacramentum Mundi*, the ten-volume *Lexicon of Theology and the Church*, and the twenty volumes of *Theological Investigations*. He was a theologian at the Second Vatican Council and also a member of the Papal International Theological Commission.

Marie-Dominique Chenu, O.P. (1895–1990), was born in France and became a Dominican priest and theologian. He taught from 1920 to 1942 at the famous Dominican school of theology, Le Saulchoir, where he was the director from 1932 to 1942. Chenu was a serious historical scholar of medieval philosophy and theology, especially that of St. Thomas Aquinas, while at the same time being fully engaged pastorally in the modern world. In 1930 he founded the Institute of Medieval Studies in Toronto, Canada, and he was involved as an advisor and theologian to the French priest-worker movement. Father Chenu wrote *Spirituality of Work* and *Toward a Theology of Work*. In 1942 his book, *On the New Theology Going on at Le Saulchoir*, was put on the Index of Forbidden Books and he was removed as director of the school. From 1962 to 1965 he served as a theologian at the Second Vatican Council.

Yves M. J. Congar, O.P. (1904–1995), entered the Dominicans in 1925. He studied under such Thomists as Jacques Maritain and Father Chenu at Le Saulchoir. In 1937 Father Congar published his *Chrétiens desunis (Divided Christendom)* in which he studied the causes of division among Christians and developed principles for Catholic ecumenism. Congar is this century's most important ecclesiologist, and much of his work was incorporated into the teaching of the Second Vatican Council. His books include *Lay People in the Church* (1953), *Mystery of the Temple* (1958), *The Wide World, My Parish* (1961) and *Tradition and the Traditions* (1961–1963). In 1952 he was forbidden to teach and publish because of his involvement in the new theology and the priest-worker movement. Father Congar was named an official theologian to the Second Vatican Council and later became a cardinal in 1994. Both Pope Paul VI and John Paul II have expressed their indebtedness to the theological work of Cardinal Congar.

Henri de Lubac, S.J. (1896–1991), a French Jesuit, was ordained in 1927 and from 1929–1950 taught at the Jesuit school of theology at Lyons-Fourviere in the fields of fundamental theology and the history of religion. Father de Lubac had served in the army during World War I and was arrested by the Nazis in World War II. He left teaching between 1950 and 1958 at the behest of an over-cautious Jesuit general lest the suppressive measures of the Roman curia reach him. Among his principal works are *Catholicisme* (1938), *De la Connaissance de Dieu* (1941), *Surnaturel* (1946), and *Le Drame de l'Humanisme Athee* (1949). He was the founder with Daniélou of the collection *Sources Chrétiennes* (two hundred and twenty-five volumes between 1942 and 1975). He also played a decisive role in the collection *Theologie* (eighty volumes between 1944 and 1971). In his works he often reflected on the role of faith, grace and unbelief as well as on the works of the Fathers. For de Lubac the church was not a closed group of elect but a community open to all who accepted its witness. Sacraments were communal events, not private individual actions. The church in fact was a community of sinners as well as a community of saints. Pope John XXIII named him to the theological commission preparing for the Second Vatican Council in which he participated. Father de Lubac was named a cardinal by Pope John Paul II.

Hans Urs von Balthasar (1905–1988) was ordained a priest in the Society of Jesus in 1936, although he later left the Jesuits and founded a secular institute. He had been introduced to the study of the fathers and the new theology by Father de Lubac, and he lived the life of a theologian and writer in Basel, Switzerland. Von Balthasar's large bibliography includes works on writers, aesthetics, spirituality, Christology, the church and the role of the laity in the church. He became a member of the International Theological Commission and was named a cardinal by Pope John Paul II.

Jean Daniélou, S.J. (1905–1974), studied at the renowned Jesuit school of theology at Lyons-Fourviere in France and was ordained in 1938. Since he was a serious literary scholar, his teachers, Henri de Lubac and Hans Urs von Balthasar, directed Daniélou's interests to a study of the Fathers of the church. He became an expert in the origins of early Christianity and co-director of the series, *Sources Chrétiennes*—a critical edition of the works of the fathers. Daniélou produced a variety of works in patristics, spirituality, mysticism, the church, ecumenics and the role of the laity. He was a professor at the Sorbonne and the *Institut Catholique* in Paris, chaplain to students, and a theologian at the Second Vatican Council. Some of his scholarly work came under suspicion in Rome, and eventually the theology school at Fourviere was closed. His work encourages loyalty to the Christian tradition while being open to the world and other churches and religions. In 1969 Father Daniélou was ordained a bishop and named a cardinal. His concern about misguided interpretations of the teaching of the Second Vatican Council led more liberal-thinking theologians to criticize him in later life.

Augustine Bea, S.J. (1881–1968), was born in Holland and was ordained a Jesuit priest in 1912. As a biblical scholar, he taught in Germany and then at Rome's Pontifical Biblical Institute, where he was director from 1930 to 1949. While in Rome, Father Bea served on many Roman congregations and was the private confessor to Pope Pius XII. In 1959 he was named cardinal and head of the Secretariat for Promoting Christian Unity (1960–1968). Both as a biblical scholar and a Roman administrator, he strategically influenced the biblical renewal movement in the Catholic Church. He had input into Pope Pius XII's encyclical *Divino Afflante Spiritu,* which clearly supported the historical-critical approach to the study of scripture. Over the years he collaborated with Protestant biblical scholars and so was well equipped to head the church's new ecumenical efforts after the council.

John Courtney Murray, S.J. (1904–1967), was an American Jesuit from New York City. After completing his studies at the Gregorian University in Rome, he became professor of dogmatic theology at the Jesuit theologate in Woodstock, Maryland. His publications addressed the questions of ecumenism, religious liberty, and church-state relations. As an American he brought a unique perspective to these issues. He and other Jesuits carried on a written discussion in the journal *Theological Studies*, asserting that the American church-state experience was most desirable. Times had changed and so theological thinking needed to change. Separation of church from state, however, did not imply a wall between them. Murray rejected secularist trends in the nation as ultimately destructive. In 1954 the Jesuit general in Rome required that Father Murray submit all of his writings to Rome for prior censorship and to cease writing on topics about church-state relations. He did not attend the first session of the Second Vatican Council, but at the insistence of Cardinal Spellman of New York he was invited to be an "expert" for the rest of the council, where he became the chief architect of the council's *Declaration on Religious Freedom*. His bibliography includes *We Hold These Truths* (1961), *The Problem of God* (1963), *Yesterday and Today* (1963), and *Problems of Religious Freedom* (1965).

21

The Second Vatican Council

Beginning with Pope Pius IX, the Catholic Church in the late nineteenth and early twentieth centuries had begun a process of renewal and revival. Pastoral, missionary, intellectual and institutional changes and growth made the church an influential presence in the world. Catholic people shared a clear sense of identity and mission. Catholicism might dialogue with the world of modernity, but it would not nor could it surrender to a secular, liberal ideology. Pope Pius XII had embraced the insights of the historical-critical approach to scripture and strongly urged liturgical renewal. He also warned of the dangers in new theological thinking in the encyclical *Humani Generis* (1950). The regal, aristocratic pope died in 1958 and was succeeded by the genial patriarch of Venice, Angelo Roncalli, who took the name John XXIII.

Pope John XXIII

Pope John brought a variety of experiences to the papacy. As a younger man he had been pastorally active in his native diocese of Bergamo. In 1925 he began a twenty-year diplomatic assignment in Bulgaria, Turkey and Greece. There he encountered a world of Slavic and Greek culture, more Orthodox Christian than Roman Catholic, more Eastern rite Catholics than Latin rite. The church was a minority presence, at times restricted in its activities. Roncalli was named papal nuncio (ambassador) to France in 1944 and nine years later became the cardinal archbishop of Venice. On October 28, 1958, he was elected pope.

John XXIII soon won the hearts of the world by his friendly, open, sincere style. He understood his role to be that of priest, father and shepherd. As pope he sought to shape his ministry after the pattern of Joseph in the Old Testament who greeted his brothers who had sold him into slavery with the words, "I am Joseph, your brother" (Gn 45:4). His diplomatic service had given him a special interest in ecumenism, and by his style he promoted better relations among Christian leaders. Pope John wrote eight encyclicals, two of which received worldwide attention and study. In the encyclical *Mater et Magistra* (July 15, 1961) the pope addressed the social questions of the modern world and developed the social teaching of the church. He encouraged the church to dialogue with the modern world because as church it was not only a teacher *(magistra)* but a mother *(mater)*, especially to the lowly and oppressed. The pope said that it was important to maximize the freedom of individuals, always respecting, of course, the common good. However, it was also necessary to recognize the dependency of individuals on social groups and organizations in a world where all human beings and nations were becoming increasingly interdependent. Wealthier nations had an obligation to help poorer agriculturally based economies through technical and scientific assistance as well as financial aid. The pope emphasized that this aid was not to be a form of economic colonialism.

On April 11, 1963, John issued *Pacem in Terris (Peace on Earth)* which was addressed not only to Catholics but to all people of good will. In this letter he listed the essential conditions for global peace: truth, justice, and mutual respect among nations and peoples. The state had the responsibility to protect the human rights of life, health, education and work for all. Discrimination, racism and sexism were affronts to human dignity. The letter taught that in an atomic age war simply made no sense as a way of promoting justice. For this defense of the human person and world peace, Pope John was awarded the peace prize of the International Balzan Foundation in 1962 with the approval of the Soviet premier Nikita Khrushchev. In 1963 he was posthumously awarded the United States Presidential Medal of Freedom.

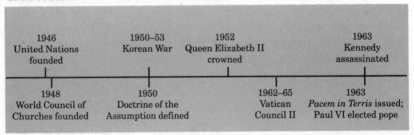

1946 United Nations founded	1950–53 Korean War	1952 Queen Elizabeth II crowned		1963 Kennedy assassinated
1948 World Council of Churches founded	1950 Doctrine of the Assumption defined		1962–65 Vatican Council II	1963 *Pacem in Terris* issued; Paul VI elected pope

The Second Vatican Council

Less than three months after his election on January 25, 1959, Pope John announced to an astonished world that he intended to convoke an ecumenical council. An ecumenical council is a meeting of the official teachers of the church (the bishops) from all over the world, to consider church matters with and under the authority of the bishop of Rome. Pope John's Council—the Second Vatican Council— would be the twenty-first in the history of the church. From the outset its agenda was *aggiornamento* (updating) and *rinnovimento* (renewal). John called the council a new Pentecost—"it is from the Spirit and doctrine of Pentecost that the great event of the ecumenical council draws its substance and life" (*Acta Apostolicae Sedis*, 52, p. 517). He hoped for a pastorally concerned council which would assist the Catholic Church to understand the "signs of the times" in order to preach the gospel of Jesus Christ more effectively. In his opening address on October 11, 1962, Pope John said that he hoped that the council would be a celebration of faith marked by optimism in the presence of the Holy Spirit. Authentic faith needed to be proclaimed in an intelligible way to modern men and women. He saw the work of the council as affirming the gospel anew rather than condemning modern errors.

The Second Vatican Council was a unique event in the history of the church for a number of reasons. It was the largest such gathering ever, with two thousand five hundred and forty voting members. They were assisted by experts or *periti* in theology, law, liturgy, etc. The final count of such advisors was four hundred and eighty. Indigenous bishops represented their own nations and cultures. The agenda of "pastoral renewal" was so broad that it allowed all dimensions of church life, internal and external, to be examined. A total of eighty observers from the Orthodox churches and Protestant churches attended the council, and their indirect participation had a significant influence on the discussions. Finally the council was covered by the media—about one thousand reporters were at the open-

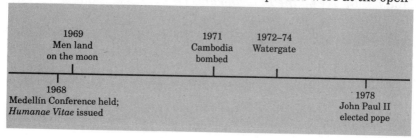

ing session. Aggressive coverage of events meant that what happened, even when not accurately reported, would be discussed and publicly debated. Language groups soon began giving press briefings, since reporters could not attend the meetings themselves.

The first session of the council began on October 13, 1962, and lasted until December 7. Not a single document was approved, but the meetings and discussions showed clearly the differences between traditionalists and progressives. The former relied heavily on scholastic theology and authority. The latter took a more historical-critical approach to the sacred sciences and valued collegiality. The texts of proposed documents were prepared and revised by commissions made up of representatives of various points of view.

Pope John XXIII died in June 1963 and was succeeded by the cardinal archbishop of Milan, Giovanni Battista Montini, who took the name Pope Paul VI. Pope Paul had worked for thirty years in the Vatican secretariat of state and then served as archbishop of Milan for almost nine years. He saw himself as an heir to John XXIII as well as Pius XII and so dedicated himself to completing and implementing the ecumenical council. His fifteen years of service as universal pastor were among the most significant in the history of the church in the modern world. He sought to guide, inspire, and institutionalize the church renewal set in motion by the Second Vatican Council.

The second session of the council opened on September 29, 1963, and ended December 4. At the beginning of his pontificate, Pope Paul VI listed his goals for the council:

1) the development of a clearer understanding of the nature of the church;
2) the renewal of the church in all aspects of its life;
3) the restoration of unity among the Christian churches;
4) a true dialogue between the church and the modern world.

The second session produced the *Constitution on the Sacred Liturgy* and the *Decree on the Instruments of Social Communication*. The third session of the council (September 14, 1964 to November 21, 1964) approved the *Dogmatic Constitution on the Church*, the *Decree on Ecumenism* and the *Decree on Eastern Catholic Churches*. The fourth and final session of the council (September 14, 1965, to December 8, 1965) promulgated eleven texts:

1) the *Decree on the Bishops' Pastoral Office in the Church;*
2) the *Decree on Priestly Formation;*

3) the *Decree on the Appropriate Renewal of Religious Life;*
4) the *Declaration on the Relationship of the Church to Non-Christian Religions;*
5) the *Declaration on Christian Education;*
6) the *Dogmatic Constitution on Divine Revelation;*
7) the *Decree on the Apostolate of the Laity;*
8) the *Pastoral Constitution on the Church in the Modern World;*
9) the *Decree on the Ministry and Life of Priests;*
10) the *Decree on the Church's Missionary Activity;*
11) the *Declaration on Religious Freedom.*

The Council's Teaching

The spirit of the documents issued by the council was pastoral. They sought to address the concerns of the church itself as well as dialogue with the world:

Now that the Second Vatican Council has deeply studied the mystery of the Church, it resolutely addresses not only the sons of the church and all who call upon the name of Christ, but the whole of humanity as well, and it longs to set forth the way it understands the presence and function of the Church in the world of today (*Gaudium et Spes,* n. 2).

The documents vary in terms of content and authority. The constitutions treat matter that is of the very essence or constitution of the church. Decrees and declarations treat special practical topics. Some of the documents, therefore, are more significant than others and have had a more profound effect on the life of the church. The most important documents of the council are:

1) *Dogmatic Constitution on the Church (Lumen Gentium);*
2) *Pastoral Constitution on the Church in the Modern World (Gaudium et Spes);*
3) *Constitution on the Sacred Liturgy (Sacrosanctum Concilium);*
4) *Dogmatic Constitution on Divine Revelation (Dei Verbum);*
5) *Decree on Ecumenism (Unitatis Redintegratio);*
6) *Declaration on the Relationship of the Church to Non-Christian Religions (Nostra Aetate);*
7) *Declaration on Religious Liberty (Dignitatis Humanae).*

The teaching of the Second Vatican Council does not represent a disruptive break with the past. Rather it develops themes and under-standings about the nature and mission of the church that presup-pose the tradition. Nevertheless, the documents do move that tradition forward. The vision and understanding of church that the council represents is a renewed and fresh vision. This is seen in some of the council's major themes.

The Church

The church is before all else a *mysterium*. God the Father calls women and men to communion with the risen Lord Jesus Christ through the Holy Spirit. Those called are in St. Paul's words "the people of God" and "the body of Christ" (*Lumen Gentium*, n. 1). The members of the church voluntarily, under grace, choose to shape their lives and destinies in terms of a relationship with the triune God. The community of believers is a sacrament or sign of humankind's oneness with God and with each other. Through bap-tism and confirmation all are incorporated into the priesthood of Jesus Christ. All celebrate the eucharist which indeed is a commu-nity celebration of thanks and a re-enactment of Christ's sacrifice on Calvary (*Lumen Gentium*, n. 10).

Only after describing the church as mystery and people of God does *Lumen Gentium* treat the hierarchical structure of the commu-nity. Clearly the church is the community of believers. Within that community the bishop of Rome, the pope, is called by Christ to be the successor of Peter, to be universal pastor. Bishops are local pas-tors who with the pope as head form a college succeeding the college of the apostles. The principle of collegiality recognizes the shared responsibility of bishops in the governance of the church while in no way diminishing the unique role of the pope as universal pastor (*Lumen Gentium*, n. 22). Collegiality then becomes a desirable way of relating throughout the entire church, for example, on the dioce-san and the parish level (*Lumen Gentium*, nn. 26–28, 30).

The church of Christ "subsists" in the Catholic Church or is most fully realized there (*Lumen Gentium*, n. 8). Nevertheless, many ele-ments of Christ's church are also found outside the Catholic Church in other Christian churches and ecclesial communities (*Lumen Gentium*, n. 8). All members of the community—bishops, priests, religious and laity are called to holiness. Given sin, weaknesses and human limitations, the community must serve its members and all the world in order to grow ever closer to becoming the mystery which is the kingdom of God (*Lumen Gentium*, chap. 5). The church, however, is at the same time holy and sinful, and so to be the body of Christ it must seek penance and renewal (*Lumen Gentium,* n. 8).

Lumen Gentium called for the restoration of the permanent diaconate for married and single men (*Lumen Gentium,* n. 29) and asked the laity to assume their proper role in the mission of the church (*Lumen Gentium,* n. 30). Mary, the mother of God, serves as a model for all. In heaven she is the image and beginning of the church and a sign of hope and comfort to all the people of God on their pilgrimage to the risen Lord Jesus Christ (*Lumen Gentium,* n. 68). She is, as Pope Paul VI declared in the council, "the mother of the church."

Church and World

Pope John XXIII, working with Cardinal Leo-Jozef Suenens of Belgium, urged from the beginning that the council treat the relationship of the church to the modern world. *The Pastoral Constitution on the Church in the Modern World* (*Gaudium et Spes,* i.e., *Joy and Hope,* from the opening words of the document) was the result. The word "pastoral" was the suggestion of Karol Wojtyla, a council delegate from Krakow, Poland.

The constitution is a positive acknowledgement of the process of modernization. It calls on all in the church to examine the signs of the times in the light of the gospel (*Gaudium et Spes,* n. 4). The church must do this since it exists in the world, not to dominate but to serve that world (*Gaudium et Spes,* n. 3). The constitution teaches:

> The joy and the hope, the grief and anguish of the men of our time, especially of those who are poor or afflicted in any way, are the joy and hope, the grief and anguish of the followers of Christ as well. Nothing that is genuinely human fails to find an echo in their hearts. For theirs is a community composed of men who, united with Christ, and guided by the Holy Spirit, press onwards toward the kingdom of the Father and are bearers of a message of salvation intended for all....that is why Christians cherish a feeling of deep solidarity with the human race and its history (*Gaudium et Spes,* n. 1).

The church is a community of conscience, not a political party, trade union or social agency. Its role or mission is to encourage or critique values—to contribute toward making the human family and its history ever more truly human (*Gaudium et Spes,* n. 40).

Every human person is innately imbued with dignity (*Gaudium et Spes,* nn. 12–22), since each is created in the image of God (*Gaudium et Spes,* n. 13). Jesus Christ reveals to all persons their true nature and destiny. The Holy Spirit thus offers the possibility of a divine destiny to all whether they be explicitly Christian, religious or neither (*Gaudium et Spes,* nn. 19–22).

The document addressed a variety of particular issues: marriage and the family, culture, economics, politics, war and peace. For instance it called upon parents to decide the size of their family—responsible parenthood—respecting always the moral order (*Gaudium et Spes,* nn. 50–51). Human persons are not pawns of an economic system; rather an economic system is meant to promote the good of persons (*Gaudium et Spes,* nn. 63–66). The council condemned total warfare, indiscriminate destruction of whole cities and civilian populations as well as the arms race as "one of the greatest curses on the human race, and the harm it reflects on the poor is more than can be endured" (*Gaudium et Spes,* n. 81).

The activities of the person in the world—personal, social, professional—are not areas separated from religion. Religion is not some private activity which is excluded from other areas of life. Christian women and men have the right and obligation to involve themselves in the temporal activities of the world in order to realize ever more graphically the kingdom of God (*Gaudium et Spes,* n. 45). The church, the people of God, is the universal sacrament of salvation.

Liturgy and Sacred Scripture

The liturgy or worship of the people of God had been done in the Latin rite more or less in the same way since the Council of Trent (1545–1563). The *Constitution on the Sacred Liturgy* called for a substantial renewal of the sacramental rites of the church. Since sacraments were signs and causes of grace, they ought to be intelligible to people (*Sacrosanctum Concilium,* n. 21). During and then subsequent to the council changes were made. There was greater and varied participation of the laity in the celebration of the eucharist (*Sacrosanctum Concilium,* nn. 26, 28, 29, 31, 47–55). The eucharist was celebrated in vernacular languages instead of Latin. Liturgical renewal had a profound impact not only on the prayer life of Catholics. The experience of liturgical change engendered a new understanding of church in general. It also caused anxiety in some quarters. The liturgy is "the outstanding means by which the faithful can express in their lives, and manifest to others, the mystery of Christ and the real nature of the church" (*Sacrosanctum Concilium*, n. 2).

The *Dogmatic Constitution on Divine Revelation* focused attention on scripture, the inspired word of God. Scripture, like the eucharist, but in a different way, is the bread of life. It should be prayerfully read by all in the church. The constitution teaches:

> In the sacred books the Father who is in heaven comes lovingly to meet his children, and talks with them. And such is the force and power of the word of God that it can serve the Church as her support and vigor and the children of the Church as strength for their faith, food for the soul, and a pure and lasting fount of spiritual life (*Dei Verbum*, n. 21).

In Catholic understanding the gospel of Christ was handed on in writing through the inspiration of the Holy Spirit and orally "by the apostles who handed on, by the spoken word of their preaching, by the example they gave, by the institutions they established, what they themselves had received—whether from the lips of Christ, from his way of life and his works, or whether they had learned it at the prompting of the Holy Spirit" (*Dei Verbum*, n. 7). This living transmission is called tradition, a theological concept which is different from a purely cultural "tradition" or custom. "Tradition transmits in its entirety the word of God which has been entrusted to the apostles by Christ the Lord and the Holy Spirit. It transmits it to the successors of the apostles so that, enlightened by the Spirit of truth, they may faithfully preserve, expound and spread it abroad by their preaching" (*Dei Verbum*, n. 9).

God's self-revelation in Jesus Christ through the Holy Spirit has two distinct modes of transmission—tradition and scripture—which are bound together and form one which moves toward the same goal (*Dei Verbum*, n. 9). This Catholic understanding of the source or font of revelation is distinctive and has ecumenical importance. It also highlights the basic ecclesiological understanding of the church as mystery.

Ecumenism

The ecumenical movement was a prelude to the council's *Decree on Ecumenism*. Originally the council considered three documents on church unity, but voted that there be one. The Secretariat for Promoting Christian Unity (today the Pontifical Council for

Christian Unity) was the main author. Division among Christians "openly contradicts the will of Christ, scandalizes the world and damages...the proclamation of the gospel." There is nevertheless a real but imperfect communion among Christian churches (*Decree on Ecumenism,* n. 3). The document calls for the restoration of unity, not a simple return to any one church. There is an incompleteness in a divided Christianity.

The council promoted dialogue among Catholics, Anglicans and Protestants. What they share in common—belief in Jesus Christ, scripture, baptism, eucharist and compassion for the poor—is more profound than are differences. The Eastern Orthodox churches share rich Christian experiences liturgically, spiritually and theologically, but as the *Decree* says:

> ...the heritage handed down by the apostles was received differently and in different forms, so that from the very beginnings of the Church its development varied from region to region and also because of differing mentalities and ways of life. These reasons, plus external causes, as well as the lack of charity and mutual understanding, left the way open to division (*Decree on Ecumenism,* n. 14).

The council urges strongly that every effort be made to restore the union of Eastern and Western Christian churches:

> If this task is carried out wholeheartedly, the Council hopes that with the removal of the wall dividing the Eastern and Western Church at last there may be one dwelling, firmly established on the cornerstone, Christ Jesus, who will make both one (*Decree on Ecumenism,* n. 18).

The broader understanding of ecumenism, reaching out to all humankind, led to a separate document, the *Declaration on the Relationship of the Church to Non-Christian Religions (Nostra Aetate).* That the conciliar fathers would produce such a document speaks to the dynamic of the council itself. A more profound understanding of the relationship of the church to the world, to all persons of good will and to other religious communions developed as the council unfolded. In May 1964 Pope Paul VI established a Secretariat for Inter-Religious Dialogue (now a pontifical council). Later he would establish an official Commission on Religious Relations with Judaism (October 23, 1974).

Nostra Aetate clearly inaugurated a new era in Catholic relations with the Jewish people. The document begins with words of respect for a deep religious sense found among all peoples. It singles out the positive values offered in Hinduism and Buddhism. Islam believes in one God, in Jesus his prophet, honors Mary and awaits a resurrection and reward in paradise. The council states:

> Over the centuries many quarrels and dissensions have arisen between Christians and Muslims. The sacred Council now pleads with all to forget the past, and urges that a sincere effort be made to achieve mutual understanding: for the benefit of all men, let them together preserve and promote peace, liberty, social justice and moral values (*Nostra Aetate,* n. 3).

The rest of *Nostra Aetate* (nn. 4–5) deals with Judaism. It teaches:

1) Christians and Jews are intimately linked in the faith of Abraham, the patriarchs and Moses.
2) The salvation of the church is prefigured in the exodus of God's chosen people from the land of bondage (n. 4).
3) Jews remain very dear to God, for the sake of the patriarchs, since God does not take back the gifts he bestowed or the choice he made (n. 4).
4) The majority of Jews then and today cannot be charged with the death of Christ (n. 4).
5) Jews should not be spoken of as rejected or accursed (ibid.).
6) All forms of anti-Semitism should be deplored anytime and by everyone (n. 4).
7) Any discrimination against people or harassment of them based on race, color, condition in life or religion is absolutely reproved (n. 5).

Pope Pius XI had said, speaking about the Jews, that "spiritually we are all Semites." The "mystery of Israel" is intimately connected with the mystery of the church. That does not mean that relations are, after *Nostra Aetate*, always smooth. It is, however, a new age.

At the fiftieth anniversary of the liberation of Auschwitz, that infamous death camp placed in Poland by the Nazis, the Nobel Prize winner, Elie Wiesel, invited those present to "close your eyes and look, and you will see what we have seen. Close your eyes, and you will see heaven and earth on fire. Close your eyes and listen to the silent screams of terrified mothers, listen to the prayers of anguished old men, listen to the tears of children....Here it is always night....The nocturnal processions of children and more children and more children, frightened, quiet, so quiet and so beautiful. If we could simply look at one our hearts would break." He prayed, "God of forgiveness, do not forgive those murderers of Jewish children" (quoted in *The Tablet*, February 4, 1995, p. 157).

For the same occasion Pope John Paul II called the *shoah* (the holocaust) "one of the darkest and most tragic hours of history." In Auschwitz and other camps "many innocents died, of different nationalities: in particular the children of the Jewish people, whom the Nazi regime programmed for systematic extermination. They endured the dramatic experience of the Holocaust...that triumph of evil which could not but fill us with deep bitterness, in fraternal solidarity with those who bear the indelible sign of those tragedies..." The pope then concluded: "Never again anti-Semitism! Never again the arrogance of nationalism! Never again genocide!" (*The Tablet*, ibid.).

In a remarkable passage in the *Pastoral Constitution on the Church in the Modern World (Gaudium et Spes)* the council spoke of atheism. It is seen as one of the most serious problems of the modern age. Atheism today is of many types, and those who simply drive God from their hearts or who ignore the question of God, notwithstanding the urgings of their conscience, cannot avoid blame for their godlessness (*Gaudium et Spes,* n. 19). It then adds:

> But believers themselves often share some responsibility for the situation....It (atheism) springs from many causes, among which must be included a critical reaction against religions and, in some places, against the Christian religion in particular. Believers can thus have more than a little to do with the rise of atheism. To the extent that they are careless about their instruction in the faith, or present its teaching falsely, or even fail in their religious, moral or social life, they must be said to conceal rather than to reveal the true nature of God and of religion (n. 19).

Atheism is rejected by the church and must be countered by presenting true teaching and by living a true authentic Christian life (n. 21). The constitution says:

> Although the Church altogether rejects atheism, she nevertheless sincerely proclaims that all men, those who believe as well as those who do not, should help to establish right order in this world

where all live together. This certainly cannot be done without a dialogue that is sincere and prudent. The Church, therefore, deplores the discrimination between believers and unbelievers which some civil authorities unjustly practice in defiance of the fundamental rights of the human person (n. 21).

Religious Freedom

For centuries both Catholic and Protestant churches throughout the world had sought advantage and a privileged position through control of the state and government. During the Enlightenment liberals sought to privatize religion so that churches would have no place in public life. In reaction to this position the churches sought to dig in where they could or reach some sort of compromise when they could not. Later, totalitarian regimes and anti-clericals often moved against the Catholic Church, especially in Europe and at times in Latin America. In the twentieth century dictatorships, state-sponsored atheism and revolutionary movements attacked the church and religion in general as counter-revolutionary.

In the 1950s the American Jesuit, Father John Courtney Murray, began to write about and defend the concept of religious freedom. His writings came under attack from other American theologians and from his superiors in Rome. Father Murray was invited to participate in the Second Vatican Council as a personal *peritus* or "expert" to Cardinal Spellman of New York. Once at the council Father Murray worked with others toward including a special statement on religious freedom among the council's teachings. The *Declaration on Religious Freedom (Dignitatis Humanae)* represents a true development in the doctrine of the church. It teaches:

1) The human person has a right to religious freedom which is based on the dignity of the human person as known through revelation and reason (n. 2).
2) No coercion is tolerable in religious matters (n. 2).
3) Governments and civil authority should look with favor on religious life and not attempt to control it (n. 3).
4) Religious communities are of the very nature of the human person and religion (n. 3).
5) Such communities have the right to honor God, to religious instruction and to establish their own institutions (n. 4).
6) They have the right to teach and bear witness to their beliefs

and establish their own educational, cultural, charitable and social organizations (n. 4).

The declaration states:

> One of the key truths in Catholic teaching...is that...response to God by faith ought to be free, and that, therefore, nobody is to be forced to embrace the faith against his will (n. 10)....The Church, therefore, faithful to the truth of the Gospel, is following in the path of Christ and the apostles when she recognizes the principle that religious liberty is in keeping with the dignity of man and divine revelation and gives it her support...(n. 11).

The church must enjoy freedom and independence and cannot be subject to oppressive policies by governments. The church similarly must recognize the religious freedom of others, especially in those areas of the world where Catholics predominate.

Eastern Catholics

The Catholic Church is a single community or people of God consisting of several sister churches. Eastern Catholic communities are churches with their own form of governance, liturgy, spirituality and tradition. The *Decree on Eastern Catholic Churches (Orientalium Ecclesiarum)* refers especially to the Chaldean, Syrian, Maronite, Coptic, Armenian and Byzantine churches. These churches clearly show forth a variety or diversity in unity without any challenge to the ministry of the universal pastor, the bishop of Rome. The council envisions Eastern Catholic churches as bridges to the world of Eastern Orthodoxy (nn. 24–25). To this end Orthodox Christians would be allowed to receive the sacraments of penance, eucharist and the anointing of the sick in Catholic churches. Catholics can do the same in Orthodox churches in the absence of a Catholic priest. As a regular practice permission for this should be sought from the bishop (nn. 26–29).

Laity

A clerical model envisions the mission of the church to be principally the responsibility of priests and vowed religious. That model was substantially modified by a number of conciliar documents. *Lumen Gentium* clearly teaches that the church is all the people of God. The laity share in the priesthood of Christ by reason of their baptism and confirmation (n. 10). "The holy People of God shares also in

Christ's prophetic office: it spreads abroad a living witness to him, especially by a life of faith and love..." (*Lumen Gentium,* n. 12). The document states that the laity

> ...live in the world, that is, they are engaged in each and every work and business of the earth and in the ordinary circumstances of social and family life which, as it were, constitute their very existence. There they are called by God that, being led by the spirit of the Gospel, they may contribute to the sanctification of the world...(*Lumen Gentium,* n. 31).

The council took up again the vocation of the lay person in the *Decree on the Apostolate of the Laity (Apostolicam Actuositatem).* There the laity are urged "to exercise their apostolate both in the Church and in the world, in both the spiritual and the temporal orders" (n. 5). To promote and facilitate lay ministry in the church, a Secretariat for the Laity (today the Pontifical Council for the Laity) was formally established in 1977. Since the council there has been an expansion of lay ministries in the church. Some of these are intra-church, for example, lectors, eucharistic ministers, parish councils and diocesan pastoral councils. Other ministries reach into the worlds of youth, the poor, the sick, the hungry and the homeless. Some lay organizations dedicate themselves to temporary missionary work, for example, the Maryknoll Lay Missioners, the Jesuit Volunteer Corps, and a host of other such agencies.

Effects of the Council

The Second Vatican Council has been the most significant religious event of the twentieth century. It profoundly affected Catholicism and consequentially the entire religious world. The council had touched in one way or another almost every aspect of Catholic life. The possibility and need for renewal were premises accepted by the majority of participants, and they went about their task in earnest. Their conclusions were almost immediately communicated by the media to the Catholic world. Karol Wojtyla, then archbishop of Krakow and a participant at the council (later Pope John Paul II), wrote in the Introduction to his book *Sources of Renewal: The Implementation of Vatican II* (Harper and Row, 1980):

> Through the whole experience of the Council we have contracted a debt towards the Holy Spirit, the Spirit of Christ which speaks to

the Churches. During the Council and by way of it the Word of the
Spirit became particularly expressive and decisive for the Church
(pp. 9–10).

The Second Vatican Council offered a new understanding and
working model for the church. The church was all the people of God—
laity, religious, priests, bishops and pope. This communion was a
sacrament, a sign of the risen Lord Jesus present to the community
through the Holy Spirit. Various ministries distinguished members,
but these ministries were seen as services, not powers. The pope himself was universal pastor and the point of unity for all local churches
as was the bishop for his own particular church. All Catholics by baptism were called to participate in the renewed liturgical life of the
community, bear witness in the world and act to promote the gospel by
serving others, especially their more vulnerable sisters and brothers.

The council cautioned that this mysterious communion would
always be in need of renewal inasmuch as the church was holy and
also sinful at the same time. As a community of conscience the
church's mission was ultimately to make an encounter with the
risen Lord Jesus Christ possible to members and to all women and
men of good will. It did this, of course, with respect, humility and
confidence that the Holy Spirit was with it.

In the years immediately following the close of the council, church
leaders sought to implement new practices and attitudes and to educate the faithful in the teachings of Vatican II. Never before in the history of the church had so many changes been set in motion so quickly.
A period of some turmoil ensued. The number of vocations to priestly
and religious life declined, especially in western Europe and North
America. Considerable numbers of priests and sisters left the active
ministry, many to marry. Legitimate authority in the church was often
criticized and openly challenged. Polarization among Catholics developed—sometimes categorized as "reactionaries," "conservatives,"
"moderates," "liberals" and "anarchists." Some people refused to recognize the legitimacy of the council and rejected its changes. Small congregations, for instance, continued to celebrate the eucharist in Latin
as it had been celebrated since before the Council of Trent. Others
went beyond approved changes and made up their own liturgy. By and
large, however, the vast majority of the people of God took change in
stride. The "sense of the faithful" moved them to adapt, acclimatize
and accept a newer vision of what it meant to be Catholic, Christian,
religious, human persons at the dawn of the new millennium.

22

The Post-Conciliar Church

The purpose of an ecumenical council is the strengthening of the faith and life of the church. In response to the challenge of the Protestant Reformation, the Council of Trent (1545–1563) inaugurated a needed reform of the church and provided a vision of Christian life that guided Catholic experience until the Second Vatican Council. During their ministry of service as bishops of Rome, Popes Paul VI, John Paul I and John Paul II have faced the formidable challenge of concretizing the vision of the Second Vatican Council and implementing its decisions on all levels of the life and ministry of the post-conciliar church.

Pope Paul VI

The last working session of the Second Vatican Council was December 7, 1965. Pope Paul concluded that session by stating that the church has "declared herself the servant of humanity at the very time when her teaching role and her pastoral government have, by reason of the Council's solemnity, assured great splendor and vigor: the idea of service has been central." The participants in the council, their *periti* and observers then returned home. It was up to the pope to implement *aggiornamento*.

Governance of the Church

Even in their last session the bishops of the world with the pope began a renewal of the Roman curia, the bureaucracy that assists the pope in his universal pastoral ministry. The Holy Office became the Congregation for the Doctrine of the Faith. Pope John XXIII had established the Secretariat for Promoting Christian Unity in 1960; Pope Paul added secretariats for non-believers and non-

Christian religions. In 1967 he also established the Council of the Laity and the Pontifical Justice and Peace Commission. Pope Paul fixed the term of appointments to curia positions at five years. Officials of the curia would now be required to offer their resignation at the age of seventy-five and would automatically resign at the death of a pope. A serious effort was also made to internationalize the curia by appointing members from America, Africa and Asia as well as Europe to important positions.

Pope Paul VI issued a rule that bishops must submit their resignation at the age of seventy-five although their ministry could be extended. He determined that only one hundred and twenty cardinals would vote for a pope and all must be under the age of eighty. In an effort to promote collegiality among bishops, he established the synod of bishops, a meeting of representative bishops and others to advise the pope on relevant issues every three years. He encouraged local bishops to serve collegiality by establishing priests' senates and diocesan pastoral councils and parish councils. National episcopal conferences (i.e., the college of bishops of a particular nation) were given greater voice and prominence in the life of the local church and in its relations with Rome.

Liturgy

The council had called for the renewal of the worship life of the people of God. In 1964 Pope Paul established a special commission to implement the renewal. The celebration of the eucharist, the heart of Catholic prayer life, would now be celebrated in vernacular languages using a newly revised missal. The rites for baptism, confirmation, reconciliation, anointing of the sick, matrimony and ordination were likewise revised. Rules for fasting and abstinence were changed. Since liturgy is both the public prayer life of the community and at the same time the most personal and intimate dimension of an individual's relationship with God, these liturgical changes deeply affected Catholic life and spirituality. For a few these changes were deeply upsetting; for most they were profoundly energizing.

Travels

Pope Paul described himself as a "pilgrim pope." He became the first pope in history to travel to various parts of the world. He visited the Holy Land, where he met and prayed with the ecumenical patriarch Athenagoras and other Christian and Jewish leaders. He also visited

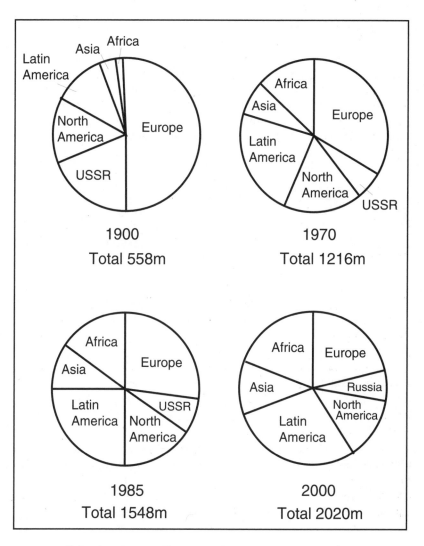

Christian Growth 1900 – 2000

India, Portugal, Turkey, Colombia, Uganda, Australia, and a number of other Asian countries. He escaped an assassination attempt in the Philippines unhurt. At United Nations headquarters in New York City Pope Paul pleaded with representatives of one hundred and seventeen nations for peace:

> No more war, war never again....If you wish to be brothers, let the arms fall from your hands. One cannot love while holding offensive weapons....Respect for life, even with regard to the great problem of birth, must find in your assembly its highest affirmation and its most reasoned defense. You must strive to multiply bread so that it suffices for the tables of mankind and not rather favor an artificial control of birth, which would be irrational, in order to diminish the number of guests at the banquet of life.

His day in New York included a visit to the World's Fair and then mass at Yankee Stadium in the Bronx. On June 10, 1969, in Geneva, Switzerland, he addressed the International Labor Organization and visited the headquarters of the World Council of Churches. To the former he stated clearly:

> Never again will work be superior to the worker. Never again will work be against the worker, but always work will be for the worker. Work will be in the service of man, of every man and of all men.

Social Teaching

Pope Paul participated in the Latin American Bishops' Conference (CELAM) meeting at Medellín, Colombia in 1968. That meeting affirmed that the church must take a preferential option for the poor. If the people of God were to be an authentic communion, they must minister to the least of their brothers and sisters. The pope warned that systems and structures which inevitably caused injustice were totally unacceptable to Christians. The Medellín conference concluded by asserting that Latin America often found itself in a situation of institutional violence, internal and external colonialism and social sin. Much of the analysis used at Medellín was based on liberation theology, a way of interpreting the gospel to serve the poor. At times some advocates of liberation theology employed a Marxist analysis of society. Such analysis, however, was not acceptable to the magisterium, which warned of the dangers inherent in such a view of the world.

Pope Paul published his encyclical, *Populorum Progressio (On the Development of Peoples)*, a year before the Medellín meeting. The papal letter called for a new "transcendent humanism" which "will enable man to find himself anew by embracing the higher values of love and friendship, of prayer and contemplation."

The poor of the world seek to escape their poverty, hunger, inadequate housing and inferior education. They "seek to do more, know more, and have more in order to be more." The pope taught:

1) No one is justified in keeping for his exclusive use what he does not need, when others lack necessities.
2) Profit as the key motive for economic progress, competition as the supreme law of economics, and private ownership of the means of production as an absolute right that has no limits and carries no corresponding social obligation lead to the international imperialism of money.
3) All nations as brothers and sisters, as children of God, are called upon to work together to build the common future of the human race.

This new world can only be realized if human solidarity is characterized by social justice and universal charity. "The world," the pope claims, "is sick. Its illness consists less in the unproductive monopolization of resources by a small number of men than in the lack of brotherhood among individuals and peoples....Development is the new name of peace."

Four years later, in *Octogesima Adveniens*, a letter marking the eightieth anniversary of Pope Leo XIII's *Rerum Novarum*, Paul returned to the social question. The Christian has the duty to foster love and human solidarity. New, urgent questions face the church, the community of conscience: urbanization, youth, women, discrimination, the right to immigrate and the environment. The church does not have ready-made answers nor does it seek to impose a particular structure on the world. Nevertheless, the person and teaching of Jesus have a unique role to play in the process of human development.

The third synod of bishops, called by Pope Paul VI in 1971, discussed social justice in its document, *Justice in the World*. It stated:

Action on behalf of justice is a constitutive dimension of the preaching of the Gospel, and a part of the Church's mission, which is to redeem and liberate the human race by manifesting and realizing God's plan for it.

The church's mission involves:

...the right, indeed the duty, to proclaim justice on the social,
national, and international levels and to denounce instances of
injustice when the fundamental rights of man and his very salvation demands it.

Other Activities

Pope Paul VI personally supported the Second Vatican Council's
efforts to establish church unity. He met with patriarchs and leaders of the great Orthodox churches a number of times. His symbolic
gestures were meant to convey his great respect for other religious
traditions while improving an atmosphere necessary for dialogue.
He sent back to the Orthodox churches the relic of the head of St.
Andrew, which had been in the Vatican since 1462. He and
Patriarch Athenagoras revoked mutual excommunications. Paul
met leaders of Protestant churches, for example, the archbishop of
Canterbury Michael Ramsey, and other religious leaders, including
the Dalai Lama.

In his efforts to promote collegiality in the church, Pope Paul took
special interest in the synod of bishops. The first meeting of bishops
took place in 1967 and considered the topic of an international commission of theologians to advise the pope and Vatican agencies.
Subsequent synods examined the questions of priesthood, social
justice and evangelization in the modern world.

On the diplomatic plane the pope established relations with more
than forty new countries, mainly in Africa. He also sought a rapprochement with communist states in Eastern Europe. This did not
entail any acceptance of communist ideology. It was rather a pragmatic effort to serve the interests of Catholics in Eastern Europe
and to perhaps lessen the dogmatism of leading communists.
Russian leaders visited Pope Paul in the Vatican, for example,
President Nikolai V. Podgorny in 1967. Hungary established diplomatic relations with the Vatican in 1966. Five years later Cardinal
Jozsef Mindszenty left his exile in the United States embassy in
Budapest, where he had lived since the 1956 Hungarian uprising.
This ultimately paved the way for naming new bishops in the coun-
try. In 1967 President Josip Tito, of the former Yugoslavia, renewed
relations with the Vatican, and in 1973 diplomatic relations
warmed with both the former Czechoslovakia and Poland. The
Croatian cardinal Josef Beran was released from prison after more

than fifteen years and allowed to move to Rome, where he died. The cardinal is buried with the popes in the crypt of St. Peter's Basilica. The *oestpolitik* of Pope Paul, while criticized in some quarters as too accommodating, remotely contributed to a new era of East-West relations and in a degree to the collapse of the iron curtain.

On July 29, 1968, the pope issued an encyclical on the regulation of birth, *Humanae Vitae*, which provoked sharp disagreement in many parts of the Catholic world. The letter portrays marriage and sexual love as a gift of God and a collaboration with God in the generation and education of new human persons. The letter reiterated the church's traditional teaching on responsible parenthood and birth control. It rejected direct abortion, direct sterilization of either spouse, permanent or temporary, as well as artificial means of contraception. *Humanae Vitae* expressed a concern that widespread use of contraceptives would encourage a cavalier secularist understanding of sex, promiscuity, infidelity and degradation of women, as well as offer governments an opening to intrude in the personal lives of married couples. The tone of the letter was pastoral. Couples were urged to pursue high ideals while not being discouraged by natural weakness. Bishops and priests were asked to be faithful to the authentic magisterium of the church.

After *Humanae Vitae*, Pope Paul VI was viewed by some as too conservative, afraid of innovation and change. He was said to be vacillating and unsure—a Hamlet. The pope saw his teaching as a defense of life and the family. In June 1978 Paul referred to the encyclical in an address to the college of cardinals as "a painful document of our pontificate, not only because the issue was serious and delicate, but also—and perhaps even more important—because there was a certain climate of expectancy" that there would be a relaxation in the church's traditional teaching about artificial contraception.

Other critics saw Paul and the work of Vatican II as a capitulation to secularism and the modern world. Archbishop Marcel Lefebvre, former missionary bishop of Dakar, Senegal, refused to accept the teachings of the council on liturgical renewal, ecumenism and religious freedom. He and his followers refused obedience to the pope, and after ordaining thirteen priests in 1967 he was suspended from exercising his functions as a priest. The archbishop continued ordaining priests without authorization and traveled the world protesting much of the council's teaching. Lefebvre found strong support in France, Germany, and the United States among traditionalists. His priestly Society of St. Pius X claims more than two hundred priests

and hundreds of thousands of members. Papal efforts at reconciliation failed, and in 1978 Pope Paul publicly warned these dissidents.
Subsequent to Pope Paul's death Lefebvre was excommunicated for
ordaining four bishops without permission. The archbishop died in
1991 but his schismatic movement continues.

Pope Paul VI was universal pastor at a unique historical moment
in the life of the church. His difficult task was to institutionalize the
renewal set in motion by the council. A deft hand was needed to
steer the church so that it would authentically renew itself and
remain a faithful people of God, sacrament of the mystery of God
and the oneness of humankind. Paul died on August 6, 1978. In a
meditation on his death the pope had written:

> As for myself, I would like, at the end to have a comprehensive
> understanding of the world and of life, and I think that such an
> understanding should be expressed in terms of gratitude: every-
> thing was given, everything was grace....One's leave-taking, it
> seems, should be one great and simple act of thanksgiving. In
> spite of its pains, its obscurities, its sufferings and its inexorable
> transitoriness, this mortal life is something very beautiful, a won-
> derful reality, endlessly original and moving, something worthy to
> be celebrated in joy and in glory....My fellow men, understand me,
> I love you all with the outpouring of the Spirit, which, as a minis-
> ter, I must share with you. Thus I salute you, thus I bless you, all
> of you...and to the Church, to whom I owe everything and who
> was entrusted to me...may the blessing of God come down upon
> you: may you have an insight into the true and deepest needs of
> mankind: and may you walk humbly—that is to say in freedom—
> strong and filled with love towards Christ....The Lord is coming.

Pope John Paul I

The conclave of cardinals meeting in the Vatican on August 26,
1978, under the guidance of the Holy Spirit, elected Albino Luciani,
the cardinal patriarch of Venice, to be pope. He chose to be called
John Paul I. Instead of a traditional papal coronation, John Paul
preferred a simple ceremony to inaugurate his ministry as universal pastor. His simplicity, sense of humor, and holiness quickly won
the admiration of the world, which was shocked and saddened by
his sudden death on September 28. John Paul I had been pope just a
month—the September pope.

Pope John Paul II

On October 16, 1978, the world was surprised with the announcement that Karol Josef Wojtyla was elected pope. The Polish John Paul II was the first non-Italian pope in more than four hundred years. At fifty-eight years of age he was also one of the youngest.

Pope John Paul II was born May 18, 1920, in Wadowice, Poland. He lost his mother when he was nine and his father when he was twenty-one, and his only brother, a doctor, died during a scarlet fever epidemic. Under the Nazi occupation of Poland he worked first in a quarry and then in a chemical plant. In 1942 the future pope began studies for the priesthood, which were done secretly since the Nazis had closed the Krakow seminary. Ordained in 1946, Wojtyla studied for his doctorate in theology with the Dominicans at the University of St. Thomas (Angelicum) in Rome. His dissertation treated the question of faith in the mystical writings of St. John of the Cross.

Father Wojtyla returned to Poland to teach philosophy and Christian ethics in Krakow and Lublin. His intellectual efforts sought to link the thought of St. Thomas Aquinas with insights from phenomenology, especially those of Max Scheler (1874–1928). Over the years he published more than three hundred articles. At the same time he ministered to the needs of university students as a chaplain, advisor, friend and pastor. The young priest, intellectual, artist, poet, and former actor immensely enjoyed skiing and mountain climbing with groups of young adults. In 1958, a priest just twelve years, Pope Pius XII named him auxiliary bishop of Krakow. Pope Paul VI named him archbishop of Krakow in 1964 and a cardinal in 1967.

Bishop Wojtyla participated in all the sessions of the Second Vatican Council. He forcefully supported the teaching of the council and its vision of the church. He stated:

> The fact that the Church emerges simultaneously along these two dimensions, *ad intra* and *ad extra*, also means that it necessarily lives *in statu missionis*: that it must tirelessly carry out the burden of the mission which wells up from the very Trinitarian depths of God, and that through this mission it must constantly penetrate man and his world as leaven, to lead him to his eschatological consummation. Vatican II reminded us that the Church is found "within" the world and that the world is not totally "out" of the Church.

For Wojtyla, the church, the people of God, was a "communion," a real interrelatedness of persons in the Holy Spirit. It was not simply

an association. The mission of that communion was evangelization—the proclamation of the gospel to a world desperately in need
of a saving, healing and liberating word. On October 22, 1978, Karol
Wojtyla, as John Paul II, inaugurated his ministry as universal pastor, stating: "Be not afraid." Jesus had spoken these words to the
apostles (Lk 24:36) and to the women who had come to the tomb (Mt
28:10) after the resurrection. In his popular book *Crossing the
Threshold of Hope*, the pope asked: "Why have no fear?" and subsequently commented:

> Because man had been redeemed by God. When pronouncing
> these words in St. Peter's square, I already knew that my first
> encyclical and my entire papacy would be tied to the truth of the
> redemption. In the redemption we find the most profound basis
> for the words "Be not afraid!" "For God so loved the world that He
> gave his only Son" (John 3:16)....The redemption pervades all of
> human history, even before Christ, and prepares its eschatological
> future....The power of Christ's cross and resurrection is greater
> than any evil which man could or should fear.

Travels

John Paul II has been the most traveled pope in history. In Rome, as
its bishop, he has visited many of its three hundred and twenty
parishes to be with his people. He has regularly traveled to other
parts of Italy for the same reason. There have been more than seventy international pastoral visitations to over one hundred different
countries. These pilgrimages have taken on a certain format. The
pope is often received as the ruler of Vatican City by the head of
state. He meets with bishops, priests and religious. Special groups
are singled out: youth, the sick, workers, the marginalized and
indigenous peoples. Ecumenical contacts with leaders of other
churches and religions are made. The pope celebrates the eucharist
in cathedrals and in open-air ceremonies, which are attended by
hundreds of thousands. At the 1995 World Youth Day in Manila, it
was estimated that between three and five million people attended
the closing eucharist. He also visits local Marian shrines and when
possible likes to beatify or canonize local blesseds and saints. John
Paul has beatified more than seven hundred women and men and
canonized over two hundred and sixty-eight, showing the church
and the world that holiness can be a way of life.

During the course of these pastoral visits Pope John Paul preaches and instructs. Often he will give more than forty prepared homilies and addresses during a trip. Since the events are covered by the media, his message reaches a wide segment of the population. He preaches the gospel of Christ and applies it often to certain concrete situations, events or issues. In June 1979 he returned to Poland and preached in Victory Square, Warsaw. At the time no public religious expression was allowed by the communist government. The pope insisted in his homily that there was no aspect of life where Christ had no right to enter. The applause of a million people lasted fourteen minutes. The Slavic pope simply waited as the fear of his beloved Polish society was unlocked. His visit home is credited with energizing and sustaining the labor movement, Solidarity, which would eventually lead to the downfall of Polish communism. In Ireland the pope condemned violence between Catholics and Protestants, clearly asserting that such fratricide could never be called Christian or done in the name of true religion.

John Paul, a promising actor in his younger years, seizes every opportunity to preach Christ's love and redemption and the sacredness of the human person. His "pilgrimages of faith" have become a dramatic way of ministering as universal pastor. He uses the media skillfully—interviews, documentaries, recordings, press releases, television, radio and film. One such interview with Vittorio Messori, an Italian journalist, became an international best-seller—*Crossing the Threshold of Hope*—published in a variety of languages.

Audiences

The pope's general audiences in Rome on Wednesday mornings have become liturgical events. Thousands gather in St. Peter's Square, the Pope Paul VI Hall, or the basilica itself for prayer, scripture and papal instruction. Often the pope will speak on a theme over a period of weeks, giving catechesis on some aspect of Christian doctrine, for example, his remarkable vision of human sexuality, the body and matrimony.

After one such audience on May 13, 1981, as Pope John Paul drove slowly around St. Peter's Square in his white jeep, Mehemet Ali Agca shot and seriously wounded the pope. After several operations Pope John Paul recovered. Agca was caught, convicted and given a life sentence in an Italian prison. It was suspected that he was part of a conspiracy promoted by the Bulgarian secret police. On December 27, 1983, the pope visited Agca in his cell in Rebibbia

Prison. A published photograph of the pope quietly talking with his would-be assassin became a powerful symbol of reconciliation and forgiveness.

Teaching

The energy and work ethic of Pope John Paul II is clearly seen not only in the sometimes grueling pastoral visits and his everyday schedule but also in the vast body of writings that are his teaching. His bibliography is enormous and varied: homilies and addresses to various groups on doctrinal, moral, cultural, pastoral and social topics. He has issued lengthy apostolic exhortations on such topics as catechetical teaching, the family, the sacrament of reconciliation and penance in the life of the church, the role of the laity in the church, and the formation of priests. He also has composed shorter apostolic letters on human suffering and the evangelical counsels, letters addressed to the youth of the world for whom he has a special fondness and on the dignity of women, and letters for special anniversaries (e.g., the sixteenth centenary of the conversion of St. Augustine). At Christmas 1994 the pope sent a letter to the children of the world explaining the meaning of Christmas and asking for their prayers. On Holy Thursday the pope generally addresses a letter to the priests of the world.

The pope's more formal instruments for teaching have been his twelve encyclicals:

1) *Redemptor Hominis (Redeemer of Man)*—March 1979—a Christian anthropology which affirms the unique sacredness of every human person redeemed by Christ and the mission of the church in support of that person.
2) *Dives in Misericordia (On the Mercy of God)*—November 1980—the mercy of God should be reflected in human conduct and mutual forgiveness.
3) *Laborem Exercens (On Human Work)*—September 1981—a theology of work, which should be for all a source of dignity, mutual care and service.
4) *Slavorum Apostoli (Apostles of the Slavic People)*—June 1985—a tribute to the Slavic missionary brothers, Cyril and Methodius, on the eleventh centenary of the death of St. Methodius. Both saints have been declared patrons of Europe by Pope John Paul II along with St. Benedict.
5) *Dominum et Vivificantem (Lord and Giver of Life)*—May

1986—a prolonged meditation on the Holy Spirit present in the church's bishops, priests and faithful, thus grounding the truth of revelation and the truth of the human person.

6) *Redemptoris Mater (Mother of the Redeemer)*—March 1987—a theological exposition of Catholic theology about Mary, her mediatorial role, as a model of motherhood and a disciple of Christ.

7) *Sollicitudo Rei Socialis (On Social Concerns)*—December 1987—a theological statement about the plight of so many poor and powerless human persons, deprived of basic human dignity by forces beyond their control. The letter calls for all peoples to be in solidarity in order to promote human development. The church's social teaching adopts a critical stance toward liberal capitalism without a moral social sense as well as Marxist collectivism.

8) *Redemptoris Missio (Mission of the Redeemer)*—January 1991—a new synthesis about the church's teaching on evangelization in the modern world. The church is at the service of the world; it imposes nothing but rather proposes.

9) *Centesimus Annus (The Hundredth Year)*—May 1991—the one hundredth anniversary of *Rerum Novarum* is celebrated. In this encyclical the pope addresses in a special way the newly liberated countries of Eastern Europe.

10) *Veritatis Splendor (The Splendor of Truth)*—August 1993— an exposition of Catholic moral teaching that goes directly against the moral relativism of the modern age, offering instead a vision of the human person who is capable of knowing and discovering the truth. In particular the countries of the West, dominated by materialism, consumerism, individualism, are addressed.

11) *Evangelium Vitae (The Gospel of Life)*—March 1995—a lengthy theological defense of life, especially against abortion, euthanasia, and the pervasive contemporary "culture of death."

12) *Ut Unum Sint (That All May Be One)*—May 1995—a lengthy encyclical on ecumenism in which the pope acknowledges that the office and the role of the bishop of Rome are problems in the search for church unity. He commits himself to exercising his office in such a way that he retains what is essential to the Petrine ministry while being open to a new situation.

Other Activities

Pope John Paul II has unabashedly embraced the ecclesiological concept of collegiality as taught by the Second Vatican Council. Critics view him as authoritarian, unbending, autocratic—a product of the conservative Polish church in a country dominated by communism and Soviet control. Yet perhaps no pope in history has consulted or dialogued or listened to so many. Formally and informally he has met with groups of the faithful, as well as non-Catholics and critics, on his many pastoral pilgrimages. John Paul has continued the synod of bishops, that is, meetings with elected and appointed bishops from all over the world, at regular intervals to treat church matters. There have been synods of bishops dealing with religious life, priestly formation, penance and reconciliation, and the role of the laity in the church. He has convoked special synods, for example, that of the Dutch bishops to examine some contentious issues in the church in Holland, and a synod of Ukrainian bishops to select a new major archbishop. There have been extraordinary synods, for example, on the occasion of the twentieth anniversary of the Second Vatican Council, which assessed the results and examined difficulties as well as made an effort to chart the future direction in line with the teaching of the council. Continental synods have been convoked to examine and plan for church life on a continent, for example, the synod on Africa and the synod on Europe. Others are planned for America, Oceania and Asia.

The pope has gathered the cardinals of the world for special consultations. The first was to consider the grave fiscal situation of the Vatican. It had been regularly running a serious deficit which threatened to affect the charitable works of the church. Another such meeting was called to suggest ways to commemorate as a universal church the dawning of a new millennium. In very dramatic ways John Paul has institutionalized collegiality, promoted it and worked with it.

There are many other unique events that have affected church life during the pastoral ministry of Pope John Paul II:

1) In 1983 he promulgated the new Code of Canon Law for the Latin rite Church, a major work begun during the papacy of Pope John XXIII.
2) In 1984 full diplomatic relations with the United States were established. The first Vatican nuncio (ambassador) was

Cardinal Pio Laghi. That same year the concordat with Italy was updated.

3) In 1986 the pope invited to Assisi one hundred and fifty members of different world religions as well as representatives of all Christian churches for a World Day of Prayer for Peace, a remarkable interfaith ecumenical event.

4) In 1988 John Paul issued the apostolic constitution, *Pastor Bonus*, which reorganized the Roman curia.

5) In 1990 a similar Code of Canon Law for Eastern Catholic churches was promulgated.

6) In 1992 a new universal Catechism of the Catholic Church was approved.

7) In 1994 the Vatican established diplomatic relations with the State of Israel.

8) World Youth Days, which brought together young people from all over the world for festive prayer, liturgy and papal instruction, have been celebrated in Rome, Poland, Spain, the United States, and the Philippine Islands.

The World Church

Catholic people, numbering almost one billion, are profoundly diverse culturally, ethnically, geographically, economically and politically. Yet they belong to a church which claims as its distinguishing marks to be one, holy, catholic and apostolic. Throughout two thousand years of history the Catholic community has struggled to maintain its unity, sanctity, universality and an unbroken line of apostolic succession.

The present historical moment for this "world church," to use the description of Karl Rahner, S.J., is most complex. Contemporary Catholics, women and men, face a host of issues as they seek to live out their lives as disciples of Jesus in the modern world. They share some of these issues in common; other issues affect some more than others. Some issues are perennial; others are new to the present age.

The Second Vatican Council inaugurated a period of renewal in the Catholic Church which continues. A living community always renews itself or risks irrelevancy. In the case of the church, believers are convinced of the presence in the community of the Holy Spirit. True renewal, therefore, is always discerned by the community and its leaders in terms of the direction of the Holy Spirit.

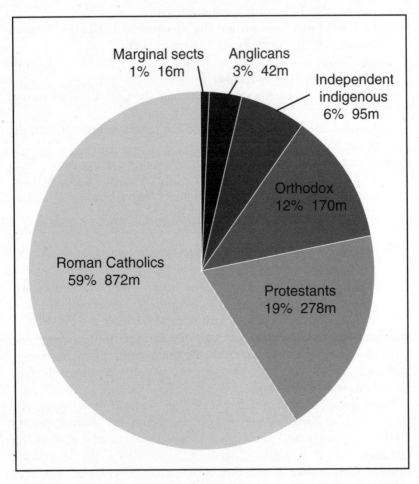

Size of Christian Denominations 1985

Issues Facing the World Church

Growth in the Holy Spirit is of paramount importance for the Catholic community. A Christian person voluntarily seeks to shape his or her life in terms of a personal and communal relationship with Jesus Christ and the gospel. Meaningful personal and liturgical prayer are indispensable for the spiritual life. Prayer and God's grace can truly transform the human person who seeks to imitate Christ in daily life. Human behavior then becomes virtuous, admirable, worthy, fully human and humane. Patterns of relationships among Catholics themselves and with others should be characterized by respect, truth, humility, compassion and courage: "See the Christians, how they love one another."

The vast, diverse people of God must work to become truly a communion. Disagreement and dissent over things that are not important and central to Catholic identity can be examined and discussed, but those things ought not to destroy community. Renewal efforts in the post-conciliar era at times produced suspicion, polarization, antagonism, division and failures in the charitable behavior that should mark the life of Christians. A task facing all in the church is to be truly united in "one Lord, one faith and one baptism" (Eph 4:5).

The historical divisions in the body of Christ are the result of many converging forces—political, ethnic and economic, as well as theological. The Second Vatican Council unleashed unprecedented ecumenical efforts in the Catholic Church. Notwithstanding great progress in understanding and collaboration, serious differences remain that separate Christians. Church leaders and communities are challenged to overcome these differences so that, in the words of Jesus' prayer, "they may be one as we are one" (Jn 17:11).

The unity of a "world church," served by a universal pastor, the pope, does not preclude distinctness. The church is the people of God in many cultures and nations. It must be inculturated, that is, the gospel must be inserted into the host culture and take root there. It cannot remain a foreign product imposed by outsiders and present only superficially. Through the process of "inculturation" the gospel transforms authentic cultural values and incorporates them into Christianity; it critiques those values or patterns of behavior incompatible with the message of Christ.

The concern for authentic inculturation is most evident in non-European local churches (e.g., in Africa, Asia, and Oceania). Great strides have been made in this area. For instance, a more African expression of Catholicism is developing since the 1994 synod on Africa. Having heard their priests, pastoral agents and people, several hundred African bishops met with Pope John Paul II to elaborate a plan for evangelization on the continent. A tension, that of "the one and the many," will always exist. How is it possible to maintain the unity of a worldwide church made up of many and diverse local churches? What are the limits of the responsibilities and actions of the Roman curia, serving the pope in his pastoral mission? What are the competencies proper to the local church in inculturating the gospel? These are the questions which in one way or another are asked by all local churches.

The church is a community of conscience and compassion. Its platform for action is the beatitudes—blessed are the poor, the hungry, the peacemakers and those who mourn. The criteria for judging the authenticity of Christian existence are found in Matthew 25:34–37:

> Come, you who are blessed by my Father; take your inheritance, the kingdom prepared for you since the creation of the world. For I was hungry and you gave me something to eat. I was thirsty and you gave me something to drink. I was a stranger and you invited me in. I needed clothes and you clothed me. I was sick and you looked after me. I was in prison and you came to visit me.

The people of God are seriously challenged because of the unequal distribution of the world's goods to take a preferential option for the poor. As members of a community called to a life of virtue, all must seek to serve concretely the needs of the poor and to work to change unjust systems and structures that cause poverty and its manifold side effects. Since Vatican II, church leaders, theologians, pastoral ministers and small basic communities in Latin America have worked effectively and prophetically to take the side of the poor, powerless and marginalized. The Peruvian priest, Father Gustavo Gutiérrez, and other thinkers have sought to articulate their vision of Christianity and the church in what is called the "theology of liberation." That vision calls upon Christians to put into practice what they believe. Rooting its vision in the bible, it seeks the empowerment of the poor and the transformation of an unjust economic order.

The theology of liberation and grass roots basic communities have at times seriously threatened the entrenched order of things and provoked fierce repression by local and/or national authorities. The number of priests, women religious, lay leaders and faithful who have been brutally tortured and murdered by other baptized

Catholics in Latin America is staggering. Archbishop Oscar Romero of El Salvador was gunned down while celebrating mass. He had consistently called for an end to the violence and social injustice in his country. Four American women, two Maryknoll sisters, one Ursuline sister and a lay missionary, who were working with the poor and refugees, were raped and murdered by Salvadoran soldiers.

Work on behalf of justice is a constitutive part of the gospel. It is not optional; it is not pre-evangelization. The social doctrine of the church, however, does not preach class warfare. Church leaders have at times become alarmed at some practitioners and advocates of liberation theology, and some of them have been forbidden to teach or lecture. Leaders have been accused of pusillanimity or siding with the status quo. The church must be an effective sacrament of Christ and a prophetic community working for justice. On the one hand it cannot become partisan, choosing one side over and against the other; on the other hand it must act in accord with the norms of the gospel. To do nothing is to collaborate in injustice. Great prudence and great courage are needed to preach the gospel of justice.

The Christian community shares a moral vision which seeks to promote the fullness of the human person. The Catholic Church, its leaders and all believers witness to a culture of life. The people of God have a stake in and a responsibility to address concrete moral issues: abortion, euthanasia, racism, sexism, capital punishment, war, unjust wages and a host of others. A secular, anti-religious climate seeks to relegate religion to the sidelines of public life. The church today by its witness in word and action must proclaim effectively its ethic of life to all. Powerful forces—governments, media, particular interest groups and individuals—oppose the church's vision and attempt to deprive it of a voice.

Within the church itself there are issues that challenge its ability to minister well. The number of men entering the priesthood and the number of women entering religious life have decreased sharply in some countries since the Second Vatican Council, for example, the United States, Ireland and other western European countries. Missionary priests and sisters from former colonies now serve the churches which once sent them missionaries. There has been, at the same time, an expansion of lay ministries in the church since the council. Lay persons, both women and men, married and single, are committing themselves in one form or another to church ministry. These events pose important questions:

1) How does the church promote collaboration in ministry between clergy and laity?
2) How are lay ministers to be adequately prepared in theological pastoral practice and to be economically supported with a just and family wage?
3) What will be the shape of religious life in the future?
4) Have older forms of religious life, orders and congregations served their purpose so that the future lies with new, enthusiastic groups that are now being established?
5) How will the church recruit suitable candidates to a celibate priesthood in a culture that does not understand or value the witness of celibacy?

The women's movement has raised the consciousness of the world to the injustices that women have suffered throughout history because of their gender. Women in the church have always been a significant force in promoting Catholic life and identity. They were the formative teachers and role models who passed on the tradition. Still women were rarely involved in church administration and decision making. The feminist movement has awakened the institutional church to its discrimination against women and the need for women's charisms. Increasingly women are assuming positions of leadership in apostolic movements and organizations, dioceses, and the Roman curia.

The question of the ordination of women and the question of a married clergy are difficult issues for the contemporary church. Pope John Paul II has declared that it is not within his power to change the tradition of an all-male clergy. He also insists as well on the value of celibacy for priests of the Latin rite. Some Catholics are silently pained by these decisions while others react with anger and bitterness. For all Catholics there must be the willingness to maintain the bonds of charity while searching for the truth of God's will for the church of the twenty-first century, which only the Holy Spirit can reveal in the unfolding life of the people of God.

In *Crossing the Threshold of Hope* Pope John Paul II urges all humanity to "be not afraid." Fear not the world! Fear not yourself! God so loved the world that he gave his only Son (Jn 3:16). Humanity is redeemed. The pope writes:

Peoples and nations of the entire world need to hear these words. Their conscience needs to grow in the certainty that Someone exists who holds in His Hands the destiny of this passing world....And this Someone is Love (cf. 1 Jn 4:8–16)—Love that became man, Love crucified and risen, Love unceasingly present....He alone can give the ultimate assurance when He says "Be not afraid."

The history of the Christian tradition is the story of a people's struggle over two thousand years to follow Jesus, who is the way, the truth and the life. It is a story of failure and sin, a story even more of grace and redemption. The people of God are a sacrament of Christ who is the sacrament of the living God, Father, Son and Holy Spirit. The church passionately believes in the possibility of being and doing good. The Catholic communion in the third millennium must continue to champion gospel humanism as servant of the world in service to the truth.

FOR FURTHER READING AND REFERENCE

Catechism of the Catholic Church (Mahwah: Paulist Press, 1994).

Edward L. Cleary, O.P., *Crisis and Change: The Church in Latin America Today* (Maryknoll: Orbis Books, 1985).

Austin Flannery, O.P., ed., *Vatican Council II: The Conciliar and Post Conciliar Documents, New Revised Edition* (Northport: Costello Publishing Company, 1992).

Thomas M. Gannon, S.J., ed., *World Catholicism in Transition* (New York: Macmillan Publishing Company, 1988).

Adrian Hastings, ed., *Modern Catholicism: Vatican II and After* (New York: Oxford University Press, 1991).

Peter Hebblethwaite, *Paul VI: The First Modern Pope* (Mahwah: Paulist Press, 1993).

———, *Pope John XXIII: Shepherd of the Modern World* (Garden City: Doubleday, 1985).

New Catholic Encyclopedia, Vol. 16, "Paul VI, Pope," by T. Early; "Humanae Vitae," by B. A. Williams.

———, Vol. 17, "Paul VI, Pope," by F. X. Murphy; "John Paul II, Pope," by T. C. O'Brien.

Karl Rahner, S.J., "Towards a Fundamental Theological Interpretation of Vatican II," *Theological Studies* 40 (1979), 716–27.

Tad Szulc, *Pope John Paul II: The Biography* (New York: Scribner, 1995).

George Hunston Williams, *The Mind of John Paul II: Origins of His Thought and Action* (New York: Seabury Press, 1981).

Index